THE AMERICAN
MUSICAL STAGE

THE AMERICAN MUSICAL STAGE

BEFORE 1800

JULIAN MATES

RUTGERS UNIVERSITY PRESS

New Brunswick   *New Jersey*

Grateful acknowledgment for its subsidy
is made to the Sonneck Memorial Fund
in the Library of Congress

√ ML
1711
. M4

To the Memory of My Father

Prologue

If the reader likes musical comedy, as I do, there are
few books he can read on the subject. If he is interested
in the musical stage generally, there are books available,
but few concerning themselves with the American musical stage. As a matter of fact, only two works deal with
the history of America's musical comedy; both begin with
The Black Crook, in 1866. Both ignore, for reasons neither
gives, the history of the musical in America up to that
date.

A few books and articles have handled different facets
of America's early drama. Yet each has missed a significant fact: America's early theatres were essentially lyric
theatres. In eighteenth-century England a new stress on
musical productions was gradually absorbed into other
dramatic traditions. In America no earlier dramatic forms
existed, and the musical stage became our only theatrical
tradition. No one work has put together all the elements
which made up America's early musical stage, and yet it
is possible that only by looking at the theatre in its en-
tirety—the entertainments related to the stage, the theatres, the theatre orchestras, the companies, the repertory,
the librettists and composers, the critical milieu—can
America's early drama be seen for what it was: the beginning of a tradition of musical drama.[1]

And so the following pages have assorted purposes.
They explore an area of American culture in which almost
no previous work has been done. They set back the date
for the first American musical comedy more than seventy
years. They suggest that today's American musicals, far

from being recent phenomena, are a heritage from the eighteenth century.

As focal point for this study of the origins of America's musical stage, as a means of making clear how all the elements worked together in an actual production, I have used William Dunlap and Benjamin Carr's musical of 1796, *The Archers*. Called an opera in its own day, it would be called a musical or a musical comedy today.

The Archers is useful for several reasons. It is the first extant musical performed in America and written by Americans. Its first performance was in the John Street Theatre, New York, which was entering its last season after having been open for thirty years, covering the most important years of the beginnings of the drama in America. The theatre orchestra was composed of the best musicians of the day and represented the culmination of efforts to build a good, professional theatre band in New York. The Old American Company, which performed *The Archers*, had been in existence about half a century, was one of the two best acting companies in the United States, and was composed of actors, singers, and dancers renowned in England and France as well as native-born Americans.

Today the musical stage flourishes. "Musical comedy is the form that makes the most extensive use of theatrical convention in our time, and something of its theatrical vitality must stem from the fact." [2] Conventions are not created for particular productions—they evolve slowly. And the conventions which fill today's musicals with theatrical vitality began their movement in time on the stages of America in the eighteenth century.

No study of this kind could possibly have been written without the generous help of many people. Professor

Lewis Leary of Columbia University devoted a great deal of time and effort both to the book and to its intractable author. Professor Eric Bentley of Columbia read portions of the manuscript and proffered both suggestions and encouragement. Research was begun at Columbia University in the seminar of Professor Maurice Valency, to whom the author owes a debt of gratitude for the interest he took in the topic and the guidance he gave in the book's early stages.

I am grateful to Dr. Carleton Sprague Smith of the Music Division and to Mr. George Freedley of the Theatre Collection of the New York Public Library for their suggestions and help, and to the staff of the New York Public Library. Valuable help was provided by Robert Barlow and the staff of the library at Yale University; Helen Willard and Mary Reardon Keating of the Harvard University Theatre Collection and the staff of the Harvard library were also generous with time and aid. The staffs of the Columbia University library, the Library of Congress, and the library of the University of Pennsylvania were unfailingly helpful and kind. Time for research and for writing was provided by a Hofstra College faculty fellowship. I should also like to thank Miss May Davenport Seymour of the Museum of the City of New York, the staff of the New York Historical Society, and the Players Club for both access to their collections and assistance.

And I am not sure there would have been any book at all were it not for my secretary, research assistant, file clerk, typist, proofreader, and editor—my wife.

J. M.

C. W. Post College
Brookville, New York
1962

Contents

THE AMERICAN
MUSICAL STAGE

I

Entertainments Related to the Musical Stage

On April 18, 1796, *The Archers, or Mountaineers of Switzerland,* a new musical, written and composed by Americans, was to be presented at the venerable John Street Theatre. The doors opened forty-five minutes before curtain time, and the wise members of the audience planned to arrive early, as places in the gallery, in the pit, and even in the boxes were unreserved. On the way to the playhouse, a theatregoer, musing upon the variety of entertainments available to him in New York, might have noted that almost all were musical. A little more reflection would have impressed upon him that all were closely related to the theatre.

The eighteenth-century musical was performed before an audience used to music in almost all of its entertainments, public and private, amateur and professional. If, in mid-twentieth century America, music has become, as Jacques Barzun has put it, a "passionate avocation," [1] it was scarcely less so in the eighteenth century. Not only were most entertainments musical, but these musical entertainments exerted a powerful influence on the growth of America's stage.

1

New York in the 1790's was an impressive city. Travellers compared it to Paris, to London, and to one it seemed like Venice, "gradually rising from the sea." [2] Its population grew during the decade from 33,000 to 44,000, and visitor after visitor found the hospitality and friendliness such as to rank New York "the most agreeable place I have visited in the United States: nor am I singular in this opinion, there being scarcely any traveller I have conversed with, but what gives it the same preference." [3] This most cosmopolitan of American cities offered an assortment of amusements. Even before the Revolution, concerts, drama (in all its forms), puppet shows, comic lectures, outdoor gardens, jugglers, musical clocks, magicians, and acrobats were available to New Yorkers; the post-Revolutionary period added wild animals for show, equestrian exhibitions, circuses, dances, and slack-rope performers. [4]

Yet New York was not the only city with a profusion of entertainments. Throughout the South one could enjoy, in addition to the theatre, dancing, gambling, hunting, cockfights, gouging matches (in which the loser could save his eyes by shouting, "King's Curse," or simply, "Enough"), horseback riding, fiddling, horse racing, festivals (which included races, fights, beauty contests, violin contests, barbecues, music, singing, dancing, and drinking), balls, illuminations, and lavish dinners. [5] Even small towns such as New Haven enjoyed an astonishing assortment of amusements; and almost any occasion was enough to bring out nascent Barnums. Commencement days at Harvard, William and Mary, Yale, Dartmouth, and other colonial colleges, for example, were festive enough to provide all sorts of entertainments.[6] In the seventeenth century public opinion had been hostile to the theatre, but by the end of the eighteenth century so many amusements had arisen that one finds a plea in 1794 for a well-regulated stage on the grounds that it helps to eradicate other, "low" forms of entertainment.[7]

These "low forms," these scattered, bastard amusements paved the way for the entrance of Melpomene and her sisters. Puppet shows, curiosities, dissolving views, and rope dancing were popular forms of entertainment here well before the beginning of anything resembling legitimate drama.[8] In fact, George C. D. Odell is right in saying that "the theatre cannot be disassociated in treatment from other forms of amusement. Actors from the earliest days here appeared frequently in concerts or in entertainments of various sorts."[9] A letter to the editor of the New York *Journal*, December 27, 1794, shows something of the nature of these entertainments: "Pursue the gay and jocular companion through his weekly round of pleasures—On Monday evening at the play, Tuesday at Piken's public dance, Wednesday at Ricketts's Circus, Thursday to see Gibonne and Coco, Friday Seely's long room, and Saturday's theatre closes the week of mirth. . . ."[10] With the possible exception of Thursday, the gentleman could attend musical programs every night of the week, and the probability is that on Sunday in church he heard a fine organist and soloists from the theatre. Theatre people performed for him six days a week, and not always in a theatre. The gentleman's week reveals both its musical nature and how close the gentleman was at all times to the musical stage.

2

The closest possible interaction existed between the concert and the drama.

Before the Revolution, concerts were given by itinerant or resident musicians. Concerts leaned heavily on operatic music, and with good reason.[11] For one thing, enemies of the stage found music relatively innocent, "and it is likely that many whose scruples would not permit them to enter the theatre were foremost in their championship of the various musical activities. . . ."[12] The result was that musicians and actors had frequently to turn to the concert hall as a means of keeping alive. "This grew into a custom, and from now on the history of our early concert-life became closely affiliated with the history of the opera."[13] And not only with the opera: magicians, readings from plays, even fireworks were used to attract audiences to concerts. All of the musicians were expected to perform both at the theatre and at concerts, and one frequently finds as many as four stars from the theatre at a given concert.[14] The concerts themselves frequently included musical entertainments from the theatre, dramatic recitations, and even the music from favorite pantomimes.[15] A visitor to New York in 1793 was delighted with the voice of Mrs. Pownall (a leading actress of the day) and was pleased to hear her sing "at the play, the concert, and at Trinity Church."[16] There were not enough well-known musicians to attract audiences to concerts, and theatre people added the necessary glitter to fill concert halls. In fact, in 1793 all four leading ladies of the Old American Company were singers (two of them having made their New York debuts in concerts), and all four appeared regularly in the concert life of the city.[17]

And so the fact that the same performers appeared both in concerts and in the theatre tended to support the union of the two forms of entertainment, with numerous hybrid results. Not only were some concerts given in the theatre, but songs and scenes from the theatre were performed at concerts; the same performers appeared in each. The marriage was a significant one.

Before 1800 a music lover had a choice of five different types of concerts to attend. He could go to individual concerts, subscription concerts, the concerts of various music societies, or outdoor concerts. And if he or his friends were musically inclined, there was a variety of private concerts given at home all the year round.

The European concert had grown from private assemblages, and indeed the very appellation "chamber" music was originally used only to differentiate between private and public music-making. In America players appeared in public as well as private performances; early in this country's history amateurs who appeared in public often entertained in private homes as well.[18] Everywhere the traveller went, he was entertained by his hosts with music. When Francis Goelet visited Boston in 1750 he was entertained by the daughter of his host performing on the harpsichord, and later by a "consort" in which his host and others played "one Indifrent, Small Oargen, one Base Violin, one German Flute, and Four small Violins. . . ." He visited a country house outside Salem and noted the fact that the house was complete with gallery for musicians.[19] When Sir John Wentworth, provincial governor of New Hampshire, visited William Bayard in 1767 he recalled especially Miss Bayard's "harpsichord and voice." That this private interest in musical matters, these private concerts, continued at least through the last years of the century, is attested to by the number of impromptu concerts mentioned in diaries of the time.[20]

But suppose the music lover had preferred to hear a semi-professional concert, one given in public. Here the music societies took over, and here the origin branches off somewhat from European music societies. The latter began as aristocratic organizations which gradually permitted the entrance of professional musicians. Eventually, the middle class, too, began to join these private academies which became the most important centers of musical life.[21] In America the way was paved, oddly enough, by the clergy, who established singing societies in an attempt to improve psalm singing in church. One immediate result was the establishment of church choirs, but the idea of music societies took root and grew until the large semi-professional organizations of the late eighteenth century were developed. Societies which were exclusively choral in nature rose quickly, such as the Uranian Society of Philadelphia and the Musical Society of Yale College. If these singing societies, formed by the clergy, are accepted as the precursor of regular music societies, then it is not surprising to find New England leading the way, with the establishment of singing societies after about 1720.[22]

But they were not limited to New England. Dr. Alexander Hamilton attended a concert by the "Musick Club" in New York in 1744.[23] The St. Cecilia Society, founded in Charleston in 1762, has been called the first musical society in America [24] (largely, one suspects, because of its fame, importance, and achievements rather than because of historical precedence). In any case, "the St. Cecilia Society formed until the end of the eighteenth and far into the nineteenth century the center of Charleston's musical life as it found expression in concerts." [25] Just as in eighteenth-century France almost every town had a concert society in which amateurs and professionals met to play together, so Philadelphia had an Orpheus Club as early as 1759, Charleston had an Orphaeus Society in 1772, and Boston had a flourishing Music Society in 1786; [26] and there were music societies in Concord, Baltimore, Fredericksburg, Boston, and Newport before 1800. There were occasional competitions between the musical societies.[27] (The practice continues today, and it is tempting to imagine a World Series between, say, the Milwaukee Mozarts and the Boston Brahms.)

There must have been intra-city rivalry, too, at least for attendance at concerts, since we know the larger cities frequently had several music societies. The New York of 1796, of Dunlap and Carr's *The Archers,* had seen the birth and death of a whole collection of these societies, but four of them were still functioning actively in the year of Dunlap and Carr's opera: the Columbian Anacreontic Society (founded in 1795 by John Hodgkinson, leading actor and singer of the Old American Company, and President during all four years of the Society's existence), the Calliopean Society, the St. Cecilia Society, and the Harmonical Society. Evidently New York found four societies not quite enough, since both the Haydn Society and the Polyhymnian Society were organized before 1800.[28]

In the last years of the eighteenth century New York's public concert life moved from winter to summer; [29] it is possible that the competition between the many winter concerts given by music societies helped to cause this shift, and helped to add to the amount of good music available to New Yorkers, at least for such citizens as were invited to these exclusive functions. The societies frequently put notices of meetings in the newspapers, and

at least one letter to the editor criticized the concert itself, thereby affording a glimpse of program and performers.[30] The program was similar to the public concerts being given at the time, and the outstanding performers
were those whose names could be read at the top of the
playbills for the John Street Theatre. There must have
been a certain satisfaction in attending these invitation
concerts and in ignoring the public ones; the fashion-
minded Miss Bleecker mentions going with her parents
to three music society concerts in four months.[31]

Another type of concert offered to an eighteenth-century audience—that given by subscription—also had its
roots fairly early in the century. The subscription concerts
presented the same performers and programs as other
concerts, but were distinctive in the manner in which
they were organized. One or a group of musicians placed
advertisements in newspapers asking for subscribers to
one or a series of concerts; they gave their presumably
well-known names, and the places where subscriptions
could be purchased. When enough subscribers had assured them of financial success, they announced the program (for the first, if more than one concert) and then
ran this advertisement until the day of performance,
hoping to fill all remaining seats. Prices were, of course,
cheaper for those who bought tickets for the entire series.
Frequently the prices were less for women, too, if they
were brought by a man.

The first attempt to establish a series of concerts probably occurred in Charleston in 1732, soon after that city
heard its first public concert. Philadelphia heard subscription concerts in the 1760's, though they may have begun
there considerably earlier; the next stride forward in
Philadelphia's subscription concerts came with John Bentley (subsequently leader of the orchestra of the Old

American Company), who in 1783 founded the "City Concerts," a series which ran fortnightly until eleven had been given in the first series. A Stephen Deblois ran subscription concerts in Boston all through the 1760's and 1770's.[32] New York's first subscription series occurred in 1760; it was started by Alexander Dienval and W. C. Hulett, the latter a dancer, violinist, and sometime orchestra leader of the Old American Company. By 1794 New York had two sets of subscription concerts and each featured singers from the theatre. These two groups united in 1795 to form New York's "City Concerts,"[33] though by 1796 two different subscriptions had again been launched.[34] At the beginning of the year, despite competition from individual concerts, the Van Hagens and Messrs. Rausch and Moller advertised their "Old City Concerts." When enough subscriptions had been received, they announced their first program; altogether, four different concerts were given in this series, running from January 12 to February 16. By December subscriptions were being taken for two series: one group called itself the "City Subscription Concerts," and was run by Hewitt, Rausch, and Saliment; the other group, the Old City Concerts, was now run by Moller alone.[35]

Open-air concerts had been popular in America since the 1760's. Most often they were mixed with so many other forms of entertainment and were so heavily theatrical in nature that they formed almost a separate category. New York boasted this form of entertainment in 1796, too.[36]

And now suppose the music lover to have decided on a public concert. He has not been invited to a society's concert; it is not summer, so there are no outdoor concerts; his friends do not play instruments, so he cannot listen to a private concert; and he does not care to buy a subscription. He, nonetheless, has a wide choice as he selects an individual, public concert to attend; here, too, he has the satisfaction of knowing that his country's public concert life extends almost as far back as that of Europe. Most European music of the past had been centered in the courts; only in England had music wandered from the court and meandered into public theatres, concert halls, and pleasure gardens.[37] On the continent, "The musical institutions of the baroque era (which ended about 1730) can be described negatively by the lack of public concert hall and the concert audience. The distribution of music relied almost entirely on private circles. . . ." [38] But in England John Banister, a violinist, arranged the first public concerts, in 1672. The form of these concerts of Banister established the basis for those later given in America, but it must be remembered that when introduced here (1729 is the earliest date we have) they were still a comparative novelty in Europe; Vienna, for example, did not have a public concert until 1728.[39]

The third decade of the eighteenth century, then, saw the beginning of public concert life in America. Before 1730 one finds only occasional references to concerts, and most of these are restricted in nature, such as the concert in Philadelphia in 1700 given by the Wissahicken hermits at the consecration of Gloria Dei, or the concert reported at Fort George by John Sharpe in 1710.[40] The 1730's found concerts launched in all major American cities. A public "Concert of Musick on Sundry Instruments" in Boston in 1729 first attested to experience with this form of entertainment. Boston and Charleston listened to public concerts in 1731 and 1732, and New York began having public concerts about 1735 or 1736.[41] Of the larger cities only Philadelphia lagged behind; her first recorded public concert was in 1757, though she had private concerts before then, such as the Handel concert mentioned in the *American Weekly Mercury* in 1734.[42] Of all the cities beginning to have public concerts, however, Charleston's growth was the most rapid. By 1737 concerts had been given in the playhouse; many concerts had been arranged by John Salter, Henry Campbell, and a Mr. Cook; Charleston had had her first song recital, and had seen the first attempt in the colonies to establish a series of concerts.[43]

The 1740's saw no new events in the history of the concert in America but instead a tremendous expansion in the number of concerts given and in the places where they appeared.[44] The 1750's revealed the tendency of concerts to rely more and more heavily upon the theatre, both for performers and for repertory[45] (it is no coincidence that this change in concerts was coeval with the arrival from England of Hallam's Company, which under the name of the Old American Company was still flourishing in 1800), and this tendency prevailed through the end of the century. The 1760's continued the trends already noted, though perhaps worthy of mention is "the first American composer's concert," featuring the music and the performance of Giovanni Gualdo, in Philadelphia in 1769.[46]

There were fewer amusements during the American Revolution, but the 1780's found the concerts picking up with increased rapidity and range and without the infusion of amateurs so common before. Opposition to the theatre forced the advertising of operas as concerts, and George Washington attended "concerts" in Philadelphia at which such "operas" as *The Tempest* (as altered by Dryden) were given.[47] By the 1790's even Boston had, reluctantly, withdrawn its objections to the theatre, and concerts went back to being concerts. The last decade of the eighteenth century saw an increased influx of musicians to the United States from all over the world, many of them men of high repute abroad. The composer of *The Archers,* Benjamin Carr, arrived in Philadelphia in 1793 and began to give concerts there.[48] In addition to their chores at the theatre, more and more actors gave concerts, and in New York during the 1793-94 season "every leading musical performer in the city indulged in at least one concert ere the winter waned." [49]

When the theatre season was over, instrumentalists and singers took to the road (when not travelling with the mother company) to give concerts in communities too small to support a theatre. William Priest, musician with the Chestnut Street Theatre in Philadelphia, gave, in August, 1794, some idea of their perambulations: "Having a few weeks vacation at the theatre, we agreed upon a scheme to give three concerts at Lancaster, a town in Pennsylvania, about seventy miles west of this city. Our band was small but select; and our singers Darley, and Miss Broadhurst. . . ." [50] The two singers named were amongst the most popular actors in America in the eighteenth century.

One finds a rich concert life all over the United States by 1796. Miss Arnold (later the mother of Edgar Allan Poe) gave concerts in Portsmouth, New Hampshire, and Newport, Rhode Island, in 1796.[51] West and Sully, both theatre managers and performers at other times, gave a "Grand Concert" in Savannah in August of this year; and Mrs. Pownall, the actress, gave a concert in the theatre on March 21. The ubiquitous Miss Arnold and her mother turned up at one of a great number of Boston concerts in the same year.[52] And New York, not content with private and subscription concerts galore, featured at least two concerts given by Miss Broadhurst,[53] the same lady who played the part of Rhodolpha in Dunlap and Carr's *The Archers*.

The theatregoer on his way to John Street passed the tavern where he was accustomed to buy his concert tickets. Generally he bought them in advance, since both theatre and concert hall discouraged purchasing tickets at the door. If he obtained a single ticket he probably paid about one dollar for it, a figure that remained more or less the same all through the eighteenth century, though, as mentioned earlier, prices were less for an entire series or for women with men.[54] Generally this dollar entitled him to listen to the music, to enjoy some refreshments, and to dance at the ball afterwards. The first English concerts had originally cost one shilling and "call for what you please," but later an annual subscription fee of ten shillings provided the concertgoer with coffee at a penny a dish. The custom of serving food at concerts evidently continued in America at least until 1799, for Miss Bleecker, in her entry for January 24, says, "Peter Stuyvesant brought me some Cakes from the Concert—." Nor was the ball after the concert original here; our very early concerts included them, though there is some evidence that the custom was beginning to die by the end of the century.[55]

If one were prompt one probably arrived a few minutes before seven. The hour from six to seven seems to have been the most desirable time for commencing a concert all through the eighteenth century; and most New York concerts in 1796 began at seven. Once inside, say, the Assembly Room, William Street, the chances of hearing the music were evidently not ideal. A letter by X.Y.Z. to the New York *Gazette, or Weekly Post-Boy*, December 27, 1764,[56] complains with indignation of

the strange Behaviour at the Concert, of a certain set of
Males and Females, to whom, out of mere Complaisance
to their appearance, I will give the soft Appellation of
Gentlemen and Ladies—I am a dear Lover of Music and
can't bear to be disturbed in my Enjoyment of an Enter-
tainment so polite and agreeable.—How great then is my
Disappointment and Vexation, when instead of a Modest
and becoming Silence, nothing is heard during the whole
Performance, but laughing and talking very loud,
Squawling, overturning the Benches, etc.

These objections were not unusual, for it was common
for conversation to continue during the performance of a
concert. Thanks to the ball after the concert, dress was
generally elaborate, though the same was not true of concerts in smaller towns. In Lancaster, William Priest mis-
took three gentlemen for servants because of their dress;
however, things were better in Hanover, he says, since no
man there could enter without breeches, and no man
could dance without a coat.[57]

As far as the music itself was concerned, the eighteenth
century managed to thoroughly blur the distinction between serious music and light music.

The most distinguished of musicians composed and took
part in the performance of dance music, out-door music
and music played during meals. Court orchestras were
at the same time the equivalent of the modern concert
orchestra, the theatre orchestra, the dance band, the restaurant band and the open-air promenade band. The
same composers wrote the music for all of them.[58]

Though mixed in nature, concert programs in the eighteenth century both before and after the Revolution offered the best foreign music of the day. An excellent
example is the fact that Handel's *The Messiah* was introduced to a New York audience in 1770, one year before

Germany heard it.[59] Many concerts revealed peculiar programs and included everything from dramatic recitations to magicians to entire scenes from popular ballad operas; but orchestral music was plentiful, and such masters as Corelli, Vivaldi, Purcell, Haydn, and Handel were well represented, as later in the century were Gluck and Mozart. Nonetheless, for most of the eighteenth century the orchestra was considered an adjunct to vocal or solo music, and this vocal music was "largely drawn from operas and oratorios, popular songs, and catches and glees." [60]

An interesting concert took place on November 15, 1796, in New York (at which no less than four members of the cast of *The Archers* performed).[61] The music included a *Sinfonie* by Pleyel, and the Finale of the concert was by Haydn; in between, Miss Broadhurst sang "The Waving Willows," a "Bravoura Song," and "The Cheering Rosary"; Mr. Tyler sang "The Cottage of the Grove" and joined Miss Broadhurst in "O come, sweet Mary, come to me"; they were joined by Mr. Johnson and Mr. Lee in a glee. In addition to all this, Mr. Moller played a piano concerto, the Messrs. Saliment and Hewitt (leader of the John Street Theatre's orchestra) played a concertante for flute and violin, Mr. Saliment played a flute concerto, and the orchestra played a "Battle Overture," probably written by Hewitt. The program was in two acts (almost all eighteenth-century concerts were in two or three acts) and was followed by a ball conducted by Mr. Hulett.

The program was probably not as long as it sounds, since the custom was to advertise an entire symphony, even though only one or two movements were actually played. The custom earlier in the century had been to play the first movement of a symphony as overture, fol-

lowed by other works, and then the final movement of
the first symphony as Finale,[62] but this had given way,
presumably in favor of more variety.

By 1800 the day of a concert given by a single individual had not yet arrived; "on the contrary, the greatest
excitement came with an evening containing both new
talent and old friends alternating and combining into a
veritable vaudeville." [63] The concert orchestras were generally fairly small, but since Concerti Grossi (concertos
for several solo instruments with orchestral accompaniment) were mostly played and these only required about
a dozen musicians, the concert orchestras did not need
to be larger.[64] That these orchestras were small from
choice rather than scarcity of talent is easily shown by
two huge concerts: a Boston concert in the 1770's featured over 50 performers, and a Philadelphia concert of
1786 managed to assemble an orchestra of 50 and a chorus
of 230! [65]

A correspondent of the New York *Daily Advertiser*
(March 31, 1796) wrote of the Columbian Anacreontic
Society's Ladies Concert (which, incidentally, included
no less than five actors from the Old American Company) [66] and gave a clue to the length of these concerts.
Advertised to start at seven, it broke up, he says, about
eleven (after refreshments, but no ball). The writer of a
letter to the New York *Argus* had attended another concert which began at seven, with dancing continuing till
after midnight; it is difficult to say when the ball began,
but three and a half to four hours is probable for the
length of the concerts themselves in eighteenth-century
America.[67] But the most interesting thing about the letter
to the *Argus* is the effect Miss Broadhurst's singing had
upon the author. She and other people from the theatre
were influencing concert life: they drew audiences to con-

certs, and they (and the tunefulness of songs from the lyric stage) helped form musical taste:

> As the directors have ever shown a disposition to give satisfaction, and as it becomes the duty of those who advocate and support the undertaking to point out the way which will most tend to promote it, I would express not only my own wishes but the wishes of a very great number of subscribers, that in a future arrangement of music for the evening, a greater share of vocal be introduced. The general taste for vocal music, and the reflection that we are not long to be delighted with the performance of Miss Broadhurst, excites the wish, that while we do possess the treasure, we may partake of its qualities in as great a degree, as her goodness is willing to indulge and gratify our desires.[68]

By 1800 concerts had been heard in New York, Philadelphia, Boston, and Charleston of the larger cities; in the small cities, concerts were given in Lancaster, Hanover, Savannah, Newport, Salem, Portland, Portsmouth, Annapolis, Baltimore, Williamsburg, Richmond, Fredericksburg, Alexandria, Norfolk, Petersburg, Bethlehem, Princeton, Newark, Trenton, New Brunswick, Albany, Cambridge, Charlestown, Providence, Concord, New London, and Hartford [69]—all this by 1800, and tied closely to the theatre. "It is safe to say that, whenever and wherever during the last quarter of the eighteenth century concerts of any importance were given in the small towns they generally were due to the enterprise of the musical members of theatrical companies just then performing at these places." [70]

3

The audience attending the performance of *The Archers* at the John Street Theatre had available other, more elaborate musical entertainment than that offered in the concert hall. Indoor circuses produced lavish musicals with the best performers of the day, combined feats in the arena with the action on stage, and in every way provided flamboyant models for the theatres' musical productions.

The eighteenth-century circus was a very different affair from the circuses of the past and the circus which was to come. Before 1700 the only meaning attached to the word was a "wall-encircled arena, with its slanting tiers of seats, its gaping multitudes of spectators, its horse, foot, and chariot races, its naval shows, its athletic combats, and its groups of gladiators clashing arms. . . ."[71] True, the component parts which make up today's circus also go far back in time; but it was the eighteenth century which began to draw the elements together, which began to establish the form.

Philip Astley, commonly considered the father of the modern circus, started as a professional soldier in the cavalry, then toured England awhile doing feats of horsemanship, and eventually set up an amphitheatre for equestrian shows in London.[72] He quickly advanced beyond horsemanship alone, and an early advertisement for one night's program clearly shows that he had soon assembled seventeen different people (and there may have been more, if outsiders were needed to work the puppets), to say nothing of horses and a zebra, to entertain in a variety of performances.[73] This early advertisement mentions, in addition to equestrian feats, slack-wire performances, puppets, animals, tumbling, clowns, juggling, and balancing, and even manages to stress new costumes and settings; the circus was launched.

The next decade formalized the circus, and the musical aspect grew from Mr. Astley's playing and singing atop a horse to the inclusion of a stage in the amphitheatre and the performance of ballets, harlequinades, and ballad operas. This form of the circus, an olio of horsemanship, clowning, tumbling, and lyric theatre, proved extremely popular in England, and almost simultaneously with its appearance there, one finds it spreading all over America. Isaac Weld, who was in America from 1795 to 1797, discovered "the amphitheatre [in Philadelphia] is built of wood; equestrian and other exercises are performed there, similar to those at Astley's." [74] The man primarily responsible for the introduction and growth of the circus in America was John Bill Ricketts, and Decastro, himself a noted performer in Astley's, said of Ricketts that his fame "excelled all his predecessors, and it is said he has never been surpassed." [75]

But if Ricketts was the first to introduce the eighteenth-century's version of the circus to America, he was not the first to introduce its backbone, fine and fancy horsemanship. Equestrian feats of all sorts had established themselves here as legitimate forms of entertainment by 1771.

John Sharp did trick horsemanship in this year as did a Mr. Faulks and "a Yorkshire man" in Boston. [76] In 1772 Mr. Jacob Bates, another equestrian, could be found in Philadelphia, whence he travelled to New York in 1773 (where he varied his performance with clowning, another essential element of the circus) and then to Boston. Thomas Pool is often credited with the introduction of the circus to America. His first circus, in 1785, was in Philadelphia, where his performances consisted of horsemanship, with a clown and fireworks thrown in for good measure. Pool opened his "Menage" in New York in 1786 (the clown giving way, later in the season, to a band of music) and another in Boston in the same year. [77]

But Ricketts, who arrived in America in 1792, combined a sense of showmanship (the circus gradually absorbed almost every extant form of entertainment during his career) with a willingness—nay, a mania—to travel and spread the knowledge of his new form of entertainment throughout America. One finds at least two circuses each in Philadelphia and New York during the eighteenth century bearing his name and at least one circus apiece in Norfolk, Charleston, Albany, Boston, and Hartford.[78] In 1798 he took his troupe as far north as Canada and gave a series of performances in Montreal.[79] From his first riding school in Philadelphia in 1792 to the burning of his Amphitheatre (which occurred inadvertently but appropriately during the Hell scene in the pantomime, *Don Juan*) Ricketts's contribution to the growth of the circus in America was both unique and important. He excelled as showman and as horseman, and his reputation was great enough so that the most eminent men of the country came to know him.[80] Ricketts constructed three different circuses in New York alone in the decade after his arrival: one on Greenwich Street, in back of his house, in 1793; one on Broadway, on the corner of Oyster Pastie Street (Exchange Alley), in 1794; and his last, on the west side of Greenwich Street, in 1797.[81] He and his chief competitor, Lailson, continued their activities to the end of the century and neither appears after 1800, when the reborn circus began to look a good deal more like that with which we are familiar today.

The New Yorker of the late 1790's probably attended the circus at the "New Amphitheatre" in Broadway, which was lighted by candles (indicating a roof) and held 1,500 spectators. Circuses must have been built large all over the colonies, since Cobbett, for example, makes reference to 1,000 spectators at a circus performance in Baltimore.[82] The success of these massive structures probably influenced the building of subsequent theatres and elicited from William Dunlap the comment that "Another evil flowing from large theatres, is that desire to fill them, which has induced the shameful exhibitions of monsters and beasts, and other vulgar shows." [83] Dunlap may have put the cart before the equestrian, but at the very least he reveals an interaction between circus and theatre.

The amphitheatre was constructed of wood, and most pictures of the circuses of the day, both English and American, indicate the fact that the building was probably circular.[84] The interiors were decorated as lavishly as possible. Charles Hughes, a rival of Astley in London (and, according to Decastro, the teacher of Ricketts), had added a stage to his amphitheatre by about 1783; in 1794, when Astley rebuilt after his circus had been demolished by fire, he, too, included a stage.[85] A picture of Astley's shows a circular ring a few feet from an ordinary stage, the space between filled with musicians and the whole surrounded with tiers of boxes for the audience. It is known that the circuses in America were also completely equipped for theatre performances.[86]

Dickens, though writing at a slightly later period, offers some help in picturing the interior of an English circus:

> Dear, dear what a place it looked, that Astley's; with all the paint, gilding, and looking-glass; the vague smell of horses suggestive of coming wonders; the curtain that hid such gorgeous mysteries; the clean white sawdust down in the circus; the company coming in and taking their places; the fiddlers looking carelessly up at them while they tuned their instruments, as if they didn't want the play to begin, and knew it all beforehand.[87]

Ricketts was also lavish in decorating his amphitheatres in America. In 1796 he advertised paintings in his Amphitheatre, the arms of each state over each box, the arms of the United States opposite the stage, Commerce and Agriculture on the front of the stage, different flags between each box round the circus, and "A toute of Scenery, extremely interesting." [88]

Tickets were generally purchased in advance (at, for example, Mr. Hunter's Hotel), though, unlike the theatre, they were also available at the Amphitheatre. The prices, in New York as elsewhere, were one dollar for box seats and fifty cents for the pit.[89] Most New York circus performances in 1796 began at seven or seven-thirty, though those given at an earlier date in New York and in smaller cities frequently started earlier. It is difficult from the programs to say how long the performances ran; however, John Anderson, who lived only a few blocks from Ricketts's Amphitheatre, mentions arriving home from the circus some time after eleven.[90] Performances were generally given three times a week, on alternate nights with the theatre; when the theatre was closed, the circus moved its nights of performance to Monday, Wednesday, and Friday.

Once inside the circus, an incredible variety of entertainment awaited the visitor to Ricketts's Amphitheatre. Just as Philip Astley's early productions had included nothing but horseback performances accompanied by two fifes and a drum, all of which gradually gave way to a wide range of spectacles (by 1799 Astley was showing pantomimes, melodramas, spectacular pieces, and ballets),[91] so in America the pattern was similar. John Bill Ricketts performed Astley's function in this country, sometimes adding innovations before Astley did; and it was the year 1796 which marked the transition in the life of the circus in America. At this time Ricketts advertised both horsemanship and stage performances, and "For years thereafter, dramatic shows formed part of the circus bill." [92] He began advertising in New York on May 5 for his first performance of the season which was to include "Equestrian Exercises, Tight rope dancing, [and] ground and lofty tumbling." [93] On May 9 his advertisement included music, and by May 17 his circus featured Chinese fireworks and a clown (Mr. Spinacuta). The omniverous circus had swallowed Italian shades by May 21, dancing by May 23, an exhibition of paintings by June 4, harlequinades by June 9, Chinese shades and pantomimes (the eighteenth-century singing variety) by June 20, and a series of "Grand Pantomimes" with new music by June 25. Other additions included more original (plus those already well-established) pantomimes, horse races, spectacles, interludes, concertos, songs. Both while the circus was in the Amphitheatre and during its absence, full concerts were given there. [94]

New York was not the only city to have drama served up in the circus in 1796; Ricketts's season in Philadelphia, which began on October 12, included thirty-two different dramatic entertainments, mostly musical in nature. Lailson opened his "New Circus" in Philadelphia in March of 1798 with a French opera by Sedaine, *The Deserter*, and Ricketts countered by opening in May with *La Servante Maitresse*, one of the most popular operas of the eighteenth century. Ricketts was not content with the presentation in 1796 of shadow figures (the last gasp of this particular form of entertainment); in 1799 he introduced puppets into his circus. Simple pantomimes and interludes gave way in the circus to concert music and full-length operas. [95] Eighteenth-century diarists referred to the dramatic piece they were going to see at the circus rather than those elements for which a circus is distinguished today. [96]

The fact that the circuses developed two separate companies, one for the arena and one for the stage, meant that several well-known theatre personalities were associated with them. The Sully family, a name important in the early history of the American drama, began its theatrical fortunes in the circus, and appeared in New York at Ricketts's in 1796. John Durang (one of the bowmen in the first performance of *The Archers*) joined Ricketts's menage and, with Mrs. Durang, stayed with the circus for years dancing, clowning, singing, painting scenery, and producing ballets. The theatre dynasty of the Placide family found Alexander Placide, the first of the line in this country, doing pantomimes in New York in 1792, a result of his training with Astley in London.[97]

The decision on the part of Ricketts to pre-empt for his circus the musical stage, hitherto reserved for the theatre, undoubtedly hurt the latter considerably. A correspondent to *The New-York Magazine* [98] noticed one night that the theatre's pit and gallery were filled but the boxes were empty and commented caustically that the "genteel" part of the community was with Mr. Ricketts. The circus's sumptuous productions hurt the attendance at those musicals put on by the theatres.[99] In Charleston "Mr. Lailson's very fine circus attractions (arranged in the bills as to be almost identical with the theatrical offerings) were such a thorn in the flesh . . ." that the theatre was finally forced to hire Lailson and get him to join the theatre company.[100] In Philadelphia, Wignell and Reinagle were forced to hire an acrobat and pantomimist in order to compete with Ricketts, and a controversy raged between the two companies over which was to have exclusive rights to Saturday night performances. Ricketts won.[101] In New York Dunlap's impractical partner, John Hodgkinson, suggested buying up all circuses as a means of cutting out the Old American Company's competition. Dunlap, unconcerned with monopolistic practices, wrote that "If *these* [Ricketts's and Lailson's circuses] were ours, cannot others be built? And if Circus's can be built which will answer as Theatres, cannot Theatres be built on similar plans?" [102]

No, the theatres could not readily provide the kind of magic that the circus was able to evoke, a magic unavailable anywhere else. And the proof was inside the Amphitheatre itself. Not, perhaps, in Swan's circus, a pathetic neophyte, which gives some idea of performances before Ricketts:

> After four, I came home and went with my brother to Swan's circus—2/ admitted us into a place call'd the Gallery, where we found ourselves amongst a parcel of Negroes and children. The equestrian hero was giving directions for mounting a horse, he next introduc'd a young lady, who rode round and leap'd a bar about two feet high,—two monkeys, who perform'd several tricks on the rope etc.—afforded us more entertainment.—Swan pretended to make his horse dance *Nancy Dawson,* which was play'd by a hand-organ and Violin. This wretched entertainment was drawn out to almost an hour and a half.[103]

But there was nothing "wretched" about Ricketts's performances. For one thing, the stage contained ramps leading to the arena, so that theatre and circus performances might occasionally be integrated, as Dickens's description of Astley's indicates they were:

> What a glow was that which burst upon them all, when that long, clear, brilliant row of lights came slowly up; and what the feverish excitement when the little bell rang and the music began in good earnest, with strong parts for the drums, and sweet effects for the triangles:

Well might Barbara's mother say to Kit's mother that the gallery was the place to see from, and wonder it wasn't much dearer than the boxes. . . .

Then the play itself: the horses . . . and the ladies and gentlemen . . . the firing, which made Barbara wink—the forlorn lady, who made her cry—the tyrant who made her tremble—the man who sang the song with the lady's maid and danced the chorus, who made her laugh—the pony who reared up on his hind legs when he saw the murderer, and wouldn't hear of walking on all fours again until he was taken into custody—the clown who ventured on such familiarities with the military man in boots—the lady who jumped over the nine-and-twenty ribbons and came down safe upon the horse's back— everything was delightful, splendid, and surprising! [104]

Delightful, splendid, and surprising! These might have been the talismans of Ricketts, too. The New York *Argus* of July 28, 1796, contains a description of Sully displaying equestrian feats at the Amphitheatre. Suddenly a voice from the audience demanded a chance to ride, too. Sully acquiesced, and a grotesque figure emerged from the audience, entered the ring, and mounted the horse with difficulty. In the midst of the audience's laughter, the figure stripped off his outer clothes and stood, atop the horse, revealed as Ricketts himself! Almost anything could happen at the circus, especially if it was colorful and musical.[105] The circus nourished America's musical stage, fed it ideas, vigor, performers, and popularity.

4

Before 1800 still another type of theatre was available. This one, it is true, opened only in the summer, but summer pleasure gardens, too, offered solid fare to those with a hunger for the musical stage.

The pleasure gardens of London augmented the theatres, circuses, and concert halls in providing scenes of musical activity; the principal gardens, Vauxhall (1732), Ranelagh (1742), and Marylebone (1738),[106] served as models for American open-air concerts. The American pleasure gardens began as imitations, but it was not long before the American variety changed the types of entertainments offered,[107] and the musical stage had found another outlet.

The history of pleasure gardens in America goes back well into the eighteenth century. New York had a Ranelagh Gardens (John Jones, proprietor) in 1766 which was laid out for breakfasting and evening entertainments; a complete band of music played Monday through Thursday evenings during the summer, and a dance hall was featured with dancing taught by John Trotter. The period from 1762 to 1767 in New York found a Vauxhall and a Ranelagh in operation, each offering food, concerts, entertainments, dancing, and so forth. Charleston's Vauxhall was open in 1767 and featured pantomimes and balls besides its concerts of vocal and instrumental music.[108] There is evidence of other summer gardens before the Revolution, though it was not until after peace had come with the British that summer gardens really began to flourish.[109]

New York had a Vauxhall in 1793, two Vauxhalls in 1797 (one of which was renamed Ranelagh in 1798), a new Vauxhall in 1798, and a Columbia Gardens in 1800, among others. There were many other gardens in New York during these years, but for the most part the kind of entertainment they provided is uncertain. Charleston's Vauxhall Gardens flourished from 1795 to 1800, with an excellent French orchestra, the whole under the management of the already-encountered equestrian and actor,

Alexander Placide. A Pennsylvania coffee house under Vincent Pelosi started summer concerts in 1786; other Philadelphia pleasure gardens included Harrowgate Gardens and Bush Hill, each of which gave summer concerts before 1800; a Vauxhall Gardens was located here, too, and was functioning by 1791. By 1800 Baltimore had competing concerts in rival gardens.[110]

The kind of entertainments seen at these pleasure gargens again brought the eighteenth-century gentleman near the musical stage. The earliest of the summer gardens featured organs, though orchestras of seven and later fifteen or more instruments were soon in use.[111] (Benjamin Carr, composer of *The Archers,* played in the orchestra of a pleasure garden in Philadelphia in the early 1790's.) Later the gardens stressed concerts and fireworks, and these concerts generally utilized theatre bands. The programs for the concerts, given in pleasure gardens were, as the regular concerts, heavily theatrical in nature and included actors from the theatre, dances, scenes, and songs from the musical stage representations. These programs usually lasted from four to five hours and cost one dollar.[112]

The competition between New York's chief pleasure-garden entrepreneurs, Joseph Corre and Joseph Delacroix, afforded the citizens of New York a rich bill of musical fare. The summer of 1798, for example, found Vauxhall (doing "grand Harmonical Music") in a competition with Ranelagh (with grand concerts "of Vocal and Instrumental Music"), and both of them nearly ousted from the field by the Columbia Garden ("The Concerts will be continued every night. . . .").[113] All three featured musicians, singers, and dancers from the theatre. Corre may have started straight dramatic entertainments (which usually meant musical comedies) at his theatre-in-gardens in 1791 (with *The Beaux' Stratagem* and *The Lying Valet*),[114] though by 1800 his Mount Vernon Garden was unquestionably giving theatricals three times weekly; summer dramatic performances generally began at nine, cost four shillings, and offered a full-length play or opera. These theatricals were always followed by concerts as well. The theatricals were frequently farces and musical shows, and the concerts were given by members of the Old American Company.[115] Theatrical performances at summer gardens proved popular enough to extend themselves well into the nineteenth century; the American musical stage had found yet another means of establishing itself.

5

The audience on their way to the John Street Theatre for the première performance of *The Archers* had still other musical stage entertainments available. They might go to a puppet show or shadow play. Puppets and shades played surprisingly large roles as outlets for the lyric theatre and as resources upon which the legitimate stage might draw for new elements.

Puppets, or marionettes, or fantoccini, or Punch and Joan (Punch's wife did not become Judy until the end of the eighteenth century) [116] were immensely popular in America almost from the time the first colonists arrived here.[117] The statement that "Puppets were to be the harbinger of the theatre in the New World . . ." [118] is probably accurate only insofar as it implies a continuing *theatrical* tradition, rather than the spasmodic early attempts of the theatre to find an outlet. In any case, almost the entire eighteenth century gives us records of puppet shows in America.

There is a record of strolling players setting up a puppet

show in New Haven in 1727 or 1737. Henry Holt's shows in South Carolina in 1734 and in New York in 1737 and the season of 1738-39 were probably puppet shows, too. And it is possible that the Playhouse in New York of 1733 was used for puppet shows.[119] There is definite record of marionettes in Philadelphia by 1742,[120] performing "An agreeable comedy or tragedy, by changeable figures of two feet high." [121] New York had a Punch show in 1743, and in 1747 saw a Punch opera—*Bateman, or the Unhappy Marriage*. Punch's Company of Comedians appeared in New York in 1749 in a specially-built room; these performances were given from July 25 through November 27, a run which tends to indicate some demand for their presence.[122] A mechanical puppet show was announced in New York by Richard Breckell, clock mender, in 1755.[123]

The 1760's disclose various puppet shows ranging the colonies: New York was entertained by one in 1767, Philadelphia in 1768, Boston in 1768, and Williamsburg in 1769.[124] The 1770's found the puppeteers in Philadelphia for the 1772-73 season, in New Orleans in 1771, Williamsburg in 1772, New York in 1770, and Annapolis in 1772.[125] New Haven saw shades exhibited in 1785, and Philadelphia in the same year. John Durang, dancer with the Old American Company, made the puppets for a series of Philadelphia performances in 1787, and Chinese and Italian shades were seen in that city in 1785 and 1790.[126] The final decade of the eighteenth century found puppets and shades performing everywhere in the colonies. In New York alone there were Chinese shades at 14 William Street in 1790, Signor Falconi's Chinese shades and Punchinello in 1795, Gonoty's Punch and Chinese shades in 1795, puppets during the 1796-97 season, Ombres Chinoises and Prussian fantoccini in 1799, as well as the fantoccini of Maginnis in the same year.[127]

Within a few months either way of the first performance of *The Archers,* there were puppets and shadow
plays in New York to add to the number of musical entertainments available. Ricketts's Amphitheatre featured
Italian and Chinese shades on May 21, and they were
still being shown by June 20. Though Maginnis and his
"Prussian Fantoccini" were in Boston in 1796, he would
perform at Ricketts's in a few years. Gonoty's Punch and
Chinese shades were also in New York, at Martling's Long
Room in Nassau Street.[128]

The puppets and shades represented still another aspect
of America's lyric theatre.

While shadow figures were old even in the eighteenth
century, it was Caran d'Arche who transformed the prim-
itive *ombres chinoises* into *ombres françaises* and Séraphin who began, in 1770, to amuse the children of Paris
with the first of these, *The Broken Bridge.* Records of
shadow plays in America go as far back as 1785, only
fifteen years after Séraphin, and in 1799 a New York playbill reveals the fact that *The Broken Bridge* was still a
major attraction.[129] Perhaps the best way to understand
the musical nature of the shadow plays is to inspect *The
Broken Bridge.*[130]

The play begins with the shadow of two arms of a
broken bridge arching over a stream, but failing to meet
in the center. (A 1790 print from Berlin shows a six-man
orchestra playing during the performance and guiding
their music to the actions on the screen in front of
them.) [131] Some ducks cross the water. A laborer enters
from the right and with his pick loosens some stones of
the bridge which fall into the water (one arm of the
laborer is on a separate pivot and is able to rise and fall).
As he works he sings, usually a traditional lyric about the
bridge of Avignon. A traveller appears on the left side of

the bridge and hails the nearly-deaf laborer who eventually notices him. The traveller wishes to cross the stream and asks the laborer how he may do so; the worker resumes his hacking away at the bridge and sings that animals swim over. The spoken dialogue and answering song continue as the traveller asks how far it is across; he is told, helpfully and in song, that "When you're in the middle you're halfway over." How deep is the stream? The sung answer informs him that if he'll drop a stone he'll soon find the bottom. A boatman (with his back on a pivot, so he can move in his boat) appears and offers the traveller a lift. Once on the water, the opportunity for slapstick situations is too rich to be missed, and the misadventures which follow include a crocodile who threatens to swallow the boat. Finally, the worker manages to dislodge so large a fragment of the bridge that he falls into the stream with it and is contentedly devoured by the crocodile. The cycle is rounded off as ducks and geese swim over the stream once more, and the curtain falls.

There were, of course, many other plays like *The Broken Bridge* (a popular English one had a collection of scenes in a haunted house),[132] but dialogue, songs, and musical accompaniment seem to have been invariable.

As far as the puppet shows were concerned, some were straight plays (with songs, and so forth between scenes), some were lampoons of popular operas, and some were operas themselves. The debt the musical stage owed to puppets is amply shown by the first presentation in Philadelphia of *The Poor Soldier*, a ballad opera so popular that not a season went by from 1786 through 1800 without at least one performance of the work by the Old American Company.[133] This work is in two acts, the first of which contains no less than ten airs (including duets) and the second nine airs (including a quartet and much chorus work).[134] Few operas contain as many arias, or musical comedies as many set numbers. And yet

> The first representation of *The Poor Soldier* in Philadelphia, was made through the medium of *puppets* [italics added] at a house in Second street . . . The puppets were made by John Durang. The dialogue and songs of the opera were conducted by some of the actors and actresses formerly belonging to the Southwark company. The puppet theatre was located in the third story, and it was crowded every night at fifty cents a ticket.[135]

Puppets and shades, then, were a great influence on the American theatre. They did not require a regular playhouse and so could spread drama throughout the colonies in "whatever assembly room, improvised hall, or barn they could find." [136] They were certainly a good deal easier to transport than a troupe of actors. The fact that puppet shows had been permitted to continue in England even after most theatres had been shut down [137] probably indicates the fact that in America, too, they were permitted in communities which banned the regular theatre. Their influence on the theatre extended into other areas. For example, "Artificial figures were another help to Ciceri [the foremost scene designer in America in the eighteenth century] and his painters in the realizing of spectacular processional effects." [138] Too, the theatre relied on the puppets' popularity and on the recognition of types in achieving such novelties as "A Punch's Dance by Master A. Hallam." [139] Even the beginnings of the minstrel show may be recognized in a puppet advertisement in 1767: "a Negro Dance, In Character." [140] The "Punch companies" did drolls and burlettas as well.[141] Operas, ballad-operas, dances, songs, drolls, burlettas—almost every form known to the musical stage of the eighteenth century, plus, as in the case of the shadow plays, some forms of their own; the American musical stage was surrounded by riches.

6

Dancing, inextricably a part of today's musical comedies, was also closely bound up with the lyric theatre in the eighteenth century. Local dances from all over the colonies quickly found their way to the stage, and audiences promptly adapted stage dances for their own amusement.

"Terpsichore usually preceded Thalia and kept her constant company in all the dramatic enterprises." [142] Certainly there was much dancing on the stage of both theatre and circus,[143] and many of the styles for social dancing were probably set in these places. The most popular dances of the day were the minuet, gavotte, sarabande, allemande, and waltz; reels and country dances, jigs and the quadrille were also performed. All concerts were followed by dances, using the entire theatre band and frequently attended by theatre people.[144]

Records of assemblies, balls, and quadrilles, go back in time.[145] In 1796 there were balls after each of the concerts already noted in addition to many assemblies given with no other excuse than themselves. "As to dancing, there are two assembly-rooms in the city, which are pretty well frequented during the winter season; private halls are likewise not uncommon." [146] By the end of the century there was no lack of dancing teachers, and most of them were people associated with the theatre.[147] For example, at least three different dancing schools existed in New York in 1796: those of Mme. Deseze, Mr. J. Mitchell, and Mr. Pickens.[148]

Aside from the fact that what was danced on the stage probably influenced what was danced at private assemblies, and aside from the fact that the same musicians appeared at each, and aside from the fact that it was theatre people, stars of the musical stage, who taught dancing to America, there is one further relationship between dancing in the colonies and America's lyric stage. John Bernard, a young actor newly arrived from England, speaks of his activities in Philadelphia near the close of the eighteenth century: "Balls and quadrilles occupied the intervening nights of the play: not to divide its attraction, but to make parties for its support. . . ." [149] Musical comedy stars had become ambassadors of good will for the adolescent theatre.

7

A few more scattered forms of musical entertainment also played a part in the development of the American lyric theatre.

Musical clocks, for example. In 1796 the New York *Argus* of July 28 noted a large exhibition of these machines and gave a rather full description of them. New York had been gazing with awe at these mechanical wonders since at least 1743, when a clock was advertised which performed the "choicest Airs from the celebrated Operas." [150] The New York *Mercury* for December 29, 1755, referred to a musical clock which depicted the puppet-opera, *Bateman*. [151] Even with clocks the musical stage breathed over one's shoulder; for one thing, these clocks performed the best music of the day (Corelli, Handel, etc.), and for another ". . . the itinerant musical clocks did much toward developing the love of good music in our people." [152]

Even readings, recitations, and lectures kept the eighteenth-century American close to the musical stage. As far back as 1767, when Douglass gave his famed lecture on heads, Mr. Woolls sang operatic music after each part.[153] Almost every extant lecture program shows that whenever the lecturer paused for breath, a singer filled the pause with song; and the lectures themselves were accompanied by music. There is some evidence that these lectures were accompanied by full bands.[154]

In the 1760's Hallam and Henry gave pre-season lectures in Philadelphia, and again Woolls sang at the lectures.[155] Boston heard Douglass lecture on heads in 1769 and in 1770 a gentleman who "read" the *Beggar's Opera* and sang the songs. "He read but indifferently but Sung in Taste." And in Portsmouth *Love in a Village* was "read" in 1769.[156] Charleston, too, had these lectures cum portraits cum "Music adapted to the subject," as did Savannah; the combination of lectures, recitations, and songs was popular in Annapolis and Baltimore, too.[157] They must have been reasonably profitable, since in at least two cases actors were permitted out of debtors' prison to deliver lectures; in both cases they were successful enough to remain free.[158]

Immediately after the Revolution, when most theatrical performances were banned, lectures "interspersed with songs, etc." served the very useful function of helping to keep the theatre alive in America. The final step in these bastard entertainments seems to have been the welding together of concerts and readings under an over-all title, such as the 1795 *Fashionable Variety, or, a Touch at the Times*.[159] As one might expect, the New York of the 1790's was not without this particular form of entertainment, either. The *American Minerva* for January 22, 1796, contains an advertisement of Mr. Powell (of the Boston theatre) for his entertainment in six parts to be given the following evening. It was called *The Brush* and included readings and songs which are listed in the advertisement.

Museums also brought a touch of the musical stage to the eighteenth century. Before the Revolution "museums were no more than cabinets of natural history or collections of curiosities . . . often assembled in fits of absentmindedness"; after the Revolution, they frequently absorbed puppet shows, curiosities, dissolving views, rope dancing, and the like.[160] New York's principal eighteenth-century museum was founded by John Pintard for the Tammany Society in 1790, though it was run by Gardner Baker.[161] An evening at Baker's Museum must have been a delightful way, musically and otherwise, to pass the time: "Here we heard some music and then proceeded to the *Menagerie,* and seated ourselves in Mr. Baker's little observatory.—Saw the exhibition of the magic lanthorn.— had mead and cakes and upon the whole passed the time very agreeably." [162]

Parades and hand organs in the streets and music clubs indoors also contributed musical entertainment.[163] Even a trained dog act could not venture far from the musical: the *American Minerva* of February 18, 1796, announced Gabriel Salenka and his trained dog; by the end of the month the dog act included "An Indian Dance. By four Indians now in the city." But in spite of all temptations the theatre remained the best place to go for the musical stage. There was one amusement for the lover of the stage on the night of April 18, 1796. A new opera was to be performed at the John Street Theatre, and the John Street Theatre was the place to be.

II

Theatres and Audiences

No composite description of eighteenth-century American theatres—the theatre season, the theatre exteriors and interiors, the stage equipment, the audiences that flocked to productions—exists, yet no understanding of the early American musical stage is complete without knowledge of these elements.

1

In 1796, when the theatregoer turned into John Street to attend the first performance of *The Archers*, one or more theatres existed in every city in the United States. William Levingston had received permission to construct the first theatre in the colonies for the Stagg family in Williamsburg in 1716; it was on Palace Green, near Bruton Parish Church, and its very first advertisements in the newspapers mentioned its need for musicians.[1] From this date, 1716, to the end of the century, new theatres cropped up all over the colonies.

At the beginning it was difficult to tell a theatre from someone's warehouse or store, and as much mist obscures the first permanent theatre in the colonies (that is, a building constructed for the purpose of showing plays) as obscures the first American play or American player. But

40

whether the first permanent theatre was built in Annapolis in 1753 or in Philadelphia in 1766,[2] theatre performances were given in some sort of building almost continuously from the 1730's until today.

After the first performances in a theatre were given in Williamsburg, a brief dramatic hiatus ensued. New York became the next city to house the fugitive drama, then Charleston, then Philadelphia,[3] then a host of smaller cities.[4] The performance of *The Archers* at the John Street Theatre had its way paved by the growth of theatre after theatre as they were permitted in cities all over the colonies.

Charleston's Court room and Council-Chamber were used for the first theatre season (1734-35), and her first theatre opened in February, 1736, on Dock (later called Queen) Street. A succession of theatres followed. The Dock Street Theatre burned down in 1740, and a new one was not built until 1754, though in the interim Shepheard's and two other taverns were used for entertainments. By 1763 Charleston had erected a new theatre on Queen Street, near the site of the old one. The largest theatre in the colonies during the early days was opened in Charleston in 1773, and *it* did not burn down until 1782. Charleston's next theatre, Harmony Hall, opened in 1786 and was placed just outside the city limits, where it functioned for two full theatre seasons before being converted to a kind of Vauxhall, although stray plays were given there occasionally through 1790. In the 1790's Charleston found herself with two theatres: The Charleston Theatre opened in 1793, and in 1794 a new Church Street, or City, Theatre raised its curtain; and the two ran stiff competition for each other through the end of the eighteenth century.[5]

Philadelphia, too, boasted (or rather bemoaned) an assortment of theatres before 1800. In 1749 a company used

Plumstead's warehouse for a theatre (though an indignant populace quickly ousted them, whereupon they made their way to New York).[6] Several companies had performed in the "New Theatre in Water Street," or Plumstead's warehouse, in 1754, for example. The "Theatre on Society Hill" was built in 1759. While the Southwark company was away, in 1769, students at the College performed plays, probably in the Assembly Room in Lodge Alley. Plays were given, or at least read, in the standard theatre substitute, taverns, when anti-theatre laws closed the Southwark after the Revolution. Harmony Hall, Northern Liberties, was used for plays for a few years after 1789.[7] But Philadelphia's two outstanding theatres were the Southwark (opened on November 14, 1766), and the Chestnut Street Theatre (opened for plays February 17, 1794).[8] A visitor to Philadelphia in 1795 found "there are two theatres and an amphitheatre . . ." though by then the Southwark was scarcely used at all.[9]

Boston had fewer theatres. That some interest in theatres was stirring early is evidenced by Increase Mather's attack on them in 1686 and the law passed in 1750 forbidding them.[10] An attempt to build a theatre in 1767 failed and was followed by another prohibitory law in 1784. The law was probably needed by that time, since Boston had tasted drama during the Revolution when Burgoyne's company turned Faneuil Hall into a theatre. Boston attempted one or two other theatres until the Blue Laws were argued to sleep in 1793.[11] Boston, like Philadelphia, possessed two theatres in the 1790's, the Federal Street (opened February 3, 1794) and the Haymarket (December 26, 1796). They went into devastating competition with each other till the Federal Street burned down in February of 1798 (though it was rebuilt and reopened by the end of October), and the Haymarket was demolished in 1803.[12]

Rhode Island, too, had its theatres in the eighteenth century. Providence provided its Court House for some performances in 1792, and Newport converted a brick market (built in 1762) to a theatre in 1793. In December of 1794 Newport had a regular theatre ready to receive actors, and Providence followed with its new theatre in 1795.[13]

Theatres sprang up in the smallest as well as the largest cities. A traveller of 1759, for example, found a company of actors performing in Marlborough, Maryland, in a theatre which was really "a neat, convenient tobacco-house, well fitted up for the purpose." [14] A greater number of actors began to be imported, and an outlet for their activities needed to be created; this outlet was found in decentralization. "Thus it happened that theatrical performances occurred in many small cities of the Union which, under ordinary circumstances, would hardly have been deemed sufficiently lucrative stations on the theatrical circuit." [15] Theatres were not always erected for these touring companies, but with surprising frequency they were.

After Williamsburg's 1716 theatre, interest waned there until 1747, when a new theatre was built near the capitol by public subscription. Williamsburg used either a new playhouse or an old storehouse for plays in 1752. Annapolis had a brick theatre by 1771, though theatre performances were seen there at least as far back as 1752.[16] Yet Annapolis audiences seemed to remain somewhat naïve in matters theatrical; when Fennell acted *Othello* there later in the century, a gentleman in a box got up and said "that he had never thought a negro could have been possessed of so much intelligence, and that if my master would sell me, he would give five hundred dollars for me that moment." [17] Baltimore opened her first theatre in 1782, and reopened it in 1793, then built the Holliday Street Theatre in 1794; and both were functioning in 1795, though "the oldest of them, which stands in the road to Fell's Point, is most wretched, and appears little better than a heap of loose boards. . . ." [18] Thanks largely to the students at Yale, Connecticut built a variety of theatres in the eighteenth century. Yale students gave performances, albeit privately, as far back as 1754; then a series of taverns were used for public performances in New Haven and Amity and Milford. A letter of 1774 indicates the possibility of a real theatre at the college in that year: James Hillhouse, writing to Nathan Hale, said, "Now we have a School of Drama and a wonderful mechanistic as well as artistic theatre to take the place of a room in a tavern. . . ." [19] Hartford opened a theatre in August, 1795. Savannah, New Orleans, Albany, New Bern, Detroit, Lexington, and Portsmouth all managed to erect theatres to house both regular and strolling companies during the late years of the eighteenth century. [20]

Finally, there is New York, where the John Street Theatre was destined to span the most important years of the growth of the drama in America and to operate regularly as a theatre longer than any other building in eighteenth-century America. But the history of the theatre in New York goes back farther than 1767. It begins in the years 1699-1702, when Richard Hunter petitioned the governor of New York for permission for himself and a company of actors to perform in New York. [21] In 1732 Rip Van Dam's warehouse (on Nassau Street near the junction of Pearl Street and Maiden Lane) was converted to a theatre, and performances were given in Hall's Long Room in 1739 and at the house of Governor Kip in 1743. Van Dam's "theatre" was evidently still in use as the Nassau Street Theatre in 1750; it was torn down in 1753 and another play-house built on the same spot. This theatrical activity took place in a city of fewer than 5,000 houses and a population of about 10,000.[22] In 1758 the Nassau Street Theatre had been put to other use, possibly as a church, and so a new theatre was erected by Douglass on Cruger's Wharf, "a large pier, with houses upon it, which at that time extended from Pearl Street into the East River, between Old and Coentries slips."[23] The Theatre on Cruger's Wharf was used for one year, and in 1761 with Governor Colden's permission a new theatre was built on the southwest corner of Nassau and Chapel (now Beekman) Streets, called the Chapel Street Theatre. It housed performances until 1766, when it was finally torn down.[24]

On December 7, 1767, the John Street Theatre, New York's leading playhouse for thirty years, was opened; it was located on the north side of the street, between Broadway and Nassau Streets, on the site of 15-21 John Street. During the Revolution General Howe's company acted in the John Street Theatre (only four months after he entered the city) until General Clinton's company took over in 1778; the theatre was in use by these military thespians from 1777 through 1783 as the "Theatre Royal."[25] After the Revolution, in 1785, it was again called the John Street Theatre,[26] and its productions were supplemented by theatrical performances in William Street in 1790 and operas in French at the City Tavern.[27] By 1796, when *The Archers* aided in rounding out the John Street Theatre's career, the roof was already on the new Park Theatre.[28] Hugh Gaine, long-time printer of tickets and playbills for the theatre, laconically noted in his journal for Saturday, January 13, 1798: "This Night the last of acting in the Old Theatre, John Street."[29] And on January 29 William Dunlap, author of *The Archers* and manager of the new theatre, noted in his diary that the New Theatre had opened. The contract for this theatre which was to function well into the nineteenth century specified that the John Street could not be used while the new theatre was in operation.[30] The old theatre was being led out to pasture. Sic transit indeed.

2

In 1796 the doors of the John Street Theatre opened, as a rule, at five-fifteen and the curtain rose at six-fifteen; the late approach of darkness as summer drew on, however, caused the managers to set curtain time back an hour; an advertisement in the New York *Diary*, April 13, 1796, announced the fact that for the rest of the season doors were to open at six and performances commence "precisely at 7." The circus, too, by late May was opening its door as late as six-thirty and commencing its performances at seven-thirty.[31] The six o'clock curtain time, usual in England in the 1700's, seems to have prevailed in all American theatres throughout the century, from Savannah to Charleston to New York, from 1735 to the end of the century. The only variation was in late spring performances, such as *The Archers,* and summer performances, such as those in Charleston in July of 1796, which began at eight.[32]

The chances are the audience would be home by midnight. A 1767 production of *The Beggar's Opera* took three hours and five minutes, *without* afterpiece.[33] John and Alexander Anderson, brothers who lived near the theatre, each occasionally noted in his diary the times he returned from John Street: on March 26, 1793, Alexander arrived home between eleven and twelve; on March 12, 1794, he got home about eleven; on February 23, 1797,

he noted that the theatre performance was over at eleven;
on February 29, 1796, John mentioned the fact that the
play was over at ten (perhaps an afterpiece was still to
come?); and on April 11, after seeing *The Maid of the
Mill* and *The Tempest,* he got home after eleven.[34] Four
to five hours was apparently the standard length of an
evening in the theatre in eighteenth-century America.

The days of performance were set with some rigidity.
From the beginning Monday, Wednesday, and Friday
were the three nights of performance each week, though
occasionally Saturday was either added to the week's performances or substituted for Friday. Thus, the second performance of *The Archers* was given on April 22, 1796, a
Saturday. When two theatrical troupes were in a city at
the same time, the second alternated nights with the first,
as Covent Garden and Drury Lane did at the start of each
season in London.[35]

The length of the season varied from city to city and
from time to time. Early in the century all companies
travelled and stayed in a given city as long, presumably,
as the receipts made it worth while. Later in the century,
when companies became identified with particular cities,
the seasons became of standard lengths. Summers might
be spent touring small cities, but the winter season found
the company home to roost. The home season, again parallel to the season in London, generally began in the au-
tumn; benefits began in the spring, and the season closed
in early summer.[36]

Prices had remained relatively unchanged throughout
the 1700's. Eight, six and four shillings (or one dollar,
seventy-five cents, and fifty cents) were the standard fees
for box, pit, and gallery respectively. These figures, with
some negligible variation, held all over the colonies. For
example: in Boston (though the Federal Street Theatre

was at one time forced to reduce its prices to fifty cents for the pit and twenty-five cents for the gallery); in Savannah (box and pit one dollar; gallery fifty cents); Charleston (six shillings, five shillings, three shillings six pence, reduced for summer performances to five shillings, four shillings, two shillings four pence); Philadelphia (seven shillings six pence, five shillings, and three shillings in the 1750's, upped to eight shillings, six shillings, and four shillings by the 1790's; Wignell and Reinagle attempted to raise the box and pit prices to a dollar and a quarter and a dollar, but lack of customers forced prices back down again); Providence (six shillings, three shillings, two shillings three pence, later raised to one dollar, seventy-five cents, and two shillings three pence, and still later forced down, in the pit and gallery, to fifty cents and twenty-five cents).[37]

Of course, the small strolling companies stopping at sparsely populated cities adjusted their prices accordingly; M'Grath, for example, charged fifty cents for all seats while in Reading, Pennsylvania, and children under ten were admitted at half price.[38] There is some evidence to indicate the possibility of season tickets being available.[39]

The New York prices had remained relatively stable; the 1735 price for a box was five shillings and remained at that level through 1751, except for a brief leap in 1750 to eight shillings, five shillings, and three shillings. In 1753 eight shillings, six shillings, and three shillings were tried, though they were rapidly forced down to six shillings, five shillings, and three shillings. In the 1760's the prices in New York had settled at eight shillings, five shillings, and three shillings; by the 1790's prices were eight shillings, six shillings, and four shillings, and they remained at this level until the end of the century.[40]

At the beginning, late-comers could pay half price for admittance, but the practice was abolished in 1753, well before the custom was given up in England,[41] and never renewed.

All seats were to be bought before the performance began, and no money was taken at the doors. A playbill for January 31, 1792,[42] states: "The Doorkeepers are positively prohibited taking Money at the Doors, unless in Exchange of Places, therefore Ladies and Gentlemen will be kind enough to supply themselves with tickets." Tickets were available at various taverns, book stores, printers (in New York at Hugh Gaine's at the Bible in Pearl Street), and at the box office of the theatre from 10 to 12 A.M. on days when there was no performance there and from 3 to 5 P.M. on days when a performance was to be given in the evening.[43] All this was a far cry from the days when actors had to go from door to door to sell tickets. Nonetheless, all problems involving tickets were not resolved by this system, since many reports exist concerning counterfeit tickets.[44]

3

A New York newspaper in 1787 had noted, "It is customary to have a dram shop in the neighborhood of theatres (as is the case in this city), where the audience, exhausted by attention to the performance, may recruit their spirits by taking a glass of gin, or something equally exhilarating, between the acts. . . ."[45] The dram shop probably added to the confusion caused by horses and carriages jamming the entrance. They had been a problem since 1767, when the John Street Theatre first opened; the New York *Gazette* of December 14, 1767, had suggested that "To prevent Accidents by Carriages meeting it is requested that those coming to the House may enter

John-Street from the Broad-Way, and returning drive from thence down John Street into Nassau Street, or forward to that known by the Name of Cart and Horse Street." [46] The problem had evidently not been solved by the last decade of the century as playbills show: ladies and gentlemen were requested "to order their Coachmen to take up and set down their Horses Heads to the East-River, to avoid confusion." [47]

When Jonathan, in Royall Tyler's *The Contrast,* attended the John Street Theatre in 1787, he had entered through "a long entry that had lanthorns over the door." [48] This entry, sixty feet long according to Dunlap, ran from the pavement to the doors of the theatre and was covered with rough wooden material. When the audience stood before the theatre prior to the performance of *The Archers,* then, they saw a walk stretching away in front of them, lighted doorways, and a theatre, "principally of wood; an unsightly object, painted red." Dressing rooms and green room were in a wing on the west side of the building, added after the Revolution. [49] It is generally agreed that the John Street Theatre was a replica of the Southwark Theatre in Philadelphia (built only a few months before the John Street), [50] and if this is true, other details of the outside of the theatre appear as the eighteenth-century audience saw it. For example, the Southwark was also painted red (the standard color for all American theatres of the time), was "principally" of wood, and was "without outward ornament, and in its appearance no ornament to the city." [51] It was a large frame building with bricks for its first story. [52] The John Street Theatre itself was probably fifty-two feet wide, by eighty-seven feet long. [53] Possibly a new coat of red paint assailed the theatregoer's eye in 1796, since a pre-season announcement had declared that "The house has been new ornamented and thoroughly aired." [54] A notice in the New York *American Minerva,* June 3, 1796, suggests that by June a thorough airing was needed again: "The ventilators on the top of the house will be opened, and every method taken to render the house as cool as possible."

But the John Street Theatre was beginning to show its age. A visitor to New York in 1796 said that "The theatre is of wood, and a most miserable edifice it is. . . ." [55] When first built, it had been of course an improvement over the pretexts for theatres seen earlier in the colonies— over the tobacco-houses, over the taverns, court houses, and the like, over earlier New York theatres: the "upper room" used in 1732, Hall's Long Room of 1739, the "rather tumble-down affair . . . not built for the purpose" in Nassau Street which was really a "two storied house with high gables," even the ninety by forty Beekman Street Theatre. [56] The wave of theatre building in the 1790's must have made the John Street Theatre look even older, even more ramshackle. In England, larger and larger theatre structures were being formed through extensive alteration and rebuilding, [57] and this trend was reflected in America.

Someone standing outside the Federal Street Theatre (erected 1794) in Boston would have seen "a fine specimen of architecture . . . a lofty and spacious edifice, substantially built of brick, with stone facias, imposts, etc." It was 140 feet by 61 feet and "In the front there was a projecting arcade, which enabled carriages to land company under cover." [58] "A very elegant theatre," said a visitor from England, "far superior in taste, elegance, convenience, to the Bath, or any other country theatre that I have ever yet seen in England." [59] In 1796 Boston put up a second new theatre, the Haymarket: "It was an immense modern pile, proudly overtopping every other building in the metropolis," and made, said one visitor, to contain one-tenth of the population of the city.[60]

Someone standing outside the Chestnut Street in Philadelphia (opened for plays in 1794) would have seen a resemblance to the Royal Theatre in Bath, with a stately front stretching ninety feet along Chestnut Street and flanked by two fifteen-foot wings. "It is an elegant and convenient theatre, as large as that of Covent Garden," said an English visitor, an opinion concurred in by a newly arrived British actor.[61]

Someone standing on Westminster Street in Providence in 1795 would have seen the new 81 by 50 feet theatre, with a canopy over its middle door.[62]

There were new theatres all over the colonies in the 1790's. By October 2, 1796, a month before the final performance of *The Archers,* the roof was put on the Park, the Theatre which was to replace the John Street. The Park opened in January of 1798; it was in Park Row, about three hundred feet east of Ann Street, and it was 80 by 165 feet.[63]

> The entrance was by a flight of six or seven steps leading from the street and extending the entire width of the structure. There were seven arched doorways, the two end ones apparently leading to the less aristocratic parts of the auditorium. Above the arched doors were two stories of windows, the whole surmounted by a pediment with sculptured device of shield and eagle, representing a national emblem. To the rear was a large four-story wing for dressing rooms and storage apartments, scenic and otherwise.[64]

However, it was to be some twenty months before this new theatre opened, and meanwhile business went on as usual at the John Street.

4

The entrance to the John Street Theatre probably had
three doors, one for each part of the house,[65] and each
guarded by a doorkeeper. Doorkeepers not only collected
tickets but showed boxholders to their boxes and opened
the doors for them. During the Revolution, when the
John Street Theatre was called the Theatre Royal, seven
doorkeepers were used, and each man was paid two dollars. The boxes were kept locked, said a notice in the
paper, "and a screw key to them deposited with the Box
Keeper, who will show the proprietor of any Box for the
Night, to his number the moment he arrives and unlock
it for him. . . ."[66] When the Park Theatre opened, doorkeepers and constables cost the manager some fifty dollars
weekly. The opening and shutting of box doors during the
performance was a perpetual source of annoyance in the
John Street Theatre.[67]

On passing through the doorway the theatregoer found
himself in the lobby. Here, on pantomime nights, "Books,
descriptive of the Pantomime," were sold. The music to
the evening's performance, for sale at the theatre (at
about twelve cents), was sold in the lobby, too.[68] A hot
stove sat here in the lobby, but many people brought their
own footwarmers, a custom no doubt dating to earlier
theatres which were prone to advertise the fact that they
were heated, but that stoves might nonetheless be
brought.[69] Something about the temperature of these early
theatres is indicated by the fact that as late as 1824, when
oil was beginning to be used, the oil in the chandeliers
occasionally thickened and the lights went out, upon
which men would go about with hot irons to thaw the
oil.[70] Also in the lobby were wooden benches lining the

walls; here people sat about before the performance, drinking and smoking.[71] Indeed, a visitor to America noted that, "The lobbies of all American theatres are provided with barrooms, to which the men resort between each act to drink, and from which the ladies are regaled in their seats with glasses of their favorite beverage." [72] The food and drink on sale in the lobby included apples, raisins, peanuts, oranges, mince pies, custards, French brandy, and Holland gin.[73]

If one ignored these treats he soon found himself in the corridor outside the boxes. "The corridors were extremely narrow, and papered. . . ." [74] The first to arrive in each box was able to take a front seat. There were bolts inside the doors "to prevent any interruption; and all those Boxes not taken, will be left entirely open for such Ladies and Gentlemen as do not take seats, or who honor the theatre casually." [75]

Light pink and gold was to be the general color scheme of the Park Theatre's interior; since this was a popular color scheme of the period, perhaps the John Street Theatre, "new ornamented" for the 1796 season, was also pink and gold. There was a pit and "two rows of boxes surmounted by a gallery." [76] The boxes probably extended all the way around the side walls, and the lower row was probably capped by two stage boxes. The gallery had two rows of benches, and space was on a first-come-first-served basis. There were no seats—only benches—in the pit.[77] The old theatres, the Nassau Street, for example, had had only "a platform and rough benches," even in the boxes, for compartments or single seats were not known to American theatres in those days.[78] But the John Street Theatre did have separate boxes, like "little cabins, just like father's corn cribs," though nothing so elaborate as Charleston's New Theatre (1793) in which every box had

a window and a venetian blind.[79] The view from the boxes
was probably obstructed by square wooden pillars, sup-
porting the upper tier and the roof.[80] All the theatres built
in the larger cities of the United States in the 1790's had
three tiers of boxes: the New York Park, the Boston
Haymarket, the Philadelphia Chestnut Street, and the
New Theatre in Charleston. Theatres in smaller cities,
such as Providence, however, continued to use two tiers
of boxes plus the usual pit and gallery.[81]

The Nassau Street Theatre had converted a hoop into
a chandelier by driving nails through the hoop and im-
paling candles on the nails; these candles had provided all
the light in the house proper, and had also provided some
discomfort for the recipients of dripping wax seated below. The John Street Theatre presumably used more
carefully wrought chandeliers, but the candles and the
discomfort below them remained; a man had to be hired
specifically to do nothing but care for the chandelier and
stoves.[82] The Park Theatre, modern as it was to be in
most respects, was not much better where lighting was
concerned. Some new theatres (such as the Chestnut
Street in Philadelphia) did have "a profusion of glass
chandeliers," but Washington Irving wrote that in the
Park Theatre the "candle-grease from the chandelier, over
the center of the pit" dropped on the clothes of those
seated below; yet, he claimed, the chandelier managed to
light the gallery, and little else.[83]

Probably there was little to see. The Park Theatre
would have had names painted on all its boxes, such as
the Shakespeare Box,[84] but the John Street Theatre confined its decorations to the motto over the proscenium.
The new theatres varied their mottoes from a simple
scroll, reading "Pleasure the means; the end virtue" in
Providence, to a painted flow of crimson drapery with the

arms of the Union and of the State of Massachusetts, blended with emblems, tragic and comic, and a ribbon on the arms saying, "All the world's a stage," in Boston. Over the proscenium of the John Street Theatre were simply the words *"Quicquid agunt homines."* [85]

The John Street Theatre held a larger audience than earlier theatres in the colonies. The "upper room" in New York which was used for the 1732-34 seasons was capable of seating about 400. The Nassau Street Theatre (1750) had room for 161 in the pit, 121 in the gallery, and contained 10 boxes.[86] It is difficult to say how many people were in each box (though some clue may be obtained from a theatre advertisement for Harmony Hall in Charleston, 1786, which shows that the front boxes seated 10 and the side boxes 6 [87]), but the total capacity of the theatre was probably between 300 and 400 people. New York's Chapel Street Theatre (1761) held a house of $450,[88] with an 8 shillings (or one dollar) top; if one dollar was the top price and the house held $450, then, logically, the capacity must have been well over 450, say between 500 and 600.

There is some dispute about the John Street Theatre's capacity, but the figure of 300 [89] is obviously wrong. Nothing is known of the capacity of any section of the house, except that a theatre advertisement of 1795 specifically includes the managers' recommendation that "no *side Box* to be taken for a less number than 8." [90] Dunlap, who after all managed the John Street Theatre from 1796 to 1798, quite specifically states that the house could "yield to the sharers eight hundred dollars when full, at the usual prices (one dollar, seventy-five cents and fifty cents)." [91] Thus the figure 1,000 is probably much closer to the truth. But in size, too, the John Street Theatre was now outdated; the new Park would hold 2,000 as the Chestnut Street in Philadelphia already did.[92]

5

As the house began to fill on April 18, 1796, attention naturally turned toward the stage itself. The "six wax lights" which served for footlights for the Nassau Street Theatre had been replaced in the John Street Theatre by plain oil lamps without glasses in the 1760's.[93] The stage of the John Street Theatre was lit by footlights, two chandeliers over the apron, and possibly hoops of candles over the stage proper.[94]

Dunlap remembered the John Street stage as being "of good dimensions," and the same was reported independently of her sister theatre, the Southwark in Philadelphia.[95] Nonetheless, contemporary reviews of plays constantly referred to the smallness of the stage where, for example, "battles almost always became so burlesqued as to destroy the effect of the best subsequent acting." [96] Other stage widths of the late eighteenth century help provide a picture of the stage as seen from out front: Boston's Federal Street Theatre had a stage opening 31 feet wide "ornamented on each side by two columns and between them a stage door and projecting iron balcony"; Philadelphia's Chestnut Street Theatre was 36 feet wide between the front boxes and ran back 71 feet from the footlights; Providence's stage was 24 feet wide, and its proscenium was 16 feet high; and Charleston's New Theatre (of 1793) had a stage 56 feet long.[97]

The stage was hidden from the audience by a green curtain. The color of the curtain was traditional. "By 1750 every travelling company in the American Colonies carried a green baize front curtain, several drop curtains, including a landscape and an interior, and, possibly, paper screens for tormentors." [98] The green curtain was not only used through the end of the century, it was forced to maintain a dual function; that is, not only did it signal the beginning and the end of the play, it also served as act drop.[99] It was not an ideal arrangement: "I wish the manager would use a drop scene at the close of the acts; we might then always ascertain the termination of a piece by the green curtain. On this occasion, I was indebted to the polite bows of the actors for this pleasing information." [100]

For scenery the groove system was popular by the end of the century, and meant identical stages in different theatres lest a travelling company be forced to create new scenery in each city on its route. Each company, therefore, tended to build or direct the building of theatres in the cities it was to visit.[101] The Nassau Street Theatre had had a green curtain suspended from the ceiling, paper screens on each side for wings, and six candles in front for the stage. This equipment was standard for travelling companies here and in England, with the addition of two drop curtains for scenery: one, an exterior set with an indefinite landscape that "could be made to serve for everything from an English country scene to the Mall"; the other, an interior "whose locale depended heavily upon the sort of furniture that was placed in front of it." These back drops and wings were flanked by vestiges of proscenium doors and balconies; drop scenes had been in use in England before 1767, and no doubt existed in America, too, although the custom remained for flats to open and close as they had done since Restoration days. Flats were usually 24 to 29 feet wide and about 16 feet high; side scenes, or wings, marked entrances and exits.

Back scenes and side wings might have been mounted on flats or back drops before the Revolution, and references to "scene opens" in pre-Revolutionary plays written in America indicate in addition use of the wing and groove system.[102] Until the last decade of the eighteenth century stage scenery in America was none too good; a letter to the New York *Advertiser* of April 4, 1787, complained of poor scenery, of dirty canvas where the author intended a beautiful landscape, "Nor is it uncommon to see the back of the stage represent a street, while the side scenes represent a wood. . . ."[103]

In the last decade of the eighteenth century in America important changes took place in the method of mounting a piece on the stage. The base (on which later developments were to be built) included four simple devices: wings, flats, flies (or borders) and drop curtains. Grooves were essential for wings and flats; they were parallel ruts in the floor and ceiling of the stage in which the flats and wings could slide. From three to five sets of grooves were used, and all scenery was pushed off and on stage by hand. Almost everything was painted on canvas, even tables and chairs. In addition to these, there were backdrops which were used with wings and borders for interiors and exteriors, mounted, early in the century, on rollers and later fastened to frames and flown to the upper part of the stage, a great convenience to strolling companies in that they could easily be carried in property trunks. This led to the gradual switch from identical stock scenes to be used in all plays to individual scenes for each production, one of the great changes in eighteenth-century stage scenery. The final distinguishing characteristic of the eighteenth-century stage was the large apron which jutted out past the second box—still, as in Shakespeare's day, used for important scenes.[104] By the end of the century, the stage settings in America were on a par with those of England, and an English visitor could say, "To judge from the dress and appearance of the company around me, and the actors and scenery, I should have thought I had still been in England." [105]

The change from a green curtain, candles, and two stock sets to the elaborate scenery and stage effects of the 1790's was brought about by only a few men. For the most part, these men were mere scene painters—the designs for sets were generally imported.[106] In 1759 David Douglass, then manager of the American Company, hired a William Williams to paint a new set of scenes, though as late as 1774 a house and sign painter was doing scenery for the theatre in New York in lieu of regular scene painters. Charles Busselot was responsible for stage illusions for Hallam at the Southwark Theatre in the 1780's, and Jacob Snyder painted scenery for the Old American Company for years. During the Revolution Major André and Captain Oliver Delancey tried their hands at scene design.[107]

Then in 1792 the Charleston City Theatre hired M. Audin, and a new era in stage design began. His specialty was transparencies, and he worked in Charleston with his son and with Belzon, Oliphant, and Schultz. Audin was probably a pioneer, in 1794, in "the lowering of lights for the shifting of scenery to music." [108] French scene designers such as Audin and Belzon, with the French meticulous attention to detail, helped the United States get away from the strong English influence on its stage. Audin did a parlor scene for *Hamlet* in Charleston in June, 1796, then went to the Haymarket, Boston; in the same year he also worked for the Old American Company in New York. He was associated with the Park Theatre when it opened in 1798.[109]

Audin's greatest competitor was Charles Ciceri, who

served as scene designer in New York from 1794 to 1800, and who "was the peer of all these first scene painters, the one man whose efforts signalized the advance of American stage decoration from the barrenness of the green curtain period to the cluttered bedizement of the early nineteenth century." [110] Ciceri was not a very fine painter, but was an "excellent machinist." He had been born in Milan and educated in Paris, had served as a soldier in St. Domingo and as scene painter there and later in Paris and Bordeaux. He had been engaged at the opera house in London; finally, he had come to the United States (in 1793) where he worked under Melbourne in Philadelphia on the new Chestnut Street Theatre, and then was hired by Hallam and Henry to serve with the Old American Company in New York. [111] He retired from the theatre in 1800, but before doing so had made scenery and stage effects an important part of the theatre in America.

> Ciceri, and his aides, often made use of the new transparent scenery, perfected in England by de Loutherbourg in 1780. From him, also, they had learned to build up their stages with scaffolding or carpentry for such elaborate spectacles that required practicable stairways, doors, windows, mountain passes, bridges, Gothic halls, and mountain torrents. The New Yorkers probably experimented with dioramic, or moving scenery; and perhaps Dunlap and Ciceri knew side walls on their stage. [112]

Ciceri also utilized artificial figures and was facile in the use of stage transformations. He and his department received one-eighth as much as the combined salaries of all the actors during the time he was with the John Street Theatre, [118] and frequent reference is made to his sets in the reviews embodied in newspapers and magazines of the time. [114]

There were other scene designers in eighteenth-century America, notably those already seen in Charleston, Mr. Milbourne and Charles Busselot in Philadelphia, Bromley, Richard Cullager, and Richard Jones in Boston, Ignatius Shnydore (who retired from the theatre in 1788 to set up as a general painter), Francisquy (more generally known as dancer and choreographer), Stewart, Petrovani, Falconi, Robins, John J. Holland, and Joseph Jefferson (primarily known as an actor and the grandfather of *the* Joseph Jefferson) in New York.[115] But Ciceri unquestionably held first place. He was to be joined by the eminent Audin to head the scenic department of the new Park Theatre in 1798,[116] but in 1796 he was unchallenged, and perhaps it was he who designed the settings of Switzerland where Dunlap and Carr's *The Archers* took place.

A good supply of fine scene designers, however, did not prevent movement and noise from backstage disturbing the audience. And no wonder. Where most modern plays call for one or two changes of setting, "in the early American theatre there was apt to be a five-act play calling for from three to ten changes of scene, a farce, and often an elaborate pantomime or interlude."[117] As curtain time drew near the backstage bustle must have been immense. The "carpenters" (scene-shifters were called carpenters because they helped to construct the settings) checked the scene plot, hung behind the first wing, then pushed the scenes out onto the stage by hand. The footlights, now lowered beneath the stage, were being lit; they were fastened to a board or tin box which could be lowered into the cellar either for atmosphere or to make the trimming of wicks less obtrusive. Most scene changes and candle-snuffing, however, were managed in full view of the audience, either by a stagehand or an actor breaking off his speech to do it himself. All stagehands were known to the audience as John or Johnny, and it was the audience's right to toss witticisms at John while he attended his business, or to demand a bow from him. The changing of scenery in full view of the audience and at frequent intervals was unquestionably disturbing, but probably inevitable in a century which saw the emergence for the first time of realistic sets and costumes plus a new stress on scenery and effects.[118]

6

It was not, however, only backstage preparations which caused the increasing din. The audience helped, too. It was a thoroughly mixed audience, representing all classes and showing a considerable change from early theatre audiences in the colonies. Before the Revolution, "Although playgoing enjoyed increasing popularity among all ranks, the wealthy effectively sought to affix the badge of fashion to their favorite diversion. As the theatre achieved respectability the snob value of being seen at a play became almost equal to the pleasure of seeing it." [119] After the Revolution, though the theatre remained a "badge of fashion," newer elements crept in, reflecting conditions abroad as well.

Because of the developments in industry and commerce, a new class of society was coming into existence [in England], one whose position and influence were based upon the merchandise in its ships and warehouses rather than upon the blood in its veins. The aristocracy was still respected for its taste and noblesse, but the middle class was getting into its hands the power formerly vested in the aristocracy. Among the new class were merchants and misers, puritans and parvenus, the conscientious and the hypocritical—men of all kinds. And among this new class were also many theatregoers—some only casual spectators, but many habitues and connoisseurs also— who made up an increasingly important part of the audience.[120]

The typical eighteenth-century audience was "both large and heterogeneous." In England, the gallery was taken over by the footmen of the nobility; merchants, clerks, and professional men made up most of the pit audience; and persons of the higher ranks of society occupied most of the boxes.[121] In America a similar division took place: ladies and gentlemen in the boxes, the pit occupied almost entirely by unattached gentlemen, and the gallery "reserved for the rabble." [122] One other element in the audience could be counted on in the large cities— visitors. From fall through the beginning of harsh weather, when New York was filled with visitors, was "the harvest time for those who have exhibitions of any kind, and especially for managers of theatres." [123] In England servants were sent to the theatres in advance of curtain time to reserve seats until their masters arrived to claim them, and the same was true in America.[124] The managers of the John Street Theatre were quite specific: "Ladies and Gentlemen will please send their servants at a quarter before five o'clock to keep places." [125] The servants remained in the theatre, and the actor faced the top and the bottom of society in the top and bottom of the house.

Brilliant audiences attended the early years of the American theatre.[126] No stigma was attached to a lady seen at a play, and, said the wife of judge-playwright Royall Tyler, "the ladies frequented the theatres constantly. . . ." [127] Magazines of the time, perhaps in an attempt to persuade, said, "We see the most respectable of our fellow citizens for taste, literature, and virtue, with their wives and daughters in our boxes. . . ."[128] Brillat-Savarin stared about him at the women of Boston and wrote that they were "excessivement belles. On en rencontre quelquefois dans les loges de théâtre qui ont des figures célestes."[129] Possibly as a means of keeping respectable women in attendance at the theatre, plays were occasionally advertised as being performed at the "particular request" of the ladies.[130] As late as 1795 a reviewer for *The New-York Magazine* felt that the theatre was "never more in fashion than this season."[131]

But there were disruptive elements in the audience as well. One of the major complaints against the theatre in America, especially near the end of the eighteenth century, was the profusion of "professional beauties and beautiful professionals" who used the theatre as a kind of stock exchange.[132] Dunlap claimed that prostitutes were so constant a section of the audience that boxes were set aside for them.[133] The prostitutes always sat in the upper boxes, and a shocked writer of 1810 indicates the ruin of the tradition by protesting vigorously against a troop of women of ill fame who had infiltrated to the lower boxes.[134] The only curb placed on prostitutes in the eighteenth-century theatre was one attempted by the managers, Hallam and Hodgkinson, of the John Street Theatre, in 1795: "N.B. No persons of notorious ill fame will be suffered to occupy any seat in a box where places are already taken."[135] "Notorious" and "already taken" seem to be the key words here: no manager in his right mind had any intention of lopping off a segment of his steady audience.

The theatre was not the safest place to be in the eighteenth century, and riots could occur at any time. Even in England, "feeling sometimes ran so high that ladies were escorted out of the theatre, and the men 'went to

work on the house.' Or in a less belligerent mood, they
were satisfied if an offending actor knelt on the stage and
begged their pardon." [136] And in America riots were almost expected. In Boston, a "Master of Ceremonies" was
hired to settle disturbances, and in New York the gallery
was kept in some kind of order by the constables stationed
there.[137] A visitor to America was incredulous at the way
audiences behaved here. He was annoyed by heckling
during a play yet said the audience would have jumped
on him if he had attempted to throw the boor out; he
attributed the behavior to a somewhat fuzzy notion of
the meaning of liberty.[138]

While evidence shows that people in the boxes and the
pit had some share in theatrical rioting, and that on occasion mobs from outside started them,[139] there is no question that most of the difficulty came from the gallery.
Pleas from managers of various theatres specifically asked
that certain items not be thrown down at the orchestra
and into the pit; these included eggs, peanuts, a variety
of vegetables, apples, stones, nuts and gingerbread.[140] The
opening address of New York's "Theatre Royal," spoken
by Captain André on January 9, 1779, referred to "mis-
sile pippins from the heights above." [141] From the very
beginning managers had threatened to close the gallery
unless the behavior of the gallery "gods" improved. Fortunately, the new Park Theatre had riot accommodations:
Ladies could be taken round to the back door of the theatre, in Theatre Alley, and let in the boxes from behind
the curtain, and presumably they could get out the same
way.[142]

Ladies contributed much to the customs inside a theatre. For one thing, they dressed brilliantly.[143] "The audiences were more careful of their dress than those of modern days, and the ladies, especially, paid that attention to

their dress which is now only bestowed when a visit . . .
to the opera is anticipated." [144] Particular reference was
frequently made to women's feathered headgear.[145] Feathers were still in vogue in 1796; an article dated April 18
(perhaps from an irate gentleman who was unable to view
all of the performance of *The Archers*) said, "Such is the
rage for feathers, that a lady's waiting maid now, instead
of the phrase *undressing* my lady, calls it *plucking* her." [146]
Boston kept a separate marshall to escort ladies to their
seats.[147] And if all this were not distracting enough, one
visitor to the theatre found "the ladies in the boxes, as
usual, studious to please; their charms were set off to the
greatest advantage; each box was a little battery in itself,
and they all seemed eager to outdo each other in the
havoc they spread around. An arch glance in one box
was rivalled by a smile in another, that smile by a simper
in a third, and in a fourth a most bewitching languish
carried all before it." [148]

The men had more difficulty maintaining their appearance. Not only did those in the pit have to worry about
missiles creasing their skulls, hot wax dripped on them
from the chandeliers; as if all this were not enough, before
the play everyone in the pit stood on the benches, thereby
affecting the condition of trousers as well. Many men
wore their hats until the performance actually began. One
possible reason for this seeming lack of manners may have
had to do with the need for keeping their hands in their
pockets, because of the presence of thieves and pickpockets in the theatre audience. Early in the theatre's
history, one of the devices used against it was advertising
for articles lost there: the implication that the theatre
housed thieves was clear. However, even after opposition
to the theatre had dwindled to insignificance, thieves and
pickpockets were to be found in the theatre here, as they

were in London and presumably in all other countries of the world.[149]

The theatre offered still other distractions. One of the worst was smoking. A French visitor to the United States in 1788 said, "This usage is revolting to the French. It may appear disagreeable to the women, by destroying the purity of the breath."[150] An English visitor in 1795 was equally revolted: "A shocking custom obtains here, of smoking tobacco in the [play] house, which at times is carried to such an excess, that those to whom it is disagreeable are under the necessity of going away."[151] Another visitor claimed that "smoking is a still greater evil in a crowded house, to prevent which, the managers are constantly making unavailing remonstrances."[152] The custom of smoking at performances was evidently only permitted in Germany[153] and in America. When the Park Theatre opened, its managers, Dunlap and Hodgkinson, pleaded with the audience to stop smoking in the house, but later reports indicate they were without success.[154]

Fortunately, some customs of the early American theatre no longer existed in 1796, such as sitting on the stage. The tradition of permitting some of the audience to sit on stage continued right through the middle of the century at least, both in England and in the United States.[155] Evidently, to get to these seats, one had to enter from backstage, and this usually entailed a visit to the dressing room of one's favorite actress. Before the Revolution gentlemen passing to their seats "were in the habit of stepping upon the stage, mingling with the performers behind the scenes, obstructing the actors, and annoying the actresses with their attentions."[156] A playbill of 1753 forbade anyone to go behind the scenes, and in 1761 Douglass also attempted to put a stop to men behind the scenes and on the stage.[157] The prohibition could not have been very effective; an advertisement in the South Carolina *Gazette and County Journal,* May 6-13, 1774, said:

> As it is almost impossible that the Performers can do their Characters that Justice their Duty to the Publick requires, when the stage is crowded, as it has been for several nights past, Mr. Douglass, at the earnest Desire, not only of the performers, but of a numerous and respectable part of the Audience, begs leave to inform the Town that—
>
> No person on any account whatsoever will be admitted at the Stage Door: and he is well assured that after this Representation, no Gentleman will insist upon it.[158]

Emphatic? Yes, but playbills for 1785 were still saying, "No person to be admitted behind the Scenes, on any Account whatever." [159] Presumably the problem had been wiped out by 1796, since playbills and newspaper notices no longer insisted on the point.

Some improvement, too, is probably in the sobriety of the audience. Theatre advertisements for 1796 insisted that door-keepers were "positively prohibited admitting porter in the house," [160] nor was liquor to be served till after the first act. "Much confusion having arisen from the introduction of Liquor into the house during the performance, the Managers respectfully hope the Gentlemen will not call for any till the conclusion of the First Piece, as the Door-keepers are, in the strictest manner, ordered to prevent its admission." [161] Comments such as "on the fall of the curtain, the dashing fellows are in a state of intoxication" and "to the people in the pit wine and porter is brought between the acts as if they were in a tavern" [162] were of no help to the theatrical or the national reputation. Fruits and liquors served between the acts had, however, always been a custom all over the states,[163] and the managers' attempts at prohibition were not always successful. This drinking plus the sounds of people cracking nuts and chewing various foods [164] must have added considerably to the melee.

The cream of society was probably not in the John Street Theatre on April 18: it was considered unfashionable to attend a première.[165]

The early custom of announcing the next night's performance from the stage may or may not have been still operative in 1796,[166] but it is doubtful whether, even if the announcement were made, it could have been heard. Some people, in an attempt to appear unconcerned with the play, looked over the audience with spy glasses; others played cards; it was customary to talk loud in the theatre, especially in the boxes; all during the first act, people wandered into the pit, and box doors opened and slammed shut.[167] Dunlap and Carr might have been forgiven for wondering why anyone would want to write for the theatre.

III

Theatre Orchestras

In the midst of the talking and the eating and the flirting and the posing, a bell rang. No one at the première performance of *The Archers* paid the least attention; servants were replaced by their masters (the former perhaps going up to the gallery to watch the performance), people bustled about, coins clinked as food was sold. There was some change, however: the bell signalled the entrance of the musicians.

The growth of the orchestra, the regular use of particular instruments, the status of the musicians—all affected the musical stage. Today's musicals may depend on the emphasizing of emotion, the creation of atmosphere, and the subtle comments on the action that an orchestra interacting with events on the stage can bring about. Yet it was the eighteenth century which was responsible for the greatest changes in the orchestra, its instruments, and its musicians, and these changes were immediately reflected in theatre orchestras. The earliest and the best orchestras America knew were her theatre bands—another reason for the unique growth of the American musical.

1

When the squealing, discordant sounds of instruments being tuned was heard, the audience delighted in the noise. In fact, as Jonathan (in Royall Tyler's *The Contrast*) remarked, they were happy to take part: ". . . and then there was such a squeaking with the fiddles, and such a tarnal blaze with the lights, my head was near turned. At least the people that sat near me set up such a hissing—hiss—like so many mad cats; and then they went thump, thump, thump . . . and stampt away. . . ." [1]

Henry Wansey notes in the Boston entry of his *Journal,* "The orchestra having played Ca Ira, the gallery called aloud for Yankee Doodle, which after some short opposition was complied with." [2] James Hewitt had been hissed thoroughly in 1794 for not being ready with a song which the gallery had called for. Ritter repeats an anecdote: "When a small band of seven or eight musicians one night [c. 1791] attempted to play in the theatre a portion of a Haydn symphony, the 'gods' in the gallery cried out, 'Stop that noise; give us Bonypart crossing the Rhine, Washington's March, or Yankee Doodle.'" [3] The right of the audience to make demands upon the orchestra seems to have continued throughout the century; almost the same words that Jonathan uttered were used again in 1802:

> I observed that every part of the house has its different department. The good folks of the gallery have all the trouble of ordering the music; (their directions, however, are not more frequently followed than they deserve.) The mode by which they issue their mandates is stamping, hissing, roaring, whistling; and, when the musicians are refractory, groaning in cadence. [4]

When the bell rang again, it was the signal for the band to play.

There must have been some trepidation and more courage on the part of the instrumentalists: simple demands were one thing; ammunition was something else. The very first speech that Hodgkinson had made as manager of the Old American Company had been a plea to the gallery to suppress their indecencies toward the gentlemen in the orchestra.[5] Pollock mentions a night in 1794 when half the instruments in the orchestra were broken by missiles from the upper reaches of the theatre. In the same year, in Boston, the musicians printed a card in the newspapers begging the "thoughtless or ill-disposed not to throw apples, stones and other missiles into the orchestra." Pelting the members of the band with a variety of objects as a means of requesting tunes seems to have been prevalent in all theatres, though Seilhamer claims that in Boston it was done for the sole purpose of assaulting the musicians.[6]

However, the musicians were not entirely guiltless. Their condition had improved considerably since the days when they were expected to dance and sing as well as play their instruments, and, by 1787 at least, they were beginning to take advantage. Odell quotes a letter to the New York *Advertiser* complaining that the musicians "instead of performing between the play and the farce, are suffered to leave the orchestra to pay a visit to the tippling houses, and the ladies in the meantime, must amuse themselves by looking at the candles and empty benches."[7] The musicians continued to show their independence, notwithstanding indignant letters to the newspapers. One furious gentleman wrote to the *Argus* in 1796 that they had refused to continue playing at a ball following a concert merely because it was after midnight.[8] But regardless of how much cause they gave, there is no question that the lot of the musicians was a hazardous one.

2

Instruments tuned to their satisfaction, the theatre band for the night of April 18, 1796, now played the first piece of the evening. Mr. James Hewitt was the leader, and his functions as conductor of the band will bear scrutiny.

Conducting, as it is practiced today, was unknown in the eighteenth century.[9] An operatic performance was under dual control: the performance as a whole, especially its vocal aspect, was guided by a man at a keyboard instrument (e.g., harpsichord, piano); the instrumentalists were guided by a violinist-leader. No baton was used (except in France, where a time-beater audibly pounded with a big stick. The same practice was followed for symphonies, concerti, and the like, except that with these the keyboard-leader took a more subordinate position).

> What the "conductor" did as he sat at the piano or harpsichord is made quite clear by contemporary writers. He played the chords, he helped the singers by giving them their notes or cues, he played the parts when they failed or hesitated, he kept an eye on the whole performance, or . . . he superintended it, leaving the instrumental playing in the charge of the violinist-leader; he moved his head, or feet if necessary, to give the time or to enforce the beat, but he did *not* wield a baton or beat time with his hands.[10]

Throughout the eighteenth century there was considerable difference of opinion in Europe concerning the advantages of keyboard or violin direction. The violinist-director was the victor, and by the 1790's violinist-conductors who stood with their instruments in their hands ready to play whenever they saw fit had become the intermediary stage to modern conductors. When they began to beat time, they began to interpret, and the bridge to today was complete.

Whatever cultural lag America may have suffered in other respects, as far as the orchestra was concerned there was none at all. Instruments were introduced here as quickly as anywhere in Europe; the finest musicians were available to play them; and these same musicians brought with them, almost as soon as they occurred, the vast changes in the conception and form and functions of the orchestra which marked the eighteenth century. It is no wonder, then, that in 1796 James Hewitt, a violinist, was the leader of the John Street Theatre's band in New York.

The keyboard-director had started to disappear in other cities as well; Gottlieb Graupner, for example, conducted in Boston from his position behind a bass viol.[11] Philadelphia alone held out awhile; when the Chestnut Street Theatre opened in 1794, it was with two conductors— George Gillingham was the leader of the orchestra, but Alexander Reinagle presided over the whole performance. "Who that ever saw old manager Reinagle in his official capacity, could ever forget his dignified *personae*. He presided at his piano forte looking the very personification of the patriarch of music. . . . It was truly inspiring to behold the polished Reinagle saluting from his seat (before the *grand square piano forte* in the orchestra) the highest respectability of the city as it entered the boxes to take seats." [12]

Only recently had the functions of the conductor become restricted merely to leading a band. In the past a band leader had been expected to do many things. All early orchestra leaders in America were expected to sing,

dance, conduct, act, and arrange the music for ballad
operas and the like; in addition, they supported themselves with concerts, music and dancing schools, and,
later, music stores. William C. Hulett, the conductor for
Lewis Hallam's original company,[13] was expected to lead
whatever musicians he could collect; he "played the violin and *danced* merrily." In addition, he ran a dancing
school in New York.[14] An advertisement of Hulett's in a
newspaper of 1770 said that "W. C. Hulet [*sic*] teaches
dancing, violin, flute, and small sword." [15] The keyboard-
director of Hallam's company was probably Mr. Love,
who gave concerts in New York and taught a variety of
instruments.[16]

Probably the greatest single function of America's orchestra leaders throughout the eighteenth century, however, was that of gathering together a group of musicians.[17] The conductor had to know how many musicians
were available in a given city, which instruments they
played, and how well they played them. The same men
appeared in many orchestras of the period, and the man
who could gather together a collection of musicians (and,
perhaps, even get them to play in unison) was the leader.

The pay of the eighteenth-century American orchestra
conductor was not extravagant. The receipt book of the
treasurer of the John Street Theatre during the Revolution
shows Philip Pfeil receiving the money for fourteen men
at one dollar a man per performance.[18] Since there is no
separate receipt for him, it may be assumed he was one of
the fourteen, receiving the same pay as the men in his
band; that is, one dollar a performance. Evidently he got
no extra pay for his duties as leader. The situation was not
much changed (though the pay had gone up a bit) when
Dunlap took over the management of the company. He
notes in his *History of the American Theatre* that he paid

a fourteen-man orchestra one hundred forty dollars a week, and the orchestra included James Hewitt as leader.[19] Each man, then, including the conductor, received ten dollars a week. Dunlap's *Diary*, however, mentions that he came to an agreement with Mr. Hewitt "who is to lead my Orchestra next season and attend to the getting up of Opera's for fourteen dollars per week," [20] or four dollars more than the players in his orchestra. Leading an orchestra and "getting up" operas was, evidently, worth four dollars a week at the end of the eighteenth century in the United States.

And yet there was no dearth of leaders. They included: Hulett and Love (or possibly Pelham) of Hallam's original company; possibly Lewis Hallam himself; John Tremaine, about 1759; Philip Pfeil at the "Theatre Royal"; and John Hodgkinson, at least during rehearsals.[21] The number of orchestra leaders multiplied as each city built its own theatre: Signor Gaetano Franceschini led the orchestra of Dennis Ryan's company; Gottlieb Graupner conducted at the Church Street Theatre in Charleston in 1795 and taught music and conducted the theatre orchestra in Boston in 1798. Graupner seems to have switched places with a Mr. Leaumont who moved from the Boston Theatre to one in Charleston at about the same time. Van Hagen conducted one of the theatre orchestras in Boston, from 1797 to 1800, after having appeared as conductor of the orchestra of the French company which visited New York in 1791. The 1790's saw Mr. Gillingham as violinist-conductor at the Chestnut Street Theatre in Philadelphia, Alexander Reinagle presiding at the keyboard. The final years of the century also saw Mr. Bellinger conducting the band in Charleston and Mr. Bergman conducting in Charleston's other theatre.[22] Almost a dozen men were closely associated with theatre orchestras, and each was responsible in his own way for helping to keep alive the American musical stage.

3

It is doubtful whether the hissing and stamping and catcalls of the gallery gods were able to drown out the sound of the orchestra; there was too variegated a collection of instruments by the end of the century. It seems strange, but there is good evidence to prove that the instruments used in the theatres were owned by the managers of the various theatres.[23] This must have been quite an expense, as many instruments were available to an enterprising theatre manager by 1796. During the eighteenth century "an increased advancement of instrumental technique, the gradual rejection of instruments which were unable to pull their weight in the growing body, and their replacement by those better fitted for the purpose" [24] were evident both in Europe and in America.

Those instruments available and utilized in European orchestras included, early in the century, one or more keyboard or chordal instruments (used to provide harmonic background), oboes, bassoons, flutes, recorders (which were gradually discarded), clarinets (which did not appear in scores until the middle of the century; for twenty or thirty years thereafter they were used in place of oboes), trumpets, drums, trombones (which appeared primarily in opera orchestras, and there not until the end of the century), the entire string family (violin, viola, cello, and double bass), and a variety of horns.[25] All of these instruments and more can be found in eighteenth-century America, some of them in use here before their first recorded arrival in European music centers.

The introduction of musical instruments to America was

gradual and took place in all sections of the country. Even the Puritans had few objections (in the beginning) to musical instruments. In a tract of 1647 entitled "Singing of Psalms of Gospel Ordinance" John Cotton wrote, "nor do we forbid the private use of any instrument of music therewithall: so that attention to the instrument does not divert the heart from attention of the matter of song." [26] And by 1635 New Hampshire had fifty-six oboes and recorders alone. Philadelphia objected strongly to music itself, though (still in the seventeenth century) German pietists near Philadelphia accompanied their singing with instruments.[27] The South, of course, provided the most congenial atmosphere for music, and, in Virginia at least, "there were few houses of those times [the seventeenth century] in which there was not a considerable variety of musical instruments, and in one or two instances the number was sufficiently great to form almost a small orchestra." [28]

By the turn of the century, the names of specific instruments begin to crop up frequently. By 1703 Philadelphia had "viol, hautboy, trumpets and kettle drums." [29] The Puritans were introduced to musical instruments in the following order: pitchpipe, tuning fork or brass reed, violoncello, flute, hautboy, clarinet, bassoon, violin, and organ, the last named appearing in a Boston church by 1713. A concert program of 1765 in Charleston listed participating instruments, and these included a French horn, cello, bassoon, and harpsichord.[30] New York newspaper advertisements for 1756-75 reveal the presence of harpsichords, spinets, chamber organs, violins, bass viols, tenor viols, Aeolian harps, English and Spanish guitars, German flutes, cellos, drums, pianos, Loutens, mentelines, mandores, welsh harps, bassoons, oboes, clarinets, fifes, bagpipes, and flageolets.[31] By 1770 none of the orchestral instruments then in use in Europe was missing from the colonies, and even an assortment of "specialty instruments" had crossed the Atlantic.[32]

There are a number of points about musical instruments in this country which are relevant to the musical stage. As is the case with every other aspect of America's musical life, the growth and development of musical instruments were inextricably tied to the musical stage. The banjo, which in the nineteenth century was to be so important in minstrel shows, made its appearance a century earlier. Jefferson, in his *Notes on the State of Virginia,* described a "banjar" which the slaves had brought with them from Africa.[33] Thomas Fairfax, visiting Richmond in 1799, was also impressed with the instrument:

> After going to bed I was entertained with an agreeable serenade, by a black man who had taken his stand near the Tavern, and for the amusement of those of his colour, sung and played on the Bangoe. He appeared to be quite an adept on this African instrument, which though it may not bear a comparison with the Guitar, is certainly Capable of Conveying much pleasure to a musical ear. Its wild notes of melody seem to Correspond with the state of Civilization of the Country where this species of music originated.[34]

Brasses, so important for theatrical effects, were available in profusion: Boston was able to assemble two brass bands in 1768 to honor John Rowe as Grand Master of the Masons. Unusual instruments were frequently featured in eighteenth-century theatres. A Savannah theatrical bill of 1785 called for musical pieces "on the *Cymbal* accompanied by the *Tambor de Bass.*" [35] Other original concoctions of the time included those of H. B. Victor, whose advertisement in the *Pennsylvania Packet* of October 17, 1774, informed the public of his intended concert on his new musical instruments, "the one he calls *Tromba doppio con tympana,* on which he plays the first and second trumpet and a pair of annexed kettle drums with his feet, all at once; the other is called *Cymbaline d'amour,* which resembles the musical glasses played by harpsichord keys, never subject to come out of tune, both of his own invention." [36] Benjamin Franklin, too, was responsible for inventing an instrument, the Armonica. It was popular both in Europe and in America, and improvements were made upon it in both places.[37] Franklin himself has left us a complete description (and picture) of his Armonica, together with instructions for building and playing it.[38] Mozart wrote an Adagio and Rondo (K. 617) for Franklin's elaborate musical glasses and the instrument was played in theatres and at concerts all over America during the eighteenth century, usually as a solo instrument.

4

The early theatrical companies contributed heavily to the cultural life of the cities in which they appeared, particularly in the appreciation and performance of music.[39] Less well known, however, are the byproducts of people associated with the theatre. Being a musician in eighteenth-century America meant being many other things as well. John Tremaine, for example, an actor with the Old American Company in the 1750's and conductor of the orchestra for awhile, built a harpsichord for the use of the company in 1759. Benjamin Crehore, carpenter for the Federal Street Theatre in Boston, was well known by 1791 in Boston, New York, and Philadelphia as a maker of violins, cellos, guitars, drums, and flutes, and, later still, he manufactured pianos as well. Some of the musicians in the theatre orchestras owned music stores, where sheet music could be purchased (often published in the same place) and all sorts of instruments were repaired and sold. Benjamin Carr, composer of *The Archers,* owned stores in several cities; both Gilfert and Hewitt, too, owned music stores in New York at various times.[40] Alexander Reinagle, composer and co-manager of the Chestnut Street Theatre in Philadelphia, had advertised in the New York *Packet* of June 12, 1786, that he gave lessons in singing, harpsichord, piano, flute, and violin, plus use of "the best instruments and music printed from London." [41] And it is probable that George Everdell, conductor, player (with the Old American Company) and arranger, is the same Mr. Everdell that Miss Bleecker reports in her diary as periodically tuning her piano in 1799.[42]

Europe had traditional occupations for the musician which America had not yet had time to build. For the European musician,

> The most regular work was found in the opera and theatre orchestras. The concert-giving societies which could not provide full-time employment for the members of their orchestras recruited their players from amongst those who were also engaged in the theatre, and the personnel of each orchestra varied more or less from time to time or from season to season. . . .[43]

In addition to playing in a variety of ensembles, European instrumentalists generally composed music and, with less talent for composing, acted as music copyists. Some peripheral occupations were the same in America. M. Gardie of the John Street Theatre orchestra, for example, acted as copyist for the company. The military band which played at the John Street Theatre when it was called the Theatre Royal during the Revolution also played in Trinity Churchyard (where benches and lamps had been fixed for evening promenades).[44] These eighteenth-century musicians had frequent concerts at which they performed, they were called upon to play for all sorts of civic occasions, the circus came to be a steady source of employment, and later in the century outdoor gardens provided a regular source of summer income. Almost every secular composition we possess from eighteenth-century America is by a man we can place in the theatre orchestra of some city.

The early eighteenth-century American instrumentalist, however, had fewer musical organizations to choose from than his European counterpart, and his income was supplemented by what, from today's standards, look like strange sources. Musicians have been observed acting as instrument repairers, music publishers, and owners of music stores. There was a tradition connecting the orchestra pit and the stage: we constantly see well-known actors and managers playing with the orchestra, and it is even more common to watch well-known instrumentalists of the day acting, singing, and dancing upon the stage.[45] There are individual records which show musicians resorting to somewhat desperate means. Two gentlemen named Johnston and Brenon juggled on a slack wire (in 1774) and then played a tune on a French horn while balancing. Odell also mentions a Peter Clores and "Music on the wire. . . ." Kidd and Godwin, who started the theatre in Savannah after the Revolution, were both dancing masters. The early history of the drama in America shows that all dancers with the companies were expected to perform in the orchestras as well. Hulett, dancer and violinist, besides teaching these accomplishments, also taught the flute and use of the small sword.[46] Newspaper advertisements show many musicians offering vocal and instrumental lessons.[47] Mr. Wall, a comedian with the Old

American Company, retired in 1773 and announced his availability as a mandolin player.[48] An additional chore musicians of eighteenth-century America took on themselves was the running of both individual and subscription concerts; they were forced to add to their musical activities those of publicists, business managers, and so forth.[49] The final attraction used by professional musicians for making the public turn out involved placing child prodigies on the stage.[50]

The men in the theatre orchestras, then, took part in every aspect of the country's musical life. It was probably a matter of economic necessity with them, since the days had passed when professional musicians were scarce. After the Revolution the need for the amateur musician disappeared, and the professional took his place. But at the beginning of America's musical history things were very different. No concert (public or private) could be given, nothing musical presented on the stage, without adding amateur instrumentalists to the available professionals. Happily, the playing of an instrument was generally regarded as essential to a proper education, and so there were always gentlemen available to sit in on performances. There was no particular instrument that fashion demanded be played: it was not until much later that the piano came to be known as a ladies' instrument, while men of mode preferred the German flute.[51] But fashion had not dictated particular instruments earlier in the century, and so a reasonably complete orchestra could be put together, even without an adequate supply of professionals. Diary after diary of the eighteenth century shows both musical interest and ability on the part of the colonists. Captain Francis Goelet,[52] for example, mentions the daughters of his Boston host entertaining him with harpsichord music after dinner; he was then invited to a "consort" at which his host (and six other men) played—this, in 1750, in a city vehemently opposed to the theatre for forty years after. The diary of John Anderson of New York[53] records an almost incredible amount of private amateur activity. John and his brother were constantly playing their violins for visitors; John occasionally fiddled for his friends' dances; visitors to his parents' house were sure to entertain (for example, in 1796 alone, Mr. Davis sang several songs "of his own composing" on February 11; on February 26 Mr. McIntosh played highland tunes on the violin; on March 9 Mr. Martin played the violin for his hosts). When John went visiting he, too, took his violin (on February 15, he visited the Van Vleets where he played the violin and Miss Van Vleet played the harpsichord; on May 3 he went to Mr. Huggett's and "Captain Bogert and some others were there—he played on the flute—two gentlemen on French-horns, and myself on the violin").

When Hallam's company first arrived in America, only one musician playing a harpsichord accompanied the ballad operas and the like. However, the company soon discovered the wealth of amateur talent awaiting them and began utilizing it almost immediately. By the 1760's newspaper advertisements show that most cities had an orchestra to accompany theatrical performances. These early orchestras were made up of professional musicians plus amateurs who played for their own enjoyment and got no pay.[54] It is possible that, in the South at least, Negro orchestras were used in the theatres.[55] The Revolution in St. Domingo and later the French Revolution drove many Frenchmen to America, and they swelled the ranks of local orchestras; and "often, the aristocratic amateurs of those days could hold their own against professional virtuosos."[56] It was a point of pride with the early theatrical companies (as well as a means of assuring others of their respectability) to mention the genteel makeup of their orchestras. An advertisement from the Maryland *Gazette* of August 8, 1752, is typical: ". . . the *Beggar's Opera* with instrumental [music] to each air given by a set of Private Gentlemen." [57] Up to the time of the Revolution, then, the custom was to use amateurs to fill out the theatre orchestras; when these "private gentlemen" could not be obtained, the company found itself in difficulty. As late as 1782, in Baltimore, an advertisement mentioned that the only obstacle in the way of opening the theatre was the lack of good musicians.[58] After the Revolution the larger cities were able to provide all the professionals needed, but right through to the end of the century one finds amateurs aiding theatrical productions in smaller cities.[59]

The amateur performers were probably fine musicians. Stokes quotes a British visitor to New York in 1796: "The inhabitants of New York are very fond of music, dancing, and plays; an attainment to excellence in the former has been considerably promoted by the frequent musical societies and concerts which are held in the city, many of the inhabitants being very good players." [60] Certainly, Odell's comment that the "amateur quality of the music in that day" was shown by the use of amateurs to fill out the orchestras seems unjustified.[61]

5

The professional musicians were a peripatetic lot. The appearance of a man in an orchestra in one year was no guarantee that he would not be in the orchestras of other cities in successive years. The best picture of the travelling musician emerges from William Priest's *Travels in the United States of America*.[62] Hired to play in the Chestnut

Street Theatre in Philadelphia, Priest went on tour with Wignell and Reinagle's company, made side trips to smaller towns to give concerts, and described his reactions to America as he travelled. This must have been a reasonably profitable means of keeping alive, since he mentions returning to Philadelphia with more than enough cash to cover his expenses. Philadelphia, Lancaster, New York, and Boston all crop up in his book in the space of less than a year.

Trips to small towns were frequently as much a test of a musician's mettle as of his ability. Dunlap mentions the enterprising manager of a provincial company who threatened to fire the horn players because their instruments did not sound for the same duration of time as the violins.[63]

Aside from periodic trips to the hinterlands, the musicians were constantly changing their permanent residences. Benjamin Carr lived in Philadelphia and New York, the Van Hagens in Charleston, New York, and Boston, the Graupners in Charleston and Boston. Only Charleston, in the early days, could afford to hire professional musicians by the season.[64] Elsewhere, a violinist-dancer and a harpsichordist travelled with the theatre company, and amateurs and professionals were picked up wherever the company decided to perform.

As the number of companies grew, and as each company settled into a specific circuit, musicians were hired to tour with them and were paid reasonably regular salaries. A letter to the Charleston *Gazette,* April 10, 1794, contains a request on the part of three musicians with West and Bignall's Charleston Theatre company to be released from their contracts and be permitted to play with another company.[65] On a recent tour their ten-dollar weekly salaries had been reduced to seven or eight dollars per week, with which they were expected to pay all their expenses, including travel costs. Too, they were paid only in those weeks when performances were given (all theatres, for example, closed for Passion Week). Ten dollars may have been standard pay all over the colonies, since Dunlap, in 1798, mentions paying one hundred and forty dollars to his orchestra of fourteen men.[66] It is perhaps worth noting that this amount represented about 10 per cent of the total expenses of the theatre. The pay of the military band of the Theatre Royal in New York in 1779, on the other hand, had been one dollar a man (just half of what each of the doorkeepers made).[67]

As jobs grew steadier and incomes higher, independence increased proportionately. The Charleston musicians cited above did not get permission to play with another company (the managers claiming they were needed for rehearsals), and it is impossible now to discover whether they left anyhow. But only two years later, in 1796, the entire orchestra of the other Charleston theatre (the City Theatre) refused to play at an actor's benefit because he refused to sing at theirs. The result was that "trios, duets, and songs were accompanied by a single violin." [68] Aside from the interesting fact that the Charleston musicians received benefits, we can see a growing confidence on their part that they were essential to the theatre. In Dunlap's diary he reports an argument that Hodgkinson had with the wind instrumentalists. The cause of the argument is not recorded, but since one of the common difficulties in all orchestras of the time was keeping the woodwinds in tune, we have at least a clue to the dispute; in any case, some of the musicians quit the orchestra, and Hodgkinson tried to get Dunlap to agree with him in a declaration that the men should never again play in the theatre. Dunlap refused.[69] By the turn of the century,

Washington Irving reported: "The gentlemen of the orchestra are very economic of their favors. . . . What I
heard of the music I liked very well; (though I was told
by one of my neighbors that the same pieces have been
played every night for these three years). . . ." Irving also
provides what was evidently the standard answer to this
complaint, that is, that there was so much noise between
the acts, no one would hear a new piece if it were
played.[70]

6

By April 18, 1796, the Old American Company had
come a long way from an orchestra composed of the
harpsichord of Mr. Pelham, later supplemented by the
violin of Mr. Hulett. Gradually both professional and
amateur musicians were added,[71] and it is frequently possible to trace the changing personnel of the orchestra on
a city by city basis. Durang, for example, lists the orchestra in Philadelphia in 1785 as containing Mr. Phile, leader;
Mr. Bentley, harpsichord; Mr. Woolf, principal clarinet;
Trimmer, Hecker, and son, violoncello, violins, etc., and
"some six or seven other names, not remembered
now. . . ."[72] Another method of assembling an eighteenth-century orchestra two centuries after it played is
to look for all practicing musicians in a city at a given
time, being fairly sure that all were sooner or later used
in the theatre's orchestra.[73] One of the difficulties inherent
in this method is the proclivity to wander which characterized most musicians of the time. How many of the
musicians available to an orchestra in a given year actually travelled with the company when it visited other
cities? How many could be counted on as residents from
year to year? John Bentley, who had given concerts in
Philadelphia in 1783, played in the orchestra of the Old

American Company two years later, then joined the company in its travels, led its orchestra, and acted as well. In the 1780's Alexander Reinagle, Capron, Bradford, and the Van Hagen family were available for use in New York orchestras. But the final decade of the eighteenth century found New York with an almost completely different set of musicians. Almost all of the above-named gentlemen had meandered off to other cities. And the men found playing at the first performance of *The Archers* would be gone, for the most part, by the turn of the century.[74]

Perhaps the easiest way to assemble the orchestra of the John Street Theatre on April 18, 1796, is to look backward from 1798. In his list of expenses for that year, Dunlap notes those members of the orchestra on regular contract; they include James Hewitt as leader, and the Messrs. Everdel, Nicolai, Samo, Henri, Ulshoeffer, Librecheki, Pellisier, Dupuy, Gilfert, Nicolai, Jr., Adet, Hoffman, and Dangle.[75] Some of these men had been in New York for a number of years. An announcement of 1792 told the public that Hewitt, Gehot, Bergman, Young, and Phillips were available "Professors of music from the Opera House, Hanover Square, Professional Concerts under the direction of Haydn, Pleyel, etc., London." [76] Hewitt, of course, stayed in New York and took over the leadership of the Old American Company's orchestra. Young played the bassoon in Hewitt's band until June, 1797, when he was arrested (and eventually executed) for killing a constable who tried to collect debts from him. Ulshoeffer had been with the band at least since 1795 (as first violin). Victor Pelissier was first horn of the company, and had played with the orchestra since 1793. George Gilfert had opened a music store in New York as far back as 1787, had been president of the Musical Society of the City of New York in 1789, and as harpsichordist early became attached to the orchestra of the theatre.[77]

The above musicians account for two violins, a horn, a bassoon, and a harpsichord for the orchestra, with the understanding that others of Dunlap's 1798 list may also have been playing in 1796.

"As New York became the main battleground for the Old Americans after their reorganization, logically the orchestral forces were principally selected from resident musicians." [78] The New York *American Minerva,* in its advertisements for concerts and music stores, yields, in addition to those musicians already noted, the names of the Van Hagen family (January 23), Benjamin Carr (February 3), Mr. Dubois playing a clarinet concerto (March 2), and the same gentleman playing a bagpipe (April 20), Mr. Bingley playing a flute concerto (September 13), Mr. [George Edward] Saliment playing the flute (November 11), Mr. Moller playing the piano (November 30), Mr. Henry (*sic;* he is probably the Henri of Dunlap's 1798 list) playing the clarinet (November 30), and Mr. Rausch (probably playing a piano [79]) on the same date. The New York *Argus* adds the name of Mr. Relain, who was to play the harp at a concert on February 2.

The orchestra included still other musicians. M. Gardie, a French nobleman and husband of the famous pantomimist and dancer, had been in the orchestra since 1794. Mr. Henry Capron (who gave subscription concerts together with Peter Van Hagen and Saliment in New York in 1796) may also have played in the orchestra.[80] Finally, rounding out the picture of available talent in New York in 1796, is the famous writer and gastronomist, Jean Anthelme Brillat-Savarin. Some dispute exists as to whether he arrived in America in 1793 or 1794,[81] but none about the fact that he played in the John Street Theatre's orchestra in 1796. Unfortunately, Brillat-Savarin himself is reticent about the time he spent in America; however, Samuel Miles Hopkins mentioned that Brillat-Savarin taught him French in New York in 1796,[82] and Arnold Whitridge found that Brillat-Savarin attended the theatre in Boston in 1795 when the Old American Company was there, and moved back to New York when the company did in 1796. "He was in New York again, probably playing in the orchestra, when the John Street Theatre Company opened its doors in 1796. At any rate he writes to his friend Rostaing that he was still living on his musical skill. . . ." [83]

Frenchmen, Englishmen, Irishmen, Italians, and Germans; noblemen, theatrical families, debtors, composers, and adventurers—the orchestra formed more of a melting pot than most other aspects of American life.

And so a wealth of musicians was available for the John Street Theatre's orchestra on April 18, 1796—strings, keyboard instruments, horns, and woodwinds. If there seem to be a good many duplicates, it is because the eighteenth century had not yet begun to specialize its musical arts: a musician was expected to play many instruments. This is particularly true of the woodwinds, where the fact that a man played a clarinet, for instance, always meant that he played the oboe and flute as well.[84] Most of the professional musicians in New York in 1796 probably played in the theatre during the course of the year, though it may never be possible to decide exactly which ones appeared on a given night.

7

During the eighteenth century American theatre orchestras constantly increased in size, and this is typical of European theatre orchestras as well. The average European orchestra (excluding the few permanent orchestras of high repute which were subsidized by the nobility)

consisted of two or three first violins, two or three second
violins, one viola, one cello, and one bass, and one or more
keyboard or chordal instruments; the proportion of woodwinds (keeping in mind the fact that woodwinds were
used interchangeably) to strings was a little over one to
three, thereby giving the orchestra about three woodwinds; brasses (which did not generally perform in concerts) were used in the theatre for special effects, as were
drums.[85] This means the average European orchestra during the eighteenth century ran about eleven to fifteen
men, with brasses and drums added to taste.[86]

In America the smaller cities fell behind this number
(for example, Patrick gives Savannah's orchestra as num-
bering nine), though the larger cities, especially near the
end of the century, had no trouble keeping up. The
Charleston Theatre orchestra was made up of at least
thirteen members in 1794, and in the following year
thirty pieces were gathered together for a concert.[87] When
the Chestnut Street Theatre in Philadelphia opened for
its first stage presentations in 1794, its orchestra num-
bered "twenty accomplished musicians." [88] When opposition to the theatre in Boston finally broke down, a large
supply of musicians was already at hand; in 1773 one
of a series of concerts in Faneuil Hall listed fifty performers! [89] New York, however, lagged behind other large
cities. This was not from an absence of musicians: the
flute, horn, drum, and violin used by the American Company in pre-Revolutionary days gave way to fourteen
musicians in the band of the John Street Theatre when
the British took over New York during the Revolution.[90]
Unfortunately, the number was permitted to dwindle, so
that when John Hodgkinson joined the Old American
Company in September, 1792, he found that "the Orchestra was composed of about six Musicians, some of whom

were incapable of their Business." [91] Hodgkinson, out of his regard for his reputation as actor (and as manager), took it upon himself to improve and enlarge the orchestra, and by 1794, "The best band [was] collected that ever had been heard in the New-York theatre." [92] Hodgkinson's reputation aside, the competition from "the excellence of this branch of theatrical arrangement in the rival company of Philadelphia" [93] was no small factor in forcing the Old American Company to improve. At least fourteen men played with the Old American Company's orchestra in 1798, and the final word concerning size in the eighteenth century comes from a Frenchman, Olive d'Auliffe.[94] He came down from his farm to visit the Park Street Theatre in February, 1801, and reported seeing an orchestra there composed of twenty-five members. The Old American Company had brought its reputation up to date.

The arrangement of the musicians in the pit, before the Revolution, was similar to that in England; after the Revolution America followed other paths.[95] The heavy predominance of European musicians in American orchestras of the late eighteenth century probably assured the same arrangement of players here as on the Continent. Just as the gradual emergence of the violinist-conductor was closely followed in America, so too, in all probability, was the placement of the various instruments in the pit. The central figures in the eighteenth century orchestra were the keyboard-leader and the violin-leader.[96] They were in close touch with each other, watching each other closely and co-ordinating their different functions. At the elbow of the keyboard-director sat the principal exponent of the bass part (this might have been a cello or a double bass, or sometimes both, with one on either side of him). The brass and drums were generally at the back, on either side of the orchestra pit, with soloists in front and close to the keyboard-director. Aside from the fact that the oboes and bassoons were generally close together, every other position in the orchestra was subject to constant change. The arrangement of instruments in a definite pattern in the orchestra was to be the work of another day.

As far as the quality of these orchestras is concerned, almost all contemporary accounts agree that the orchestras played well and were comparable to those in Europe. Even visitors from other countries were surprised and impressed.[97] And no wonder. "The musicians who came to America in those days were unusually talented" (as suggested by their backgrounds and the variety of musical affairs they were concerned with), and "many of them were drawn here by the reputed excellence of theatrical companies." [98] In Charleston alone, in 1795, there were "two fine theatre orchestras, the highest grade musicians in the St. Cecilia Society, and a number of fine singers. . . ." [99]

This, then, was the eighteenth-century American theatre orchestra in all its aspects: its conductors and their functions, its instruments and their history, its musicians and the conditions they worked under. Its size had changed as well as its quality, and there was arranged in the pit of the John Street Theatre in New York on April 18, 1796 an excellent orchestra. The "very solemn and important phizzes" [100] of the instrumentalists while tuning their instruments gave way to "queer grimaces and contortions of countenance" as they played some introductory pieces. The audience was probably still shouting for favorite airs, when the bell rang again, and the orchestra swung into the lively Overture to Dunlap and Carr's *The Archers.*

IV

Companies

One way to comprehend the musical nature of the eighteenth-century American stage is to examine the theatrical companies themselves. In the early companies singers and dancers made up a strikingly high proportion of the troupe, and actors known for their histrionic skill contracted to perform in musicals. Further, they all exhibited their much-praised competence in an amazing number of communities.

1

The audience was still applauding the overture and calling for an encore when an actor, probably the star, John Hodgkinson, came out on stage and began the Prologue to *The Archers:*

> We tell a tale of Liberty to-night;
> How patriots freely bleed, and freemen fight;
> How men, though few, united in one cause,
> May, 'spite of millions, for themselves form laws;
> And though an union'd world their rights oppose,
> May still support the government they chose.[1]

After the Prologue, Lewis Hallam entered in the role of Conrad, and the action must have halted as the audience greeted an old friend. Hallam had been an actor for forty-four years in America and had been a part of the first important acting company to arrive in the colonies, the troupe whose descendant was on the stage of the John Street Theatre for *The Archers.*

Some plays had been produced and one or two minor companies had existed in America before the Hallam family arrived on the *Charming Sally* in 1752. What has been called the first play in English, *Ye Bare and Ye Cubb,* was performed in Accomac County, Virginia, in 1665. The students of Harvard appeared in a play in 1690. Richard Hunter petitioned the Governor of New York to permit actors to perform about 1699-1702. The Assembly of Pennsylvania passed an anti-theatre law in 1700, presumably because they were threatened by the drama. Anthony Aston, later "Mat Medley," wandered to the colonies in 1702-3 and reported on his performances here before he returned to England, where he wrote several plays and at least two operas.[2] Other pre-Hallam drama included a professional company of strolling players in Philadelphia in 1723, acting, either amateur or professional, in Williamsburg, about 1716-18, and a play in Boston in 1714. The students of William and Mary put on a "Pastoral Colloquy" in 1702 and plays in 1736. New York had a brief season of plays from 1732 through 1734. Performances took place in Jamaica in 1733 and 1745, and these actors probably migrated to appear in early colonial productions. Charleston advertised opera performances in 1735 and began regular productions in a theatre in 1736. Virginia, too, announced plays in 1736, though these were probably acted by amateurs. New York supplied employment for thespians again in 1739, again in 1743, and again in 1749.[3]

What Seilhamer calls the "regular theatre," however,

began with the Murray and Kean company in 1749; [4] and
the only other company before Hallam was that of Robert
Upton, who evidently joined forces with those actors
left behind by Murray and Kean to give performances in
New York in the 1751-52 season.[5] These early theatrical
companies had no permanent home, but wandered from
city to city, from town to town, playing in any excuse
for a theatre the populace could provide, and staying as
long as the receipts held good. The company always
travelled with character references from the governors of
the colonies in which they had appeared [6]—a necessary
expedient in a country largely opposed to the theatre.
The eighteenth century brought the gradual identifica-
tion of some troupes with particular cities. The company
became a "permanent group much like a modern opera
company. It was attached to some theatre, which it considered its home, and where it gave performances the
greater part of the year. At other times it visited elsewhere as a whole or in sections." [7]

As he sang, Hallam may have thought back to the days
he had begun in America with a group of itinerant players
who had gradually become entrenched as a permanent
institution. The entire history of the drama in America
could be traced in the history of the Old American Company, and this must have been a great source of pride
to the man who was about to retire as its manager. Not
only is the history of the Old American Company the history of drama in America, it is the history of the American musical as well.[8] For one thing, the Old American
Company, in its early years, perambulated all over the
colonies disseminating both dramatic and lyric theatre.
The original troupe arrived in Yorktown in 1752 and
opened in Williamsburg. The company performed in

Annapolis and probably in smaller cities as well during the eleven months in the South.[9] Also in the 1750's, in addition to two stays each in New York and Philadelphia, the company appeared in Marlborough, Charleston, and Jamaica.[10] The 1760's found them playing in such widely scattered cities as Albany and Alexandria, Boston and Upper Marlborough; they acted in Newport and Providence, in Annapolis, Williamsburg, and Charleston, and, of course, in New York and Philadelphia.[11] The company retired to Jamaica in 1775, and remained there until 1782. It emerged from Jamaica in 1782 as two separate companies, but the parts were rejoined as the Old American Company in 1785.[12] During the 1780's the company added Richmond and Albany to its itinerary, but a change had become apparent: the South was too far off route, and, besides, possessed companies of its own. A regular circuit was gradually established by the Old American Company, and the last years of the 1780's found them appearing in New York, Philadelphia, Baltimore, and Annapolis, establishing what amounted to a theatrical monopoly of these cities.[13]

In addition, when the Old American Company settled finally in New York in the 1790's (forcing other companies in the city either to retreat or be absorbed),[14] it continued to tour in the summer on a route which enabled small towns to see a wide range of productions by the best performers of the day.[15] Groups which split off from the mother company formed the basis for theatrical companies in other parts of the United States.[16] Strolling companies were not altogether replaced by the larger troupes [17] and may even have been aided by the opportunity to appear before audiences with thoroughly whetted appetites.

2

Before the 1796 season ended, the most important position in the Old American Company was held by a new man, William Dunlap, librettist of *The Archers*. Dunlap became manager of the company, a position he held into the nineteenth century. The duties of an eighteenth-century theatre manager were varied, exasperating, and difficult, for the manager was responsible for whatever direction the stage took. Managers such as Dunlap served as midwives to the nascent lyric theatre.

The influence exerted upon the early American theatres by managers is suggested by a glance at the numerous duties attached to the post.[18] Early in the eighteenth century the manager gave instruction in dancing and fencing and sometimes music in order to support himself; he was forced to find or erect a theatre in every town he came to; he searched for musicians in each town; he foraged for actors to supplement his company; and he was responsible for importing actors and scenery from England when he needed them, and transporting them throughout the country.[19] Later in the century he made all arrangements for renting theatres when his company toured; he generally acted himself; he cast and directed all plays; and he served as treasurer and bookkeeper.[20] John Hodgkinson, one of the Old American Company's managers, gives this picture of the manager's assorted functions:

> And here I hope it will not be deemed an unnecessary Digression, if I mention what my situation exactly was. I had to cast and arrange the Business of every play brought forward. I had the various Tempers, Rivalships, and Ambitions of thirty or forty People to encounter and please. I kept all the Accounts; I made all the Disburse-

ments, and was made, in all Money Transactions, solely
responsible. My professional Labours were extreme, and
I never finished them for the Evening that I did not attend to take the State of each Night's Receipts. . . . I
had a Check Account to take, and to make the regular
Entries in my Books. I wrote and corrected every Play-
Bill for the Printer. I planned and copied every Scene-
Plot for the Carpenter. I attended every Rehearsal, to
give Directions. I went through a varied and extensive
Line of Characters on the Stage, I found principally my
own Wardrobe for them.[21]

But the most crucial function of the manager as far
as the American musical stage is concerned was his influence on the repertory. He had to "get up what new
Pieces he shall think best. . . ."[22] From the beginning
in America the drama adapted itself "to the practical
necessities and the personal interests of the manager."[23]
Under the aegis of Dunlap, for example, the Old American Company stressed native plays and musicals, made
scenery prominent, and introduced Continental writers
(such as Kotzebue, Schiller, Robineau, Mercier, Pixéré-
court) to the American stage.[24] And, as did all leading
theatre managers of the day, Dunlap devoted half his
repertory to musicals.[25]

3

But the actors also exercised some control over the
repertory. The Old American Company, and especially
the cast of *The Archers* on the night of April 18, 1796,
illustrates very well the interaction between the actor
and the beginnings of America's musical stage.

Early troupes had been sharing companies: the manager got one or more shares, and those remaining were
"divided among the members of the commonwealth ac-

cording to ability, reputation in the profession, or the influence obtained by becoming favorites with the public." [26] A portion of the shares was assigned to the property (that is, for use, deterioration, etc., of all equipment belonging to the company). Hallam's original company, for example, had a total of eighteen shares: there were twelve performers (including Hallam) and each got one share; Hallam got another as manager; four shares were assigned to the property; and the last share was given to the manager's three children, probably for their performances in minor roles. As shareholders, the actors obviously had great influence in determining the company's repertory. Gradually, the number of sharers diminished, and actors were engaged on weekly salaries.[27] In 1797 Williamson, actor and manager at the Boston Haymarket, engaged Mrs. Whitlock for twelve special performances, and the star system in America (in effect in England since the mid-eighteenth century) was inaugurated.[28]

When the first performance of *The Beggar's Opera* took place, in 1728, ". . . actors who had never before dabbled in opera were soon making music all over Great Britain." [29] The growth in popularity of musical pieces forced actors to sing, and all early American actors were singers as well as tragedians.[30] The audiences everywhere in America expected "that all the performers should be able to sing, and there was no company of respectability that could not perform the old English operas." [31] The result is that even late in the century, when singers were hired principally to sing, contracts continued to refer to the functions of the actor in his singing capacity. Generally, the straight actors took small parts in the musical pieces, and the singers small parts in the plays, but they all sang, and their contracts were quite clear about it.[32]

Perhaps the best way to understand the lot of the actor, both in his dramatic and in his singing capacity, is to look at the contracts he signed or the agreements he made with his managers. Mr. Munto, one of the Pikemen in *The Archers,* had got into debt to Hodgkinson and Dunlap (probably from the failure of a benefit), but was willing, he said in a letter to Dunlap, to stay with the company ". . . provided he is no longer to be *insulted* by the business which is given him, that he must not be expected to play such parts as Woodville, *Wheel of Fortune,* Captain Dudley, Colonel Dormont, etc. etc. etc. that he must have the *whole* second line of opera. . . ." [33]

A word about possession of parts and "lines" of characters may help to make Munto's words clear and subsequent contracts more understandable. In America as in England, "The possession of parts was chiefly the result of the actor's peculiar talents in certain roles, although it depended sometimes merely on seniority." [34] The actor's line of parts referred, in a narrow sense, to the type of part he performed (old men, for example), and in a broader sense to all of the parts he was capable of taking.

In 1798 Dunlap hired the famous Mrs. Oldmixon, and her contract ran as follows:

> Mrs. Oldmixon engages for the ensuing season at New York: to play the first line of Opera, or such characters as she has given in a List of, the best of the Comedy Old Women, the best of the Chambermaids, or at her choice in Comedies the same as Mrs. Mattock's line of playing: Salary seven Guineas per week—she finding her own Wardrobe, and having a benefit free of the Charges on benefits. Stipulating not to sing chorusses, unless in certain circumstances of the Company she may herself choose so to do. . . . [35]

Mrs. Oldmixon's contract raises questions concerning benefit arrangements, provision of wardrobes, and requirements about singing in the chorus.

On a benefit night an actor paid the expenses of the house (other actors' fees, rent, and so forth) and collected everything over expenses for himself. Of course, if the size of the house fell below the number necessary to meet expenses, the actor went into debt for the difference. Early in the history of the theatre in America, "The beneficiaries visited the houses of the principal citizens to dispose of tickets," but the consequent degradation of the actor caused Douglass to abandon the system in 1762. Amusingly enough, the situation was completely reversed by 1796: when an actor was to have a benefit, he listed his address in the newspapers, so patrons could come to *him* to buy tickets. From 1762 on there was an attempt to show that benefits were not merely gratuities but means of showing approval and favor to actors.[36] A full benefit house was supposed to show the estimation in which the actor was held by the public; but benefits were more generally, in America at least, "gull-traps"—every theatre art and every art of the press agent was resorted to fill a house.[37] In England benefit performances began in mid-March and rarely was any new work given so late in the season. In fact, a new work was seldom performed as a benefit. In America benefits began in the spring, but they were almost always the means of giving new works to audiences—beneficiaries profited by getting up novelties,[38] and the repertory in America expanded most in benefit time. The actor chose the work to be given at his benefit, and to the actor must be given a large share of the responsibility for the increasingly musical repertory.[39]

Complaints all through the century indicate weak costuming, and it was not uncommon for actors in the same play to wear the dress of widely differing periods.[40] Since actors' contracts stipulated that costumes were to be provided by the performers, the reason for poor costuming is not difficult to fathom.

As for singing in the chorus, how common this was can be seen in even a cursory examination of playbills: if an actor had no part in the piece, he was expected to "swell a progress," as Stephen Woolls did by appearing in the chorus of Burghers in *The Archers*. And even stars might take two or more parts in the same play.[41]

Many factors influenced the quality of the performance the actor gave. Beginning in 1796 no performer could be "required to study more than four Lengths, from Play-Night to Play-Night, and in the same Proportion for a longer Time."[42] Considering that the play-nights occurred about every forty-eight hours and that a "Length" was forty lines, this does not seem excessively generous.

Perhaps as a result of long parts and little study time, the actor was frequently unprepared. Opening nights were notorious examples. When the Old American Company reopened the John Street Theatre for the 1796-97 season, however, they were the exception which proved the rule: a reviewer for the New York *Argus* (September 29, 1796) was astonished, because "we had no right to expect, in a first night's performance, so much regularity and verbal exactness." "Dramaticus," reviewing for the New York *American Minerva* of September 28, 1796, was also surprised at how good opening night was, considering it was a "first night's representation."

Lack of preparation caused another complaint: actors habitually changed the lines of the author.[43] A letter to the Pennsylvania *Gazette* concerning a production of the pasticcio, *Love in a Village*, in Philadelphia in 1767 unhappily mentions that "The Practice of altering the Author's Expressions is so universally condemned by all Men of Sense, and leaves no excuse for the Vanity or Neglect of the Actor; and I hope this little Hint will be sufficient to guard our Actors against anything of the like Nature for the future. . . ." [44] Forgetting of lines or not knowing parts to begin with were also common. Admittedly, a fairly long part might entail twenty lengths; [45] admittedly, an actor might take different parts each playing night for weeks; nonetheless, no audience was likely to be happy with an actor reading his part. The indisposition of an actor might cause an emergency situation, but the preferred answer seemed to be in substituting another piece.[46] Unfortunately, this was not always done, and frequently the ailing actor's place was taken by an actor who read his part.[47] Once Hallam became ill and his part (Prospero in *The Tempest!*) was read by Marriott. Something of the quality of these impromptu substitutions is suggested by James Fennell, who recalled being asked to replace an actor at the last minute. He pleaded that he didn't remember the part. He was then asked to read it. He continued to refuse, then finally consented, although he had not acted the role for three years, and "Having prepared myself as well as possible *during the first act*, I performed it with tolerable correctness." [48] [italics added]

Still other factors tended to influence the quality of performances. One undoubtedly was the "kindly custom" of permitting actors, of whatever ability, to make their debuts in leading roles. Another, was that songs could be encored.[49] Wood, recalling this era, said that "As a natural consequence, each artist insisted on a share of this privilege, until the merciless introduction of songs, encored by admirers of the several singers, protracted the entertainment to so late an hour, as to leave the outstanding songsters to a show of empty benches, and a handful of tired-out hearers; the audience preferring to retire at a reasonable hour." [50] One other mildly irritating habit of the actor must have been the occasions when he turned his back on the pit and recited his lines "to the dignitaries who occupied the boxes or balconies above the proscenium doors." [51]

Yet despite his weaknesses, most visitors and critics were pleased with the quality of the American actor. Certainly the pay an actor was able to command was good; the performer arriving from England found the pay scale higher on this side of the Atlantic. Most English actors who came here stayed, or if they went back to England, shortly returned, as did, for example, Mr. Johnson of the cast of *The Archers*. John Bernard admitted that he came to America only because he needed the money, and Wignell's offer of "a thousand pounds for a twelvemonth, with the option of signing an article for five years (upon my Covent Garden terms) at its expiration" was evidently too strong a temptation.[52] He was somewhat surprised on arriving to learn that no actor's salary was under four pounds per week, that many were as high as twelve and fifteen, and that benefits (at least twice a year) added about one-third to the amount. The remark with which he was greeted by a friend on arriving in America, "Ah, John, have you come to make your fortune like the rest of us?" was not wholly ironical.[53] By 1798 top stars commanded even more favorable terms. Dunlap sent Hodgkinson, leading man in *The Archers*, a contract (which Hodgkinson claimed was an insult) that indicates something of the actor's elevated status:

> For your services and the services of Mrs. Hodgkinson the ensuing season, in Tragedies, Comedies, Operas, Farces, Interludes, Pantomimes, unconditional and without reserve relying upon my sense of Justice and pro-

priety in casting characters, both finding your own wardrobes servants and dressers, and you superintending
the musical department I offer you weekly salary one
hundred dollars—.[54]

4

No picture of the early American lyric theatre can be
complete without a glance at the lives, the careers, and
the critical reception of the performers who gave it life.
Almost the entire Old American Company appeared in
The Archers; members of the cast were typical of the
actor-singer-dancer of the eighteenth century and included some of the most popular stars of the period. It
is almost impossible to separate singers from actors from
dancers, since most performers did all three, but some
members of the company were known primarily as one or
another.[55]

First, the actors. JOHN HODGKINSON, "the Atlas of the
American stage," who took the part of William Tell in
Dunlap and Carr's "opera," was born John Meadowcraft
in 1767 in Manchester, England.[56] Apprenticed to a manu-
facturer, he ran away, and he used to say that it was his
ability to sing and play the violin that gave him hope of
being hired by some theatrical troupe. His audition with
the Bristol theatre did revolve around a song, and his
acting apprenticeship was served "by speaking a few lines
now and then, singing in choruses, marching in processions, and snuffing candles. . . ."[57] He gained considerable reputation in England, especially in low comedy
roles, and on September 5, 1792, arrived in the United
States, where he made his debut on September 26 in Philadelphia, where everyone was astonished at the "singular
spectacle of a man at once combining a *first* singer with
a first-rate actor."[58] [emphasis added]

As far as his character is concerned, he was "a fine actor, with a boundless ambition, bottomless ignorance, and tremendous energy." [59] His ambition is borne out by Dunlap, who claimed that Hodgkinson's desire for "playhouse applause was inordinate, and he was as rapacious for characters as Bonaparte has since been for kingdoms." Something of his ignorance is demonstrated in not knowing the author of a play at a time he was performing the central character in it; or, again, in being asked facetiously who the "anon." was in a bill for poetic recitations, he seriously answered, "Oh, sir, he is one of our first poets." [60] As for his energy, perhaps it is enough to note that in Charleston, in the 1803-4 season, he performed at least eighty-eight different parts! [61]

He was five feet ten inches tall, was somewhat heavy at his debut in America and got fatter as he got older. "He was strongly and well-formed in the neck, chest, and arms, but clumsily in the lower limbs, with thick ankles, and knees slightly inclining inward." He had a round face, broad nose, white, colorless complexion, dark brown hair, and grey eyes, one larger than the other. There was no possibility of missing him on the street: the citizenry wore short hair of natural color; Hodgkinson wore powdered curls at the sides and a braided club or knot of hair behind; nonactors wore pantaloons and boots; Hodgkinson affected breeches and stockings and shoes. [62]

But his reputation was built on neither his appearance nor his clothes. When he died in 1805 he had the satisfaction of knowing that he had played "tragedy, genteel and light comedy, opera and pantomine, with almost equal ability," and that "probably, no performer on the American Stage, has ever equaled him in versatility and general excellence." [63] A fellow actor said of him, that his well-defined features showed every minutest change of thought or throe of feeling; while his voice could be compared to nothing but a many-stringed instrument which his passion played upon at pleasure. While such were his endowments, his method was to work himself up to a certain pitch of excitement which rendered everything he said or did the direct prompting of impulse.[64]

Although a visitor from England said that ". . . as a general actor, Mr. Hodgkinson was the best performer I have seen in America," later in his career, criticism began to mount: Washington Irving saw him in 1802 and described him as "a portly gentleman" and commented about his acting that he "fumed his hour out," and slapped his breast and drew his sword half a dozen times.[65]

Dunlap said of his performance in *The Archers* as William Tell that he was "forcible," but the reviewer for the New York *Diary* said, "We were much disappointed to see him so cold in some of the scenes which required much animation; particularly in the meeting with the Burghers. . . . In the scene where he cleft the apple from the boy's head, he was again himself." [66]

LEWIS HALLAM took the low-comedy lead in *The Archers*, playing the character of Conrad. His first appearance on the stage had coincided with the first appearance in America of his father's original American Company. Lewis was twelve, and he distinguished himself by forgetting his one line and running off the stage in tears. But by 1769 (well before Hodgkinson's arrival), he was the principal tragedian and comedian in his company.[67] Alexander Graydon, in recalling Hallam in the sixties, said that he was the Roscius of the theatre (as what popular actor was not?), that all dramatic heroes were his without a competitor, that he "had merit in a number of characters, and was always a pleasing performer. No one could tread the stage with more ease." [68] And Graydon was not alone. Another report of the 1760's said, "Mr. Hallam is the best Actor according to Common Opinion. . . ." [69] In the 1780's he was still a strong force in the theatre: Wood, in his *Personal Recollections,* said that Hallam was a "formidable rival of Henry in tragedy, and greatly esteemed as the high comedian of the corps." [70] Three sources indicate flaws in his histrionic ability: a letter to the *Pennsylvania Gazette* says, "I am sorry Mr. Hallam, who is genteel in his Person and Actions, could not speak plain English, whenever he assumes a character that may be supposed to understand the language"; another letter to the same paper complains of his habit of seeming "to suck in, or at least not to utter the first letters of the words he speaks"; finally, "In tragedy it cannot be denied, that his declamation was either mouthing or ranting; yet a thorough master of all the tricks and finesse of his trade, his manner was both graceful and impressive." [71]

In appearance, Hallam had a slight cast in one eye, and "he was slightly above the middle height, erect and thin, but strong, vigorous and graceful—being an accomplished fencer and dancer," [72] both fencing and dancing, with singing added, being the *sine qua non* of the dramatic hero. He was a thoroughly irascible person, and stingy when dealing with actors under him. He, too, had great versatility, was a great favorite as a pantomimist, and starred in almost every play, musical and nonmusical, given in America in her early years.[73] A letter to the *Philadelphia Chronicle* in 1772 proclaimed him "the best Mungo [in the musical, *The Padlock*] upon the British stage," and with the part something resembling Negro minstrelsy got under way.[74]

Soon Hallam was to be forced out of the theatre, and

soon he would try again as manager, this time of the old
Southwark Theatre in Philadelphia, and soon, in 1808,
he was to die; but in the 1790's, though he "presented only
the wreck of his former capacity," yet he "still was a
various and elegant actor. . . ." [75] He was not, originally,
to have been given the role of Conrad in *The Archers,*
but nonetheless Dunlap found that his part "told well." [76]
The New York *Diary* (April 23, 1796) claimed that he did
"perfect justice" to his role.

JOSEPH JEFFERSON was born in Plymouth, England, the
son of an eminent actor and manager, and was only
twenty-one when he arrived in America in 1795. The
company he was hired for in Boston (seventeen dollars
per week plus passage) having failed, he signed with
Hallam and Hodgkinson, appeared with the Old American
Company in Boston, then made his New York debut in
February, 1796.[77] "In Mr. Jefferson," said the New York
Daily Advertiser (February 13, 1796), "was discernible
a rich and happy vein of humour. . . ." Four days later
the critic for the same paper found that "There is a
naïvete in this gentleman's acting very pleasing," though,
of all things, he is "too uniformly comic." *The New-York
Magazine* felt that he "promises much." [78]

And so on April 18, many people were probably seeing
Jefferson for the first time; they saw "a small and light
figure, well formed, with a singular physiognomy, a nose
perfectly Grecian, and blue eyes full of laughter, he had
the faculty of exciting mirth to as great a degree by power
of feature, although handsome, as any ugly featured low
comedian seen." [79] Despite a "rather large and pointed
nose," said another admirer of his, "never was a human
face more plastic. . . ." [80]

When singing, his voice was a rich baritone; [81] he was
known primarily as an actor rather than a singer, yet it

comes as no surprise to find Dunlap saying (after another of his operas, *Sterne's Maria,* was performed in 1799), that "It is not necessary to observe to those acquainted with any part of American theatrical history, that the music of the piece was confined to Messrs. Tyler and Jefferson among the males." [82] Winter, too, says of him in the role, "As La Fleur in Dunlap's opera of *Sterne's Maria,* a singing part, he was especially brilliant." [83] He danced, also, and not only with the corps, but even did solos occasionally.[84] "To an excellent ear for music, he added no inconsiderable pretensions as a painter and machinist." [85] His mechanical abilities included the invention and execution of his own wigs, including one whose hair stood up in fright. When first hired by the Old American Company it was primarily as scene-painter, and he was considered one of New York's outstanding scenic artists, even getting separate billing for those pieces, such as the opera, *Siege of Belgrade,* for which he designed the scenery.[86] Later, when melodramas became important on the stage, "Much of their success was owing to the taste and skill of Jefferson, in the construction of intricate stage machinery, of which, on many occasions, he proved himself a perfect master. . . ." [87] He served as manager for a while, too.[88]

Jefferson played the mildly lecherous Lieutenant in *The Archers* and was not reviewed in the role. But it is safe to assume, from the comments of those who saw him at other times, that he did at least a competent job. An *"acteur distingué, à quelque chose de touchant,"* said one; one of "the best ornaments of the American stage," [89] said another. "Light Comedian, Low Comedian, Youthful Tragedian, Harlequin, and Feeble Old Man—and good alike in all,—pre-eminent in eccentric Comedy of every description," Joseph Jefferson died in 1832, after thirty-seven years on the American stage.[90]

The role of Walter Furst was played by JOHN JOHNSON. Johnson had two outstanding merits: he was brilliant at acting old men, and his wife, hired with him, was one of the finest and loveliest actresses of the period.[91] Before coming to the United States he had been successful on the London stage, and he was thirty-seven when he made his debut here ("entitled to great praise," said the reviewer).[92] Later in his career he managed the Park Theatre, and, though not primarily a singer, he occasionally appeared in concerts.[93] A "good, useful" actor, a confrère said of him, and he remained a favorite on the New York stage until his death in 1819.[94]

MR. CLEVELAND (Gesler in *The Archers*) was only a casual visitor to the New York stage. He had been one of the Banditti in *The Castle of Andalusia,* the opera which opened the Chestnut Street Theatre in Philadelphia in 1794,[95] and he acted there before coming to New York. While in Philadelphia, he and his wife "were a useful couple, but not principal performers. Mr. C. was engaged as a walking gentleman, and Mrs. C. in the role of minor and smart chambermaids." [96] They were in Boston in the summer of 1795, and it was there that Cleveland developed his reputation of theatre "apologist":

> Mr. Cleveland was a good actor, and very prepossessing in his personal appearance, gifted also with an agreeable address. He was the apologist of the theatre. If an actor was sick, no one could state to the public the substitution of another with so much grace; if a play was not ready on the night announced, no one could lay the case before the audience with such certainty of having the piece proposed in its place so warmly applauded—in fact, he had a peculiar knack for making apologies, and rarely did he

retire from the execution of this, to him agreeable task without receiving a round of applause.[97]

The story is told that, having died on stage, he rose during another's speech to tell the audience not to worry about the pealing of the Old South bell, then contentedly sank down dead again.[98]

He and his wife appeared at the John Street Theatre for the 1796 season, then left New York for good. Dunlap says that they were "genteel and useful performers;—young and handsome, but in talent not above mediocrity."[99] The review of his initial appearance in New York was kinder to him: "Mr. Cleveland is not a Common actor; His person is interesting; his voice is excellent; he appears to possess warm feelings, and a strong desire to please. . . ."[100] By the end of 1796 he had carried his warm feelings, his desire to please, and his wife back to Philadelphia. There, a systematic critic in the December 16 issue of *The Gazette of the United States*, in grading actors on the basis of fifteen as a perfect score, gave Cleveland five.[101] Charleston was evidently more appreciative of his talents, for in 1797 he and his wife took the title roles in *Romeo and Juliet* at the City Theatre there.[102]

WILLIAM KING had the somewhat dubious distinction of being the only performer to get a downright bad review for his work in *The Archers:* "The author was very unfortunate in the cast of Leopold—had the man who attempted it been perfect in his part he could have played it well: but he seems determined to try the patience of the public to the utmost."[103] In fact, very little good was said of Mr. King all through his dramatic life, except for those praises he managed, probably, to heap on his own head. At least twice in 1796 letters to newspapers, one signed "Melpomene" and the other "Thespis," spoke of his merits and, incidentally, of how desperately he and his wife needed and deserved a successful benefit.[104] He was damned with faint praise in his infrequent New York write-ups, and even in his previous work in Philadelphia he had been "without much talent or originality." [105] At one point in 1796 Mr. King challenged all of his critics, severally and individually, to mortal combat, but happily he was ignored.[106]

> He was uncommon handsome, but had not the skill that might entitle him to the rank of an artist. He could do nothing but as instructed by Hodgkinson. Sometimes his tall manly person, and fine face, under tuition and drilling, had an effect that might be called imposing. But he was dissipated and negligent of every duty.[107]

Apart from the theatre, he occasionally aided at concerts before he died (in the summer of 1796), in the euphemistic if somewhat ambiguous phrase of Dunlap, "in the flower of his youth, a victim to vice." [108]

W. H. Prigmore, the Burgomaster of *The Archers,* had acted with the company of Joseph Jefferson's father in England. He made his American debut in Philadelphia in 1792.[109] "He became the comic old man of the company, and with grimace, antiquated wigs, painted wrinkles and nose, became a favourite for a time of the gods and the groundlings. . . ." [110] He was evidently slightly offensive, both onstage and off, because of his firm conviction that no woman could help but fall in love with him. He had a knack for revising plays and pantomimes for his own benefits, and he could be counted on to help with a catch or a glee at concerts.[111] Critics were divided about Prigmore in 1796: some seemed fonder of him than in previous years,[112] but some "desisted from remarking on our old acquaintance, Prigmore, in the hope he might (at least

by accident) afford us something to applaud. But that
same uniformity of acting, which has ever characterized
him, still continues. . . ." [113] Prigmore trudged elsewhere
in his quest for appreciation: he appeared in Philadelphia
in 1797, in Charleston in 1799, and was seen for the last
time in New York in 1806, before fading out of sight. [114]

MR. LEE had no doubt practiced with the bow and
arrow when serving as an Archer in *Robin Hood* in Philadelphia in 1794; perhaps this was all the preparation he
needed in order to act a Bowman in *The Archers*. As a
member of the chorus, he had to dance and sing, so it
comes as no surprise to find him dancing in pantomimes
and singing in concerts. [115] In Philadelphia he was praised
as being "useful and respectable in the minor depart-
ments," and the same kind of limited praise was bestowed
in New York. [116] He continued to take minor roles with
the New York company for a few years, though he was
probably kept quite busy with his other work—his salary
of twelve dollars per week, it seems, was his recompense
"as performer and property man!" [117]

MIRVAN HALLAM, known professionally as Hallam, Jr.,
for obvious reasons, added little glory to the family name.
Hallam not only introduced his son to the stage, he
played opposite him occasionally as a method of enhanc-
ing the young man's reputation. [118] Born in the West Indies,
Mirvan "had neither talents nor education, and sunk into
that insignificance which mediocrity in the fine arts must
experience." [119] Aside from his work in New York, his
name cropped up in theatres in Philadelphia and Charleston before he died in 1811 at the age of forty. [120] Though
he "never possessed merit enough to be more than tolerated by his audience," though he spoke in too "high a
key," [121] the grandson of the founder of the Old American
Company fared well as Werner in *The Archers*. "*Hallam,*

jun. spoke some of his speeches with feeling," said an astonished if somewhat snide review in the New York *Diary* (April 23, 1796), "and was good throughout."

On the distaff side, three women in the cast were known primarily for their histrionic skills, Mrs. Melmoth, Miss Brett, and Miss Harding. Miss Brett and Miss Harding were children, hence able to get away without a "Mrs." in front of their names; almost the only concession to convention made by the early actors was the aura of respectability surrounding marriage, at least in name.[122]

In 1782 MRS. MELMOTH was a member of the Cork company in Ireland (supposed to be the best outside of London), and she played in Dublin, in Edinburgh, and in both Drury Lane and Covent Garden before coming to the United States. She gave readings in New York in 1792 and made her American debut the following year; she "was the best tragic actress the inhabitants of New York had ever seen. . . ."[123] Her first performance in the United States was almost her last: she appeared in Murphy's tragedy, the *Grecian Daughter,* as a singularly overweight Euphrasia; in attempting to save her father, the girl cries, "Tyrant, strike here!—here's blood enough." At the adipose Mrs. Melmoth's cry, the house was convulsed with laughter. A sign of her greatness lies in the fact that she pulled the evening out of the fire without ruining either the play or her future popularity in America.[124] She called herself "retired" in 1797, though she was still acting occasionally in 1812 in addition to conducting a small seminary. She died in 1823, at the age of seventy-four.[125]

Her range was typical. In Europe she had acted comedy, tragedy, and comic opera; she did the same here, although "judicious limit of her performance to characters not wholly unsuited to her size, secured general attention and respect." [126] She sang on the stage, albeit infrequently, and in concerts.[127]

Despite an almost incredible speech defect for an actress (she could not pronounce the letter *r*) [128] and despite her everywhere-noted surplus fat, there was complete unanimity as to her merits. One Hodgkinson (no relation to the actor) said her "declamatory powers are considerable." [129] All who saw her had praise: "one of the most popular Actresses in the United States," said one; she "had taste and judgment, which combined with her beauty, had always made her a favorite," said a second; "to a fine face and powerful voice, she added an exquisite feeling of the pathetic, which . . . years fail to efface," said still another.[130]

In *The Archers*, Dunlap found her "forcible," [131] and the New York *Diary* (April 23, 1796) said she "performed *Portia* with sound propriety," good qualities for the wife of William Tell.

Mrs. Brett had three daughters: one was the wife of Hodgkinson, the other the wife of Mr. King, and the third as yet unmarried. MISS ARABELLA BRETT danced and sang as one of the Maidens of Uri in *The Archers*. She had made her New York debut in February of this year,[132] and *The New-York Magazine* commented, "We are told that Miss Brett is yet a child in age: her appearance was that of a woman of powerful talents as a singer and speaker." [133] Arabella was "youthful and accomplished," "greatly admired as a vocalist," "an acknowledged favorite," and as an actress she was "rapidly improving" when she died of consumption in 1803.[134]

MISS HARDING, who acted Tell's son, was another child actress and another in the family Hodgkinson toted about with him, which included his wife, her mother, her two

sisters, at least two children of his own, and his ward, Miss
Harding. She did boy's parts in the John Street Theatre
in 1794, and a critic found that too much praise could not
be bestowed upon her for her speaking, singing, and action, all of which surpassed anything he could have conceived for a child her age.[135] In 1796 she had made great
improvement, and somehow managed to look "as if she
might be destined to a life of purity and happiness." [136]
As she grew older she graduated from playing "boys and
second-rate chambermaids" to "a popular personator of
old women in the Boston and southern theatres." [137]

5

Most of the remaining cast of *The Archers* were primarily singers. Vocal lines were divided much in the same
fashion as dramatic, and singers were hired for the first
or second line of opera in addition to whatever their
straight dramatic contracts called for.[138] The singers were
expected to do many different *kinds* of songs. In the 1790's
all comic opera was popular; "English opera, of course,
with a slight ingredient of French and Italian operas,
was steadily gaining in power." [139] And so in addition to
ballads (mostly from the ballad operas) and patriotic
songs, singers had to be ready with Italian operatic arias
and songs, patter songs, solos, duets, catches, and glees.[140]

Musically, these singers had responsibilities beyond the
evening's performance. Music publication in America, for
example, "awaited the development of the theatre and
the popularity of the singing actor." [141] The singers' responsibility extended into commissioning songs that they
could sing in the theatre, and in a sense they were frequently responsible for the quality of the music sung.[142]
Wood reminisced about the worst fault of the singers:

As most of the operas had been composed with a view
to the peculiar powers and voices of some original representative, it frequently happened that these pieces
were not suited to the ability of later singers, and it became necessary to omit much of the composer's music,
substituting such popular and approved airs as were
most certain of obtaining applause.[143]

While abusing the singers, we might mention that they
were probably no better at remembering their words
than the actors—at least one female was known to have
written the first words of each line of her songs on her
glove. Nevertheless, the singing-actor became so important to dramatic companies that by the end of the century
he received the highest salary of the entire troupe.[144]

Despite employment in concert halls and churches, it
was in the theatre that the singers' reputations were made
and sustained, and the cast of *The Archers* again offers a
good sampling.

Miss Broadhurst was one of the finest singers in the
company in 1796. Born in London, she had studied there
under Mr. Percy, and in 1791 she made her debut at
Covent Garden as Polly in *The Beggar's Opera*. She was
hired to sing in America at Wignell and Reinagle's Chestnut Street Theatre in Philadelphia where she sang Catalina
in 1794 in the opera which opened the theatre, *Castle of
Andalusia*. She gave concerts in New York before her
debut at the John Street Theatre, and alternated concerts with theatre appearances with singing and piano lessons in many cities for years to come before she died in
Charleston.[145] Musical ability plus an inheritance made
her to some extent independent of the theatre, and many
a manager's hair must have grayed as she "retired from
dramatic engagements whenever terms, situation, or other
circumstances were not agreeable to her wishes." [146]

She used her voice in varied styles "from the ballad to the Italian bravura," and she sang the airs of Handel quite beautifully. Her voice was "remarkably sweet and clear— her time exactness itself—her intonation correct, rather inclining to sharp without being positively so, a quality said by some late critics to give great brilliancy of effect. . . ." And, of course, her singing was made lovelier in eighteenth-century ears by her "charming and modest deportment." [147]

At her Covent Garden debut she evinced "that artless simplicity which is the charm of youth; possessing a good figure, pleasing face, and a voice clear, sweet and of great compass," [148] she brought a growing reputation to America. Her New York critics were scarcely less enthusiastic; after her concert debut, a letter to the New York *Argus* (January 19, 1796) said:

> The introduction of Miss Broadhurst to the Citizens of New-York, through a channel, which, while it evidences their exertions to give general satisfaction, opens a wide field for the full display of her unrivalled talents cannot fail of procuring that general approbation which an attention to the public taste and amusement justly deserves.
>
> The songs of "Amidst the Illusions" and "How can I forget the fond hour" were warbled in a tone of melody and softness which extracted from the most callous the undeniable confession, that "music has charms to soothe the savage breast."
>
> The bursts of applause which re-echoed from every corner of the room, and the universal cry of encore to the last song, will be the best testimony Miss Broadhurst can receive of the admiring sentiments produced from the excellence of singing, and convince her, that the citizens of New-York know as well how to distinguish merit as to give it its true reward.

Her voice must indeed have been fine, especially when one considers that despite being "a genteel and amiable young lady," she had "not personal beauty, or skill as an actress to recommend her." [149] The *New-York Magazine* remarked hopefully that "Miss Broadhurst improves upon us fast as a player," though unfortunately she was not fast enough for *The Archers* where "Miss Broadhurst exerted herself to play Rhodolpha, to the dramatic part of which she is incompetent. But she sang—and she delighted us." [150] Evidently the "little timid gentle creature" with her "modest diffidence," charmed away all critical faculties: even "Philo-Theatricus," the score-keeping critic in Philadelphia, gave her ten out of a possible fifteen. [151]

MRS. HODGKINSON was at least as good a singer and a far better actress. Her father, Mr. Brett, sang at Covent Garden and the Haymarket in London, and he taught his daughter to sing and to play the violin. Dunlap saw her at the Haymarket in 1784, but Hodgkinson met her in Bath and brought her with him to New York, where they were married. She made her American debut in Philadelphia in 1792, her New York debut at a concert in 1793, and her debut at the John Street Theatre later in the same year. [152]

In England she was "one of the loveliest young ladies on the British stage." [153] She had a pale complexion, blue eyes, and yellow, almost flaxen hair; her Roman nose was prominent, her face oval and a little long for her rather short stature.

She was very fine in opera, comedy, and tragedy, [154] although especially fine in "girls and romps . . . In Ophelia she was touching in a powerful degree, as her singing gave her advantages in this character which tragic actresses do not usually possess." Her specialty, however, was opera, and "her voice, both in speaking and singing, was powerful and sweet." As an actress, her versatility was as great as her husband's.[155]

By 1796 New York was in love with her. The *Daily Advertiser* (e.g., February 17, 1796) had nothing but praise and *The New-York Magazine* could not get over the luck in having both Mrs. Hodgkinson and Miss Broadhurst: "Two of the first singers in America, both amiable in private life; each doing justice to the other's merits; rare examples to the stage of talents without envy." [156] Propriety and chastity were the ideals, and Mrs. Hodgkinson seems to have been able to convey both to her audiences: *The New-York Magazine* raved about her "propriety" and delightful singing; the *American Minerva* found that she was "distinguished by that peculiar, chaste and correct manner of acting, which characterizes all her performances . . .;" the *Argus* said she was "remarkable for the correctness and unaffected chastity of her manner." [157] Even in her concert work she had maintained some standards of her own, and sang parts of *The Messiah* along with other, more typical concert pieces.[158]

Dunlap said that, as Cecily, Mrs. Hodgkinson's comic part in *The Archers* "told well." [159] The New York *Diary* (April 23, 1796), too, agreed that she had done "perfect justice" to her part. The *Daily Advertiser* of February 17 had said of her, "Long, very long, may the public be happy in the exertion of such talents." But the length of her public's happiness was short: she died on September 27, 1803.[160]

STEPHEN WOOLLS did not last even that long. Bath, the city whose theatrical troupe housed so many emigrants to America, was his birthplace, in 1729. His musical training in England was under the famous Dr. Arne, and it was put to good use in America, both in concerts and on the stage. One of the earliest sharing members of the

Old American Company, he sold his rights later in his career and was paid an annuity for years by the managers. He died on June 14, 1799, at the age of seventy.[161]

In his early days on the American stage Woolls was a "tower of strength" in musicals; or to switch the figure, he was a powerful enough magnet that people were drawn by his name alone on theatre advertisements.[162] One found him doing lead musical roles such as Macheath in *The Beggar's Opera* and Hawthorn in *Love in a Village,* and secondary roles in nonmusicals, such as both Northumberland and Douglas in *Henry IV.*[163]

Durang reported, on the evidence of his father, that Woolls was a good vocalist, an "honest, good man—so Mr. Hallam ever said." [164] He was first singer of the company for many years, "continuing to figure as such long after all voice had left him, and snuff and snuffle characterized his attempts." [165] He must have known his star was fading when his benefit failed in 1790, and he was forced to try another; he "subsided into 'old men'" and was still clinging to the stage in 1796.[166] He sang one of the Burghers in *The Archers,* and the "pitiful and mean appearance of the *Citizens*" was mentioned in a review.[167] He had now been connected with the company for over thirty years, and when he died, in 1799, a benefit was given for his wife and daughter, and the advertisement for the bill said in part:

> In announcing the occasion of this representation, it is a duty to mention, that the character and conduct of the deceased, was undeviatingly irreproachable, and the disposition of his mind highly amiable; it is now thirty-six years since he first appeared on the American stage, in all which time he acquired many friends and no enemies; in his professional capacity his powers of voice have frequently pleased both here, and in many other parts of

the continent; it is therefore hoped that the attendance on this charitable occasion will evince, that in the public estimation this character is just.[168]

JOSEPH TYLER, Arnold in *The Archers*, made his American debut in 1795 and his New York debut the following year. His background in England included good practice in the provinces as actor and singer, for which he had been, inadequately one hopes, prepared by a brief career as a barber.[169] He was universally praised, both for his voice and his histrionics: by the *Argus*, the *Daily Advertiser*, *The New-York Magazine*, and his contemporaries; [170] in *The Archers*, the New York *Diary* (April 23, 1796) found that "Mr. Tyler played with his usual correctness."

His work outside the theatre consisted of the usual concerts [171] plus a few not so usual occupations, the latter chargeable to some extent to his appearance. At the time of his New York debut he was "a manly figure," and was, as he got older, especially good in "serious elderly characters, requiring an aristocratic bearing." [172] In fact, he was frequently put into tragedies because he looked like George Washington, "which made it good policy to array him in powder and small-clothes as often as possible." [173] In 1798 he supplemented his theatrical income by opening a restaurant, the Washington Gardens; it is probably no coincidence that the man who packed houses by looking like Washington on the stage, should have attempted to pack his appropriately-named restaurant by the same happy resemblance. Certainly his "voice of rare excellence," which gave him most important singing parts in the theatre (*all* after Hodgkinson left the company), attracted musical New Yorkers, and his Washington Gardens served as locale for the meetings of various music societies. In 1805 he and Johnson took over, for awhile, the management of the Old American Company. He died, at seventy-two, on January 26, 1823, the day after having performed, in *The Glory of Columbia,* the part of George Washington.[174]

MR. MUNTO, one of the Pikemen, played the "second line of opera. . . ." He appeared among the "Bacchanals" in *Comus* in Philadelphia, 1794, before moving on to New York. *The New-York Magazine* found his person "manly and pleasing," noted that he spoke too low but had a good voice, and hoped he would improve. Later, that same publication was furious with Munto for being in no way prepared for a part.[175] Dunlap said he was "merely tolerable" in his New York debut, and he was, in general, "nearly worthless" to the company.[176]

6

As the last notes of the full chorus Carr wrote for the finale of Act I of *The Archers* faded away, many in the audience went to the lobby for food and drink. For those who remained behind, however, between-the-acts entertainment was offered.[177] One of the most popular entr'acte entertainers was the dancer, John Durang, and his famous hornpipe. Quickly removing his Bowman's costume, he stepped before the curtain to fill in those minutes before Act II of *The Archers* could begin.

Dancing had been intimately tied to the drama from the beginning in America. The earliest companies were able to do pantomimes in addition to operas and plays, the earliest theatre was converted from a dancing school, the earliest musicians were dancers as well as instrumentalists and vocalists, and the earliest managers were also dancing masters.[178] Everywhere in the colonies dancing preceded both the drama and music, and when the drama arrived it seemed natural to include dances in the reper-

tory, and even to put them in the plays and between the
plays.[179] As the century progressed, scattered troupes of
French dancers also began to appear throughout the
colonies.[180]

These French dancers were nothing if not versatile. As
a rule, in addition to dancing, they sang French opera,
performed on the tightrope, did acrobatics and tumbling,
and juggled, too.[181] At least five French companies appeared at the John Street Theatre in the last decade of
the eighteenth century alone: those of Donegani, Placide,
St. Aivres, Des Moulins, and Francisquy. While a French
company appeared at a theatre, a curious interchange of
actors took place: regular dancers with the theatre's company were utilized by the French to fill out their casts,
and the French took small roles in straight dramatic productions. Frequently, when the French corps departed,
some dancers remained behind to swell the ranks of the
acting company. In 1796, the cast of *The Archers,* for example, contained DES MOULINS, who had brought his
troupe to New York some years before, and M. FRANCISQUY
and M. and MME. VAL, whose company had arrived in
March and been hired to perform with the Old American
Company.[182]

By 1796 dancers had established for themselves an important niche in the growing lyric theatre. Harlequin himself was not merely an acrobat, but had a speaking part;
and "a resourceful Pantomimist and good dancer was a
power in the theatre and always ranked high on the pay-
roll." [183] Even as singers supplemented their incomes with
concerts, so too did dancers occasionally appear at concerts, either performing in the program, or leading the
Ball which followed the concert.[184] Even a dancer's children could be utilized in the theatre. As a matter of fact,
minor business in ballets and dramas were performed by

children rather than supernumeraries. Charles Durang, put on the stage himself by his father, reported that extras "were not resorted to, even to fill up a procession"; instead,

> The very minor business, and the ballet performances, were executed, principally, by the sons and daughters of the performers, who had received a suitable education in all of these requirements. . . . The children, thus employed, were taught dancing and music, and the accomplishments necessary to a theatrical education, and which would make them, afterwards, acceptable in society. The theatre was then a school; they were, of course, placed out of the theatre, under masters, to learn other branches of education. . . .[185]

Too, in the theatre a dancer got a chance to do choreography as well; even minor members of the ballet corps occasionally arranged productions, and the four best choreographers of eighteenth-century America, ALEXANDER PLACIDE, M. FRANCISQUY, JAMES BYRNE, and WILLIAM FRANCIS, were all dancers.[186]

The cast of *The Archers* contained a large number of dancers, and the first-night audience saw "incidental ballets [which] must have been rather elaborate."[187] The eighteenth-century musical included much dancing, and performers in *The Archers* typified the terpsichorean talent available in America's early lyric theatre.

JOHN DURANG was the "first American by birth who acquired reputation on the stage as a dancer."[188] Born in York, Pennsylvania, in 1768, he made his stage debut in Philadelphia, 1784, commencing a career which was to find him dancing, acting, miming, singing, designing and painting scenery, making and operating puppets, clowning in a circus, writing plays, managing a theatre, and functioning as choreographer, property man, tightrope

performer, and acrobat. About 1787 he married MARY
McEwen, also a dancer, and also in the cast of *The
Archers* (one of the Maidens).[189]

In New York in 1789 John Durang's dancing was much
stressed in advertisements, probably because of the popularity of his hornpipe.[190] He danced with the Old American Company from 1789 through 1796 and was with the
company when the Placide troupe joined it.[191] When
Placide and his troupe moved on, poor Durang began to
suffer by comparison: a critic in 1793 wondered "whether
the managers suppose we can be amused by the agility
of Mr. Durang, or whether we should be diverted with
him as the character of a clumsy stage dancer." [192] Later
in 1796 Durang moved over to the circus where he spent
his professional life until the end of the century. He retired from the stage in 1819 and died in 1822.[193]

> It would be foolish to claim that he was a great artist, or
> that he made any distinctive contribution to the art of
> the dance. Evidently he had a certain amount of skill,
> a great deal of charm, and that indefinable something
> called "box-office appeal," or his popularity would never
> have been able to survive the fierce competition to which
> it was subjected.[194]

If Mr. Durang was the most popular dancer with the
company because of his birth, MME. GARDIE was the most
popular female dancer because of her beauty and talent.
In fact, "she was the most beautiful woman at that time
on the stage" and "a fascinating dancer and pantomime
actress." [195] She had met M. Gardie in St. Domingo, and
he took her and her son back to France with him; his
father refused to accept her; they came to America, and
she made her debut in Philadelphia in 1794 and in New
York later the same year.[196]

John Durang, who danced frequently with her, told his son how lovely she was, and Charles said that "She was a fine serious pantomimist and opera dancer. This lady's brilliant talent lent a fascination to these performances, and her amiable deportment won the respect of all her acquaintances, in the social circle." [197] The New York critics were scarcely less enthusiastic:

> She gave us a delight altogether new. Her figure, face and action, were enchanting; and the mute eloquence with which she communicated to the audience every varied emotion of her soul, scarcely allowed us to regret that she was unable to express them in our native tongue. The appearance and manner of this lady are prepossessing beyond any example on our stage. . . .[198]

When she acted, her broken English was a source of delight; when she sang, her voice charmed; in fact, one critic with an eye for the cliché was content to have her merely walk across the stage.[199]

M. Gardie, in debt and unable to support wife and son by playing in the orchestra and copying music, wrote to his father in 1798 and resolved to return to France. Mme. Gardie refused to accompany him. He circumvented the impasse by murdering her and committing suicide.[200]

Mme. Gardie was one of the Maidens of Uri in The Archers. Miss Brett, the singer, was a second Maiden, and a third listed in the advertisements was MME. VAL. Mme. and M. VAL (he, too, was in The Archers—one of the Pikemen) played in Charleston with Placide's troupe before coming to New York.[201] Val was another in the line of French nobles who lost their fortunes during the French Revolution. "He and the others were gentlemen of fine manners, and true artists." [202] They arrived in New York in March of 1791 and were quickly absorbed by the Old

American Company. Their primary function in the company seems to have been to support Mme. Gardie in her pantomimes.[203]

Other minor dancers in *The Archers* were DES MOULINS, a Burgher, TOMPKINS, a Pikeman, and LEONARD and M'KNIGHT, Austrian soldiers. Des Moulins (also spelled De Moulin, Du Moulain, Dumulain, Dumoulain, and De Moulins) and a company of French rope dancers from St. Domingo appeared in the Northern Liberties Theatre, Philadelphia, in 1791, performing pantomimes and acrobatics in addition to rope dancing. He danced in the chorus of the Chestnut Street Theatre, Philadelphia, in 1794, and made his New York debut in February, 1796.[204] "Useful and respectable," he nonetheless drew fire for his work in *The Archers*.[205] Mr. Tompkins, a Pikeman, drew no notice at all (nor did MRS. TOMPKINS, a "Female Archer"); he appeared in the chorus of several works in the 1796 season at the John Street Theatre, then took his talents to the circus in 1797.[206] Leonard and M'Knight appear suddenly with the Old American Company in 1796; M'Knight had disappeared by 1797, though Leonard continued acting small roles with the company into the nineteenth century.[207] Since no other word is heard of either of them, it is at least possible that they were stage hands.

The only other member of the cast to be mentioned in advertisements for *The Archers,* and the chief choreographer for the company, was M. FRANCISQUY. He was merely a Pikeman in Dunlap and Carr's musical, but while he was with the Old American Company he was also chief choreographer, and "the inventive Francisquy staged a seemingly endless procession of ballets and pantomimes."[208] He had brought his own company from Richmond to New York early in 1796 and rented the John

Street Theatre for nights when the regular company was
not performing; John Durang and Mme. Gardie began
to dance with them immediately, and the popularity of
their troupe caused Hodgkinson and Hallam to announce
the hiring of the entire entourage by the Old American
Company. Francisquy's advent was formally recognized
by the announcement of a dance between play and afterpiece (a situation which had existed informally before the
illustrious name of Francisquy legitimatized it).[209] Aside
from his choreographic and chorus work, he danced solos,
especially the hornpipe and a "Negro dance." [210] Dunlap
found him "useful and attractive"; he left the Old American Company in 1796, however, and the rest of the century found him dancing and arranging dances for Ricketts's
and Lailson's circuses.[211]

7

The intermission between Acts I and II of *The Archers*
was almost over. The doormen had been busily distrib-
uting porter in the interval, while, backstage, "carpenters"
were changing the set from the Lake of Uri to the front
of the Castle of Altdorf. It was almost time for the prompter's whistle to suggest that the actors hurry to their places.
Doorkeepers, carpenters, prompter—it took many men besides actors and managers to keep the Old American Company running.

In the last years of the eighteenth century, the manager
of the company was also stage manager, but up to that
time the stage manager had been called the prompter, and
the entire backstage activity was centered around him.[212]
The prompter prepared the scene plot for the carpenters
and gave all cues for the action both of cast and of stage
hands; most of his signals were managed by ringing a bell,

though he used a whistle as well.[213] In addition, he prompted, no easy task in a repertory company. He was also required to make up a "Bill of Properties" for the property man. He was in charge of the company's theatrical library. He was also, of course, frequently called upon to take a role.[214] MR. RYAN was prompter at the John Street Theatre. In addition to his other functions, Ryan occasionally substituted for Faulkner at the box office.[215] He was even, on occasion, noticed by the critics:

> We beg permission to observe to the Manager . . . that it is rather too much to be obliged to hear a long part of any play twice over the same evening, once from the prompter, and once again from the player; we hope he will not put our good nature to so severe a trial again.[216]

The property man of the theatre was required to produce anything that the prompter needed for the play, and his odd jobs ran to supplying occasional dinners for the manager and, of course, acting. MR. LEE, property man of the Old American Company, was a Bowman in *The Archers*. The callboy summoned performers from the greenroom by the name of the character they were to impersonate, and sought out the more important actors in person.[217] The theatre was also forced to keep a good supply of doorkeepers (approximately seven at the John Street Theatre), constables, and general attendants to watch over stoves, candles, refreshments, and the audience.[218]

The Treasurer and Box-office Keeper of the Old American Company for over thirty years was JOSEPH FAULKNER.[219] In 1798 Dunlap found him "intelligent" and paid him a salary of fourteen dollars weekly; he had been receiving a benefit for some years. Just as Drury Lane in London gave benefits to its prompter, doorkeeper, and

other attendants, so too did many members of the Old
American Company take benefits during the course of the
season.[220] Faulkner's functions were not as arduous as
those of Mr. Barrow (of the "Theatre Royal" in New
York), who was treasurer, submanager, and did the gild-
ing and painting for the theatre, but Faulkner did have
to sell the songs of the operas as well as tickets in his box
office.[221]

MR. LUKE ROBBINS, who was merely one of many scene
painters helping to comprise "Mr. Ciceri and his department," was also an actor and singer with the company.[222]
Add a watchman, a tailor (Weston), someone to copy
music (M. Gardie), a flock of children of the actors for
small roles and processionals, dressers and a wardrobe
keeper, some general laborers, and the company was complete.[223] The total number of people employed regularly
by the Old American Company was at the very least fifty,
exclusive of the members of the orchestra.

The year 1796 brought in a "remarkable era in the history of the theatre of New-York," a "memorable year" to
those who attended the John Street Theatre.[224] Some dispute exists over whether the company that put on *The
Archers* was the best in America at that time; certainly
the Philadelphia company under Wignell and Reinagle
was at least as good.[225] In 1797, when the company of the
Chestnut Street Theatre and the Old American Company
both played in New York, there is no question that "there
were first-rate players in New York . . . even judged by
contemporary London standards." [226]

The audience on the night of April 18 was seeing excellent professional entertainment by an outstanding company. Some of the finest singers, actors, and dancers then
alive were now ready to begin Act II of *The Archers*.

V

Repertory

Act II, scene 1 of *The Archers* contains a long stretch of dialogue unaccompanied by music, an unusual occurrence on the American stage in 1796. Just as all actors were expected to sing, so all plays were expected to contain songs. If the original author had been so careless as to omit songs, an "alteration" of his work thoughtfully included them (in the eighteenth century, an "alteration" was a reworked play, as opposed to an "adaptation" which merely meant a cut play).[1] The history of American drama is inseparable from the history of American musical stage forms. By the 1790's, over one half of the American repertory was both musical and rich in ideas for the growing lyric theatre.

1

The first works America saw on her stages were by English dramatists,[2] but the plays being written at the time contained surprisingly large amounts of music. Farquhar's comedies are good examples. Four of his plays had been acted in America even before Hallam's original American Company arrived. His *Recruiting Officer* was performed in New York in 1732, helped initiate the drama in Charleston and Williamsburg, and was one of the plays our troops performed at Valley Forge during the Revolution; it was given continuously throughout the century.[3] There is no question that the *Recruiting Officer* is a comedy— nowhere does anyone list it as anything else. Yet it begins with a march, contains one song involving a soloist and full chorus, and three other songs (some repeated in different parts of a scene). How many additional songs would have been needed to make it a "musical"? None, probably, if a musical were needed on a given bill, or if the work had originally been called, say, a "comic opera."

As the eighteenth century progressed, American stages also felt the influence of Continental drama. French plays (introduced by Beaumarchais' *Eugénie,* Prologue by Philip Freneau, in Philadelphia, 1782) were performed in their original language as well as in translation.[4] "The great masterpieces of French dramatic literature appeared here . . . along with many plays now forgotten, all schools of the drama as they were developed in France being represented."[5] Native American translations and adaptations were written in abundance, and at least one (by William Dunlap) was performed in London in 1799 with success. German drama appeared in America (in 1795) with Lessing's *Minna von Barhelm.* Schiller's plays (adapted by Dunlap) were performed here, too, although the majority of German plays acted in America in the eighteenth century were Dunlap's adaptations of the works of Kotzebue. Kotzebue's dramas, as immediate precursors of melodrama, were heavily musical.[6]

Long before the end of the eighteenth century Americans began to write their own plays, and the usual series of "firsts" surrounds the beginnings of American drama. William Berkeley, Governor of Virginia in the 1640's, had written a play before coming to America, and wrote another, *Cornelia,* here. The first extant play written in America, *Androboros,* was penned by another Governor, Richard Hunter, Governor of New York, in 1714. James Ralph, if he was born here, was the first native-born playwright, though his plays were written after moving to England. Godfrey's *Prince of Parthia,* written in 1759 and produced by the American Company in 1767, represents another first—the first play written by a native-born American and actually put on the stage here.[7] Five native stage works were produced before the Revolution (two of them musical), closet dramas and Revolutionary satires and operas were written during the war, and afterwards neophyte American playwrights became prolific as American plays become the fashion.[8] The librettist of *The Archers,* William Dunlap, helped influence the vogue by popularizing the "noble savage" theme and the Gothic terror literature of England.[9] This heterogeneous repertory was rounded out by a variety of bastard entertainments such as lectures with songs and dances, literary exercises at colleges, and vaudevilles.[10] Throughout the 1700's the number of different pieces performed in America increased. In England "a new play was seldom performed as a benefit";[11] but in the United States benefit times (near the end of each theatre season) were considered the best of all possible times for new pieces, and the American repertory expanded rapidly (at precisely the period when musicals reached their quantitative peak). Early companies performed approximately thirty-five different works, New York saw sixty-four different productions in the 1767-68 season, and by 1796 Philadelphia enjoyed one hundred forty-nine different pieces of dramatic entertainment (and New York over one hundred).[12] The circus, incidentally, adds no small number to the totals: from

December 22, 1795, to April 23, 1796, Philadelphia's
Pantheon gave about twenty-two different entertainments,
and from October 12, 1796, to February 23, 1797, Ricketts
gave thirty-two different entertainments, all in Philadelphia.[13]

The repertory not only expanded, it was seen everywhere. Towns as small as Hartford (population 3,000)
had regular theatre seasons. By 1800 musicals had been
heard in every large city in the United States, and even in
such smaller communities as Savannah and Augusta in
Georgia, Columbia in South Carolina, New Bern and
Wilmington in North Carolina, Richmond, Fredericksburg, Norfolk, Petersburg, and Alexandria in Virginia,
Newark in New Jersey, Harrisburg and York in Pennsylvania, and even in such "insignificant . . . villages" as
Lansingburgh and Dumfries.[14]

Musical forms stood beside the purely dramatic forms
to make up the vast repertory. And not in a subsidiary
role. If Salem, Massachusetts, had a theatre season of
fifteen nights, nine operas were heard in that period; if
Baltimore had a summer season, musicals were produced
three and four times per week, sometimes with two on
the same bill.[15] By the 1790's the Old American Company
had in its repertory fifty to sixty tragedies, comedies, and
farces, and an equal number of musical entertainments.[16]
The proportion held elsewhere.[17]

Analysis of eighteenth-century musical stage forms is
particularly challenging: no work exists which analyzes
them as separate entities or separates the forms one from
another. The following sections attempt to establish dis-
tinctions between assorted musical stage types in order
to facilitate the study of the types and to emphasize the
nature of America's early theatre.

2

If the audience watching Act II of *The Archers* was at
all typical of American theatre-goers, one of their favorite
musical stage forms was the ballad opera. Whether the
form originated with the French comédie en vaudevilles
(involving songs set to known airs) or whether its roots
extended back to the Elizabethan jig (which used popular ballad airs but rarely employed any dialogue) or to
the masque, is relatively unimportant in the history of the
ballad opera; what is important is that with John Gay's
The Beggar's Opera the form was popularly launched in
England.[18] A variety of circumstances (objections to the
popular Italian opera, political satire, sheer novelty of
form, use of realism, use of good, long-familiar tunes, and
fine acting) combined to make *The Beggar's Opera* a hit.[19]

Although a new dramatic form had been born,[20] there
was some doubt as to what kind of baby it was and more
as to what to name it. Some eighteenth-century names for
ballad operas included: Opera; Comic Opera; Opera-
Comedy; Farcical Opera; Ballad-Opera; Burlesque Opera;
Tragi-Comi-Farcical Ballad-Opera; Tragi-Comi-Operatic
Pastoral Farce; Tragi-Comi-Pastoral Farcical Opera; His-
tori-Tragi-Comi-Ballad Opera; Comic Masque; Comedy;
Farce; Interlude; Dramatic Piece; Musical Entertainment;
Dramatic Fable; Pasticcio; Burletta.[21]

"Ballad" in 1728 was defined as a "Song, commonly sung
up and down the Streets." [22] Strictly speaking, therefore,
the name ballad opera is applicable "only to comic operas
with spoken dialogue in which new song texts are set to
old tunes." [23] But original songs began to be added in
1729, and *The Beggar's Opera* itself, the prototype of the
form, used airs by known composers (indeed, stole them

from the very best sources).[24] Since there never was a
"pure" ballad opera, and since ballad operas overlap at
least half a dozen other dramatic forms, perhaps they are
most easily recognizable by certain outstanding characteristics. They may have some new music, but they *must*
have old; they must have spoken dialogue, rather than
recitative, and a comic rather than a tragic plot; music
must hold a wholly secondary place and must be able to
be omitted without spoiling the plot. Dances may appear
frequently and spectacular scenes occasionally. The accompanying dialogue may be in prose, blank verse, or
rime, and the subject matter may adopt "nearly every
species of comic invention from farce to sentimentalism
to Arcadian refinement." Generally, they can be broken
down into types: satirical, pure burlesque, farce, sentimental dramas, and pastorals. A good part of their effect,
of course, had to come from music familiar to the audience set to new lyrics.[25]

The Beggar's Opera [26] is too familiar to warrant recapit-
ulation. But it is worth noting that there was an overture
and that during the brief three acts, sixty-nine songs were
sung in addition to incidental music to three different
dances. Regular comedies were accustomed to using five
acts, though operas employed the three-act structure, and
Gay probably had this in mind when writing his "New-
gate Pastoral." [27] Instead of hunting for songs, he wrote
his lyrics to tunes he already knew, and

> The music suits the scene and moment exactly, and the
> songs seem naturally introduced. . . . His experiments
> with duets and trios are interesting. Some of them seem
> close forerunners of modern operatic styles. The choruses
> are scarce, but they break the monotony of the solo
> work.[28]

Dr. John Christopher Pepusch wrote the overture and arranged the songs. Since Gay had already chosen which tunes to use, Pepusch probably did nothing but attend to the "mechanics of presentation." [29]

Immediately after *The Beggar's Opera* a regular school of ballad opera was developed, though it was a short-lived one.[30] In its first flush of success, other plays were hastily converted to ballad operas (and such writers as Fielding contributed to writing them); but later (as the demand for three-act ballad operas waned) they suffered the ignominy of being cut down into afterpieces, one-act "ballad farces," in which guise they were long demanded and written, and, incidentally, easily transported to such far-flung stages as those in France, in Germany (where they helped create a new form, the singspiel), and in America.[31]

The first ballad opera to be advertised by title for performance in America was *Flora, or Hob in the Well* in Charleston in 1735 (really a one-act ballad farce condensed from the longer *Country Wake, or Hob in the Well*).[32] Although *Flora* broke ground, it was *The Beggar's Opera*, in most places, which introduced the musical to America; there was ". . . no American company so 'mean and contemptible' as not to sing or attempt to sing it." [33] It was found not only "in the repertoire of every theatrical company, British or American, in the colonies during the eighteenth century," but it was used to get around blue laws by being read, and was performed by such eminent amateurs as Nathan Hale.[34] Ballad operas and ballad farces were performed by every company in America at least through the end of the eighteenth century.[35]

It was not long before an American tried his hand at a ballad opera. In 1767 the American Company accepted

and "put into rehearsal for speedy production" [36] Andrew
Barton's *The Disappointment: or, the Force of Credulity*.[37]
The title proved accurate and, just before performance,
the work was withdrawn, possibly because the satire was
too sharp.[38] Nonetheless, it was the first American ballad
opera,[39] and a good, lively one, to boot. It is in two acts
(plus prologue and epilogue), contains eighteen airs and
a country dance, and musical background (unspecified)
for a couple of additional scenes.

Four "humorists" decide to ridicule the then-current
idea that the pirate Blackbeard had buried his treasure
on the banks of the Delaware. Their four dupes include
Raccoon (an old debauched Negro), a Barber, an Irish
cooper, and a Scotch tailor. Not the least of the merits of
the opera is the fidelity to assorted dialects of Barton's
pen. Air IV is sung to the tune of "Yankee Doodle," the
earliest American reference to the song.[40] The humor is
always full-bodied and occasionally bawdy: Raccoon's
mistress, Moll Placket, has hidden a sailor, Topinlift,
under her bed and tells Raccoon that he is a spirit which
she has raised.

Raccoon:	Can you lay him down, my dear pet?
Placket:	Why I've raised and laid five hundred in my time—don't be afraid.
Topinlift (*Peeping*):	That's true for you, my girl—I'll swear for fifty.

A weak love plot gives opportunity for duets, and much
drinking for full-chorus work. No harm has been done
anyone at the conclusion, and the piece ends good na-
turedly enough as, after the dance which concludes the
ballad opera, the epilogue is delivered with the entire
cast giving the moral in sung couplets.

3

After the demand for ballad operas had fallen off, it was not until the 1760's that the musical stage came vitally alive again. Isaac Bickerstaffe began to turn out a kind of musical production very much like the ballad operas but without ballad airs—instead he used tunes not specifically composed for the occasion but from known composers, "providing as a result an intermediate form between ballad and comic opera which has sometimes been given the name of pasticcio." [41] The pasticcio, extraordinarily popular in the eighteenth century, formed the link for the comic stage between works with unknown composers and works in which one composer took all responsibility for the music.

The English pasticcio, not as formalized as the Italian (to which it traced its origin) though not dissimilar,[42] was introduced with Bickerstaffe and Arne's *Love in a Village* in 1762.[43] Bickerstaffe's book contained traces of Charles Johnson's *The Village Opera*, Wycherley's *Gentleman Dancing-Master*, and Marivaux's *Jeu de l'amour et du hasard;* Arne's kaleidoscopic score used an overture by Abel, thirteen of Arne's songs from previous works (plus six composed for the occasion) and music from Handel, Boyce, Howard, Baildon, Festing, Geminiani, Galuppi, Giardini, Paradies, Abos, Agus, Gardiner, Carey, and Weldon.[44] The story, two plots involving disguised young men and women, all escaping from despotic relations and all happily and sentimentally married at the end, is not brilliant enough to account for the overwhelming popularity this new stage form immediately achieved.[45] Perhaps the novelty of the genre in addition to the quality of the music helped. These works, though not labelled "pasticcio," always clearly stated that the music was "compiled from the most eminent masters," or "from the best composers." [46]

The pasticcio, too, quickly found its way to America. *Love in a Village,* for example, was first performed in Charleston and Philadelphia in 1766 and continued popular in the United States throughout the century.[47] Having already tried a ballad opera, America quickly attempted the new form. "Not infrequently the work was a genuine pasticcio, the musical numbers having been borrowed from various composers." [48] On May 19, 1787, Wignell chose for his benefit a new work by Royall Tyler, author of *The Contrast.* It was called *May Day in Town, or New York in an Uproar;* the composer was unknown, though he did compile his music "from the most eminent Masters. With an Overture and Accompanyments," and the music was sold in the theatre on the night of performance.[49] Apparently a true pasticcio, the two-act libretto is unfortunately lost.

Other pasticcios were written and performed in eighteenth-century America,[50] and they stood side by side in the repertory with ballad operas and with a new form which achieved great popularity in the last years of the century, the comic opera. Yet comic opera is understandable largely through its relation to its serious counterpart, and serious opera in the eighteenth century was an important part of the lyric theatre.

4

"Serious" operas constituted one of the more clear-cut forms in the eighteenth century. They might have comic themes, yet the distinction between a comic and a serious opera was obvious. As with the French opéra and opéra comique, serious opera used recitative between airs where comic opera used spoken dialogue. This distinction helps the patriotic super-moral *Archers,* for example, to be seen as a comic opera.

In the late 1600's and early 1700's Italian operatic influence [51] slipped into England, took a foothold in 1705 (with operas after the Italian models), and ousted native efforts by 1710. The Italian operas helped, perhaps, to prepare the way for English operas by providing an audience attuned to the conventions of sung drama, as English audiences had already been partially prepared by songs inserted into regular tragedy.[52] But whatever effect foreign opera had on English audiences, its effect on English serious opera itself was minute. "Whatever its foreign relations may have been, native English opera continued the traditions of the masque and the romantic drama, moving serenely in its own exotic world of absolute unreality, if not always of absolute nonsense." [53] J. Aiken, in his *Letters From a Father to His Son* (*1792 and 1793*),[54] expressed clearly the English attitude toward serious opera: "But the Italians, in their operas, have employed throughout the same artifices of recitative, song, and measured action, that were used by the ancients. A true-bred Englishman laughs at all this, or yawns. Some of our first wits have not disdained to point their ridicule against heroes stabbing themselves in cadence, and lovers expiring with a quaver."

The few serious operas written in England in the eighteenth century (those not specifically "in the Italian manner") were closer to masques in form than to operas. But serious operas were written in other countries in the eighteenth century, and Continental operatic activity was quickly reflected in America.

Unfortunately, however, serious operas were only infre-

quently sung on the American stage; instead, they were
mostly heard in concerts, and their music was frequently
used for pantomimes and ballets and for both English and
American pasticcios.[55] Though a singer's contract in America might call for the first line of serious or the second line
of comic operas,[56] only comic operas (according to the
definition established above) were meant; that is, a woman
assigned the first line of serious opera sang the highly
moral, frequently sanctimonious heroines of comic opera.
Dunlap, who was largely responsible for determining the
New York repertory in the last years of the century, admitted that serious opera was a fine thing, but "my taste
was for simple melody, and I received more pleasure from
the airs in *Rosina* [a comic opera by F. Brooke and W.
Shield, 1782] than from all the bravuras of the Italian
opera." [57]

Nonetheless, some serious operas were sung on the
American stage before 1800, and it was these which established a tradition: when Italian, French, and German
operas were performed in America in the nineteenth century, they were mounted in the regular theaters and,
mostly, by the regular theatre companies.[58] The German
singspiel did not appear at all in eighteenth-century
America's repertory; there were "exceedingly few Italian
operas performed on American soil until 1800," but from
1794 on, French actors, escaped from St. Domingo, did
sing the operas of Cimarosa and Paisiello.[59] A proper Bostonian voiced indignation: "banished forever, should be
all unintelligible Italian airs, trills, affected squeaks and
quavers, nothing but the deep-felt voice of nature, in harmonic sounds (vocal and instrumental united) can convey
with fullest energy, the powers of music to the enraptured
soul." [60] French opera, too, appeared before 1800, first
in Baltimore; the second attempt was at City Tavern, in

New York; then, New Orleans and Charleston started the first permanent French theatres in this country, and French operas were sung, and in French.[61] In 1796 a French company, alternating with the regular company at the John Street Theatre, performed French operas, including the work of Rousseau; Grétry, too, was represented.[62]

The Haunted Tower, by Cobb and Storace, was an English attempt at grand opera. "Instead of single airs to relieve the dialogue, customary in English musical pieces, the story of *The Haunted Tower* was told in music, and the success of the opera was extraordinary." It ran for sixty nights in the 1789 season at Drury Lane, and it became the Old American Company's first real attempt at serious opera.[63] *The New-York Magazine* in 1795 said of it that it was "truly a modern opera, with all the insipidity and departure from nature thereunto appertaining," though the critic hoped people would put up with the book for the "exquisite gratification" offered by the music.[64] But even before *The Haunted Tower* was put on the stage, an American had written and produced privately the first American serious opera.

The Philadelphia *Columbian Magazine* of April, 1787, announced the publication of "The Temple of Minerva, a Musical Entertainment performed in Nov., 1781, by a Band of Gentlemen and Ladies, at the hotel of the Minister of France in Philadelphia." [65] Francis Hopkinson's libretto [66] is in two scenes and contains four characters and a chorus. Scene 1, following an overture, takes place in the Temple, with the doors of the Sanctuary shut. Two trios, a duet, and some solo work tossed back and forth among the Genius of France, the Genius of America, and the High Priest of Minerva result in the determination to ask Minerva what America's future will be. In scene 2,

William Dunlap, librettist of *The Archers*

Benjamin Carr, composer of *The Archers*

Interior of Ricketts's Amphitheatre

Arnold's song from the first act of *The Archers*

lued by thy friends

fall the death of all our foes. If thou shouldst fall the death of all our foes can

never make amends then huntress why wilt thou thy life expose.

Ah! think what pangs thy Father still must feel
What pangs must Arnold know
When then expos'd unto the biting steel
Shall rush amid the foe
Then huntress why &c

Librettist William Dunlap's drawing
of Mrs. Hodgkinson (Cecily in *The
Archers*)

William Dunlap's drawing of
Hodgkinson (William Tell in
Archers)

William Dunlap's drawing of Miss Broadhurst (Rhodolpha in
The Archers)

the doors of the Sanctuary are open, and after a prelim-
inary prayer, Minerva's answer, in part, says:

> In a golden balance weigh'd,
> Have I seen *Columbia's* fate,
> All her griefs shall be repaired
> By a future happy state.
> She with France in friendship join'd,
> Shall opposing pow'rs defy;
> Thus united, thus combin'd
> Heav'n will bless the sacred tie.
> *Freedom* on her happy shore
> Shall her banners wide display;
> Commerce shall her richest store
> Through her numerous tides convey.
> *Joye* declares his high command
> Fate confirms the great decree;
> *If our sons united stand*
> *Great and prosp'rous shall she be.*

After another stanza the Genius of America sings, then
the full chorus joins in praise of Washington (who, with
his wife, was present at the performance) at the final
curtain. Though short and obviously belonging to "those
mythological-allegorical-political operas, so fashionable
at the European courts during the seventeenth and eighteenth centuries," the *Temple of Minerva*, with all of its
dialogue either sung or delivered in recitative, is "laid out
in true operatic style," and is unquestionably America's
first operatic effort.[67]

5

Despite the significance of serious opera, it was comic
opera which emerged as one of the eighteenth century's
most characteristic forms. The comic opera had extensive
antecedents in Europe [68] and England,[69] but the mold set

in Britain after 1750, thanks to the enormous popularity of works with books by, among others, Bickerstaffe, Dibdin (who composed most of his own music), O'Keeffe, and Sheridan, and music by Storace, Arnold, Arne, and Shield.[70] The vitality of the form is seen in musical comedies on the American stage today.

Two of the elements necessary to a comic opera are original music and songs relevant to the action.[71] As the eighteenth century progressed these elements were added, and "If we would look for sparks of brilliance [in the late eighteenth century] we must turn to the comic operas and the operatic farces, where . . . we may discern a few elements of greatness." [72] The addition of original music, music as a main rather than a secondary concern, these helped make comic operas not a development of ballad opera, but "in reality a separate form of dramatic art." [73]

Typical of the comic opera is John O'Keeffe and William Shield's *The Poor Soldier*.[74] Its first performance in England was in 1783, and two years later it arrived in America, where not a year went by until after 1800 that the Old American Company alone did not perform it.[75] It is in two acts, contains nineteen airs (about half original and half set to specified music) including duets, a quartet, and much chorus work. Fitzroy, an officer, has permission to marry Norah, who in turn loves a poor soldier, Patrick. Darby and Dermott, comics, love Kathleen. Father Luke, a priest, is Norah's guardian, is a snob, and is, furthermore, open to bribes. Fitzroy discovers that Patrick has saved his life in battle and helps get the lovers together, both by persuading Father Luke and by giving Patrick a commission. Dermott gets Kathleen, and Darby decides to travel and get a reputation for himself as the opera ends.

Comic operas did not survive long as main attractions,

possibly because their substance was too thin to fill up
the required number of acts. They were quickly abridged,
and as afterpieces happily lasted into the nineteenth
century.[76]

Abridged comic operas and short comic operas, written
to be used as afterpieces, form a clear sub-heading under
comic opera—the operatic or musical farce.[77] Indeed, by
the end of the century, musical farces were as numerous
as full-length comic operas and certainly as popular.[78]
Many of the comic operas were first cut down to musical
farces on their arrival in America. *The Poor Soldier,* for
example, was not only popular in its uncut form, but also
in a version (based largely on its subplot) called *Darby
and Patrick.*[79]

Another popular musical or operatic farce was *Edgar
and Emmeline,*[80] and the audience had this work by John
Hawkesworth and Michael Arne to look forward to on the
night of April 18, 1796, as afterpiece to Dunlap and Carr's
The Archers. Act I begins in a dark part of Windsor
Forest where several Fairies enter, moving to light music
and then dancing. Another Fairy enters and, after recitative and air, disperses the Fairies, then outlines the plot:
Edgar and Emmeline are each to marry the fairest in the
land only if and when they meet, they meet as friends and
not lovers. One act, two dances, and three songs later
(one for full chorus), the comic disguisings and ludicrous
discoveries over, and the lovers united, Edgar rounds off
the comic opera:

> O! might each pair thus work what fate intends,
> And none be lovers but who first were friends!

The comic opera was not quite finished with its proto-
zoan activities: it next divided itself into the interlude.
Though interludes had an extensive history,[81] little re-

mained of their past glory in eighteenth-century England. Where the operatic farce had utilized a brief plot, the musical interlude generally presented only a brief episode,[82] a brief excuse for a song or two and a dance. Again, some interludes were original, and some were abridgements of larger works. Sheridan's comic opera, *The Duenna*, for example, was also given as an operatic farce, *The Elopement*, and, in America at least, the operatic farce was occasionally compressed into "a comic opera interlude called *The Duenna, or The Double Elephant* (taken from Sheridan's *Elopement*)." [83]

Still another form of comic opera, this time a kind of "poor relation to an opera," was the burletta. Technically, the term should have been used only for burlesque comic operas (that is, those dealing in a ludicrous way with classic legend or history) and occasionally it was; they were short pieces containing a number of songs. But the term came to be used for any work accepted for performance at a minor theatre after the Licensing Act of 1737. Kane O'Hare's *Midas* (1764) was one of the more popular burlettas on both sides of the Atlantic.[84]

Beginning in the late 1760's, comic operas began to be introduced to America at a rapidly increasing rate, and the demand increased with the supply.[85] O'Keeffe and Shield's *The Poor Soldier* was put on eighteen times in its first season here, and to O'Keeffe "may be accorded the distinction of being the first dramatist to obtain extraordinary success in the United States." [86] Typical both of this opera's popularity and of the way new theatre territories were opened, is the fact that *The Poor Soldier* and a musical interlude were the first recorded performances in Cincinnati, in 1801. The immediate popularity of comic operas here is further reflected in such peripheral activities as parodies of comic operas and straight versions of them done by puppets, and even performances by children.[87] Often English comic operas were performed here under new titles, and often their books were revised and new accompaniments or new music added,[88] but even so, English importations soon were insufficient to fill the demand. And so, just as original American ballad operas, pasticcios, and serious operas fast followed the introduction here of corresponding foreign forms, so too did comic operas. Full-length American comic operas began to be written.[89]

Probably the first-written comic opera was *Edwin and Angelina; or, The Banditti* (book by Elihu Hubbard Smith in 1791, music by Victor Pelissier), though it was not performed until 1796, eight months after *The Archers*.[90] In his Preface (pp. 5-6) Smith says he wrote the principal scenes in 1791, added more scenes in 1793, got it accepted by the managers of the Old American Company in 1794 and then, in one month, converted a two-act drama in prose into an opera in three acts. As "the first opera of which all parts are known to have been created in America, and which then came to public production," *Edwin and Angelina* was also "our earliest contribution to the drama of outlawry." [91] Possibly because of its partial adherence to some of Goldsmith's lyrics if not their spirit, a British review of the printed libretto said, "Although this production is highly romantic and unnatural, as most operas are, it has had the power of interesting us in the perusal." [92] The English reviewer was easily interested, since the story of the evil Earl Ethelbert's machinations and the pure, chaste lovers is not only wildly improbable but dull.

Tammany: or, The Indian Chief, produced in 1794, "was the earliest of American operas on Indian subjects." [93] The book and the music, both lost, were by Mrs. Anne Julia

Hatton and James Hewitt. Dunlap found the story "seasoned high with spices hot from Paris, and swelling with rhodomontade for the sonorous voice of Hodgkinson, who was to represent the Indian saint." [94] The Tammany Society urged the managers of the Old American Company to put it on, and despite Dunlap's label of "a melange of bombast," and *The New-York Magazine's* epithet "that wretched thing," it was well received and was given performances in New York, Philadelphia, and Boston.[95] The words to some of the songs were printed [96] and sold both at the printing office and at the theatre, and they vindicate Dunlap rather than the audiences of the day, although it is possible that with music they were bearable. The patriotic element is strong, as seen in a duet between Tammany and Manana:

> Farewell then ye woods which have witness'd our flame.
> Let time on his wings bear our record of fame.
> Together we die, for our spirits disdain,
> Ye white children of Europe, your rankling chain.

And the quality of the whole unfortunately shines through the final chorus which pleads with humanity fervidly to glow, "Shewing soft mercy to the vanquish'd foe."

The Archers, too, has its share of firsts—the first extant all-American opera to be put on stage by a professional company.

American comic operas were as subject to being cut down for afterpieces as European, and *Tammany,* for example, continued its career as the short *America Discovered.*[97] The list of original eighteenth-century American musical farces is a long one,[98] and it includes the familiar interlude.

Interludes, or musical episodes, came between play and afterpiece, or between acts of a given piece, or in the piece itself; they were usually a brief pantomime or song or dance, and were sometimes quite elaborate.[99] They "were generally satirical dialogues on the vices and follies of the times, shorter and less ambitious in construction than a play, but filled with simple wit, which appealed to all classes, though often rude and racy in tone."[100] Almost anyone might rush an interlude to the stage to comment on a recent event. One actress, Mrs. Pownall, who broke her leg, quickly threw a piece together with plot by Mrs. Hatton and original songs by herself, a work in which she appeared, crutches and all.[101] William Dunlap, *hic et ubique*, was also adept at converting events to interludes; his *Yankee Chronology, or Huzza for the Constitution* (1812) was written upon receipt of the news that the *Constitution* had won a victory over the English frigate *Guerriére*.[102] Three characters discuss the victory, then a song follows with eleven stanzas, each ending with

Then huzzah! for the sons of Columbia so free!
They are lords of the soil—they'll be lords of the sea!

Not only were contemporary events used for interludes, but here, as in England, the interlude frequently represented an abridgement of an abridgement, or a brief continuation of a popular piece. *The Poor Soldier,* seen in America in its original form (as a comic opera) and as a musical farce, *Darby and Patrick,* was also extremely popular as Dunlap's interlude *Darby's Return.*[103] Darby, who at the end of *The Poor Soldier* was going to travel and build his reputation, here returns and tells his adventures to his former associates; his description of the Revolution in America and his two solos with chorus must have been pleasing, though the topical references to Anglophobia have little validity today.

The burletta remained a poor relation of opera in America, too, and although many pieces were advertised as burlettas, the most enduring were the *Poor Vulcan* of Dibdin and Kane O'Hare's *Midas*.[104]

6

Ballad opera, serious opera, pasticcios, and comic opera (in all its Protean guises) were not the only forms the musical stage took in eighteenth-century America—pantomime and dancing were almost as important.

Theatrical dancing became a separate form very late in the history of dance, and by then pantomime had been long established in the field.[105]

> . . . as a matter of historical and esthetic fact, ballet and pantomime are no more synonymous than are opera and ballet.
>
> A pantomime may contain a good deal of dancing and a good deal of singing (the "speaking pantomime"), and still the pantomime, if representative of its genre, is not a ballet, much less an opera. It may be likened, notwithstanding such ingredients, to living pictures, moving or not, the appreciation and understanding of which depend on ready symbolic association and ready solution of allegorical puzzles. Exactly because the ballet, from mere danced symbolical action, developed almost into a danced pantomime, it becomes difficult to keep the two apart for historical purposes.[106]

The eighteenth century, as it did with all stage forms, thoroughly blurred the distinction between the two; but the effort to look at dancing and pantomiming separately can be helpful in making clear an important aspect of the theatrical repertory in eighteenth-century America. First, the pantomime.

Eighteenth-century English pantomime was a new stage

form.[107] Whether or not the new form was created by
Weaver in 1702, it is certain that John Rich formalized
and popularized it, first at Lincoln's Inn Fields and later
at Covent Garden.[108] Rich had tried pantomimes in 1717;
it was not, however, until his *The Necromancer, or History of Dr. Faustus* that he captured the popular imagination; from then on the prices of admission to the theatres
were raised on the nights pantomimes and harlequinades
were to be shown, indicating something of the eagerness
of the eighteenth-century audience to see them.[109]

In Thomas Davies's *Memoirs of Garrick* (1808), Rich's
harlequinade is described:

> It consisted of two parts, one serious, and the other
> comic. By help of gay scenes, fine habits, grand dances,
> appropriate music, and other decorations, he exhibited a
> story from Ovid's Metamorphoses, or some other fabu-
> lous writer. Between the pauses of acts of this serious
> representation he interwove a comic fable, consisting
> chiefly of the courtship of Harlequin and Columbine,
> with a variety of surprising adventures and tricks, which
> were produced by the magic wand of Harlequin. . . .[110]

In *Tom Jones* (1749), Fielding presented a somewhat
less euphoric view of the proceedings:

> The entertainment consists of two parts, which the
> inventor distinguished by the names of the serious and
> the comic. The serious exhibited a certain number of
> heathen gods and heroes, who were certainly the worst
> and dullest company into which an audience was ever
> introduced, and (which was a secret known to few) were
> actually intended so to be, in order to contrast the comic
> part of the entertainment, and to display the tricks of
> Harlequin to the better advantage.
>
> This was, perhaps, no very civil use of such person-
> ages; but the contrivance was, nevertheless, ingenious

enough, and had its effect. And this will now plainly appear, if, instead of serious and comic, we supply the words duller and dullest; for the comic was certainly duller than anything before shown on the stage, and could be set off only by that superlative degree of dullness which composed the serious. So intolerably serious, indeed, were these gods and heroes, that Harlequin (though the English gentleman of that name is not at all related to the French family, for he is of a much more serious disposition) was always welcome on the stage, as he relieved the audience from worse company.[111]

The serious part (involving Greek or Roman myth, or some nearly contemporaneous legend) was shorter than the comic; the latter always involved the pursuit of Harlequin and Columbine by Columbine's father or guardian or suitor (Pantaloon) into unlikely places. And Harlequin's magic bat produced all sorts of transformations and enchantments. Rich's pantomimes were without dialogue and depended heavily upon scenery, costume, machinery, and the acting of "Lun" (Rich's stage name).[112]

Possibly because of Rich's unrivalled superiority, his competitors were forced to change the form. Garrick wrote of him after his death:

> When Lun appeared with faultless art and whim
> He gave the power of speech to every limb.
> Though masked and mute, conveyed his quick intent
> And told in frolic gestures all he meant;
> But now the motley coat and sword of wood
> Require a tongue to make them understood.[113]

The "tongue" that Garrick refers to was speaking and singing, both of which were added to the form by Henry Woodward in an attempt to draw audiences away from Rich.[114] Music was used extensively and helped bring

about the unique quality of eighteenth-century pantomime: the elaborating of Harlequin's unspoken movements into a regular plot told by "heel" instead of
"head." [115]

The drawing in of other elements became pantomime's
trademark as the century progressed. Spoken and unspoken action, duets sung, dancers, acrobats, scenic effects—all contributed a share.[116] Richard Brinsley Sheridan
lengthened the pantomime and expanded its very conception. Until his *Robinson Crusoe* (1781), the Harlequin
story had had no connection either with the title of the
pantomime or with its "serious" theme (in fact, Harlequin's story usually interrupted the progress of the action);
but *Robinson Crusoe* was in four acts and was the first
pantomime in which Harlequin and his friends took part
in the actual story. Crusoe's man Friday was now Harlequin, and English pantomime had arrived at a new
stage.[117]

Toward the end of the century pantomime began to
include more and more spectacle, new themes crept in,
and Harlequin himself became a different man. James
Byrne (newly returned from America where, as choreographer for Wignell and Reinagle and later for Ricketts,
it is at least possible he tried out his innovations) gave
Harlequin, in about 1799, a tight-fitting costume, expanded
his five basic positions (Admiration, Flirtation, Thought,
Defiance, and Determination) so as to include other emo-
tions, and gave many new meanings to Harlequin's postures and dress.[118]

Harlequin arrived in America with the very first plays
and operas; only a very few years were needed to give
him uniquely American characteristics. By 1740 New York
and Charleston had seen pantomimes, and Hallam's original company arrived in 1752 with at least one pantomime

in its repertory.[119] Although the company advertised itself as "being perfect in all the best Plays, Operas, Farces, and Pantomimes," the plural may be an exaggeration; Dunlap says one pantomime, *Harlequin Collector, or The Miller Deceived,* was all the American Company had for many years.[120] The 1760's found new pantomimes being added to the repertory, the inclusion of songs in the pantomimes, and even puppets performing them.[121] By 1771 pantomimes were so much a part of the repertory that William Eddis could write of the new Annapolis theatre that "the stage is well adapted for dramatic and pantomimical exhibition. . . ."[122] Baltimore saw several full-length "dance-pantomimes" in the 1782-83 season, and in December, 1782, two pantomimes of French origin were presented there. When the circuses went into competition with the theatres, pantomimes formed the battleground, and rarely did a day of performance go by when Ricketts did not advertise a new pantomime.[123]

In March, 1783, in Baltimore, *Columbus, or the Discovery of America, with Harlequin's Revels* was done, and "this represented a new manifestation—pantomime with national themes, later a major part of American entertainment."[124] These national themes in pantomimes became so popular, that "It is a curious fact that American patriotic and historical drama at this time took the form of pantomime."[125] The expanded pantomime which Sheridan had devised, *Robinson Crusoe,* was produced in New York and Philadelphia, and John Durang blackfaced to act the part of Friday.[126] "Speaking-pantomimes" began to be produced in great numbers; their origin was French; they were notable for their mixture of all the arts, and their popularity in America really grew with the French companies and French refugees who arrived here in the 1790's.[127] American pantomimes of that time were usually

given French titles. Two of the four best choreographers
in eighteenth-century America were French, Alexander
Placide and M. Francisquy, and both were adept at "composing" pantomimes. Although the French troupes performed operas and plays, their repertories were primarily
arranged to suit the dancers and mimes who made up
their companies.[128] These French actors often turned
French operas into "pantomime-pasticcios"; [129] "pasticcio"
meant the same thing it did with operas, and the pantomime-pasticcios might use a story popular in France or
England, with original choreography composed for each
company, and with music (and songs) by Pleyel, Grétry,
Giornowiski, Giordani, Shield, Reeve, Morehead, etc., and
all for the same pantomime! [130] The importance of the
book is shown in the fact that a well-known pantomime
might be advertised with "music, entirely new" or "entire new music." [131] Language barriers may have helped
kill off French opera in America until well into the nineteenth century, but French pantomime and ballet remained throughout an influence on the American stage.
The increased stress on new music gave native composers
an opportunity to do more than arrange others' music for
pantomimes, and before the century was over, an American concert could advertise on its program a collection
of music especially written for pantomimes.[132]

Other changes took place in the subject matter of
pantomimes: they became nautical as well as patriotic;
and as with today's musical comedies, no novel was safe
from being converted into a pantomime. Susannah Rowson helped the range of pantomime's interest by becoming
the first female Harlequin in America. And it was with
pantomime that the first flowering of America's scenic art
arrived.[133] Just as in England Rich for the first time began
to clear spectators from the stage in order to make room

for the machines in his pantomimes, so in America the
rage for spectacles which were a part of all pantomimes
was "the greatest single influence toward moving the
action behind the proscenium arch. . . ." [134] The French,
here, too, were a strong influence, for "the French Pantomimes were always elaborately and beautifully staged and
they excelled in the minutiae of stage-settings. . . ." [135] As
scenic realism, especially in pantomimes, grew stronger,
the following became the kind of performance admired
by New Yorkers in 1796:

> The wonderful specimens of Theatrical Art, which are
> exhibited in Mr. Ricketts' new pantomime [The Triumph
> of Virtue] or Harlequin in New-York; and the great
> variety of interesting changes makes it appear like en-
> chantments, to the astonished audience. Amongst the
> scenery, there is an elegant painting, comprehending a
> perfect view of the governor's house, the circular inclo-
> sure opposite to it, and a part of Broadway. Mr. Sully,
> as Harlequin, leaps over a house adjoining the gover-
> nor's, and goes through a number of changes with a
> facility that is surprising. [136]

Further changes in pantomime were probably brought
about by James Byrne. He had been ballet master at
Sadler's Wells and Covent Garden before coming to
America (where he and his wife worked for the theatre
in Philadelphia and the circus in New York); his pantomimes were as good as those seen anywhere else in the
world—no less an authority than Grimaldi claiming that
he was the best Harlequin on the boards. The changes
in the costume and conception of Harlequin that he inaugurated in England in 1799 (changes which were followed by all Harlequins thereafter) were probably the
results of experiments conducted in America. [137]

A reasonably good picture of the "speaking-panto-

mimes" which were, up to 1796, the most serious form
of pantomime seen on the American stage emerges from
a playbill for the performance of April 16, 1796 (two
days before *The Archers*) in Charleston. After *Richard III*
came "A Grand Allegorical Pantomime called the Apotheosis of Franklin, or His Reception in the Elysian Fields."
The cast included Houdon, a sculptor; Diard, Houdon's
pupil; Countryman; Envy; Spirit of Philosophy; Charon;
Franklin; Goddess of Fame; Clio, "Goddess of History";
Euterpe, "Goddess of Music"; the spirits of Voltaire,
Shakespeare, and Sir Isaac Newton; and Furies. Harlequin
has been ignored, but the elaborate stagecraft he brought
to pantomimes becomes apparent in the summary of
scenes:

[Act I]

The first Scene represents the statuary, Houdon, at
work on the tomb of Franklin; the tomb adorned with
two beautiful statues. The first represents the United
States holding in its right hand the American Eagle; on
its left arm a shield and buckler inscribed with these
words: "Unitate populoque Americano."

The second [scene] represents the Goddess of Pru-
dence holding a tablet with this inscription "Prudentia
direxit eum," and on the panel of the tomb "Eripuit
fulmen cielo sceptrumque tyrannis."

[Act II]

First scene represents a gloomy cavern through which
is seen a view of the river Styx, Charon in his boat and
the banks of the Stygian Lake.

Second Scene

Represents the Elysian Fields; the Goddess of Fame
descends and proclaims the virtues of Franklin, who is
conducted to the abode of Peace by Philosophy; he meets

with Diogenes, the Cynic, who introduces him to all the wise and learned men who inhabit those seats of eternal rest.

The Last Scene

Represents the Temple of Memory adorned with statues and busts of all the deceased Poets, Philosophers and wise Men. Franklin's bust is placed on a vacant pedestal, facing that of Sir Isaac Newton.[138]

Finally, the whole affair is concluded with a dance and then a "Triumphal Hymn, In honor of Franklin sung by the Goddess of Fame and the Goddess of History." New Decorations, new costumes, new music, and a grand overture were also featured.

7

In 1794 a new form arrived in America. The new form was closely akin to ballet, and it becomes necessary to glance briefly at theatre dancing in Europe and America before looking at *La Forêt Noire*, America's first "serious pantomime."

In the early 1600's dancers' dress began for the first time to be different from that of the spectators, and theatrical dancing as a separate form of the drama got under way.[139] A new form, the comédie-ballet (a play with singing and dancing relevant to the action between scenes) was invented by Lully and Molière in 1661, and this helped widen the schism between social and theatre dancing; in fact, by the middle of the seventeenth century, social dancing had nothing to do either with serious or with comic ballet.[140] In England in the seventeenth century some imitations of the French court dances were performed, as were occasional odd works such as the Shadwell-Locke *Psyche*, though in Elizabeth's time there had been stage dances which were sung, or merely played, or sung and danced at the same time. But eighteenth-century England's dancing in the theatre came not so much from France as from Italy, the kind of dancing which was done as part of a pantomime. It was this latter kind of dancing, mostly pantomimic in nature, which appeared frequently in, for example, ballad operas. *The Beggar's Opera* has a dance of prisoners in chains, a drill of highwaymen, a cotillion of ladies of pleasure [141]—none exactly a ballet. In America, the two kinds of dance were to join happily together.

Much dancing was performed on the American stage before the introduction of ballet. Records of rope dancing go back as far as 1724, and rope dancing remained popular in the theatre through the end of the century.[142] Boston's Exhibition Room opened, in 1792, with "Tight and Slack-Rope Performances," and Ricketts's second Philadelphia circus featured tight-rope performers who doubled in pantomime and ballet. When Hallam and Henry hired Placide's company, the New York *Weekly Museum* announced the engagement of rope dancers. As late as 1797 William Dunlap insisted that no competing company in Boston was to perform rope dances.[143] Something of the formal nature as well as the beauty of these rope dances may be gleaned from Henry J. Colton, who saw Placide himself in action:

> The first time I saw him was at Charleston . . . dancing the tight rope. At that period it was considered a great and graceful feat of address, and always drew crowded houses. Placide had with him a pantomime dancer. . . . The preparations for the Dance were always imposing. The attendants, in livery, carried the rope to the center of the pit, where it was duly attached and drawn upon the stage. A palace scene was set for

the rope dancing, and a row of wax candles were placed
at equal distances near the rope. Placide, habited in a
light silk Spanish dress, with silk stockings and pumps
and two watch chains, then greatly in fashion, made his
appearance amid shouts of applause, Spinacuta playing
the clown, with chalked face and parti-colored pants.[144]

The theatre absorbed all sorts of dances. When, in 1735,
Charleston saw the ballad opera, *Flora, or Hob in the
Well*, a pantomime was on the same bill, as was the
"Dance of Two Pierrots." [145] The "Two Pierrots" indicates
that mingling of pantomime and dance had already begun, as the familiar, standard postures of pantomime
characters came to be used frequently for brief dances.
The Murray and Kean company, in Williamsburg in 1751,
performed a "Grand Tragic Dance" "composed [eight-
eenth century for "arranged the choreography"] by M.
Denoir [and] called 'The Royal Captive.' " [146] When Hallam's company arrived, between-the-acts entertainment
included "A Punch's Dance" (probably in imitation of the
popular puppet shows) and "A Tambourin Dance." In
addition to the hornpipe and "a Negro Dance," and Irish
and Scotch dances, full dance productions were coming
into vogue; dancing between acts or between play and
afterpiece came to be a regular part of the evening's entertainment.[147]

The 1780's, thanks largely to John Durang, were the
heyday of the hornpipe. Though hornpipes had been popular for years (Durang himself had been dancing them
between parts of puppet and theatrical shows before
1785), it was in 1785 that he had one especially composed
for him by Wilhelm Hoffmeister, "Billy the Fiddler," a
former drummer in the army.[148] "The hornpipe is, of
course, an acknowledged ancestor of the modern tap

dance," [149] and the line of descent is easily seen in a list
of directions for doing "A Sailor Hornpipe—Old Style,"
a list which probably comprises the original "Durang's
Hornpipe" and which passed from John Durang to his
son, Charles, and is contained in the latter's book on theatrical dancing (1855). Each step takes up one strain of
the tune:

1. Glissade round (first part of tune).
2. Double shuffle down, do.
3. Heel and toe back, finish with back shuffle.
4. Cut the buckle down, finish the shuffle.
5. Side shuffle right and left, finishing with beats.
6. Pigeon wing going round.
7. Heel and toe haul in back.
8. Steady toes down.
9. Changes back, finish with back shuffle and beats.
10. Wave step down.
11. Heel and toe shuffle obliquely back.
12. Whirligig, with beats down.
13. Sissone and entrechats back
14. Running forward on the heels.
15. Double Scotch step, with a heel Brand in Plase. (*sic*)
16. Single Scotch step back.
17. Parried toes round, or feet *in* and *out*.
18. The Cooper shuffle right and left back.
19. Grasshopper step down.
20. *Terre-a-terre* (*sic*) or beating on toes back.
21. Jockey crotch down.
22. Traverse round, with hornpipe glissade.
                    Bow and finish

Assorted dances over eggs were also popular on the
stage in eighteenth-century America.[150] While no account
of them is available, one from *Wilhelm Meister* for the
same period helps in visualizing this popular stage dance:

She [Mignon] carried a little carpet below her arm, which she then spread out upon the floor. . . . She thereupon brought four candles, and placed one upon each corner of the carpet. A little basket of eggs which she next carried in, made her purpose clearer. Carefully measuring her steps, she then walked to and fro on the carpet, spreading out the eggs in certain figures and positions: which done, she called in a man that could play on the violin. . . . She tied a band about her eyes, gave a signal, and, like a piece of wheel-work set a-going, she began moving the same instant as the music, accompanying her beats and the notes of the tune with the strokes of a pair of castanets.

Lightly, nimbly, quickly, and with hairsbreadth accuracy, she carried on the dance. She skipped so sharply and surely along between the eggs, and trod so closely down beside them, that you would have thought every instant she must trample one of them in pieces, or kick the rest away in her rapid turns. By no means! She touched no one of them, though winding herself through their mazes with all kinds of steps, wide and narrow, nay even with hops, and at last half-kneeling.

Constant as the movement of a clock, she ran her course; and the strange music, at each repetition of the tune, gave a new impulse to the dance, recommencing and again rushing off as at first. . . .

The dance being ended, she rolled the eggs together softly with her foot into a little heap, left none behind, harmed none; then placed herself beside it, taking the bandage from her eyes, and concluding her performance with a little bow.

A playbill for the John Street Theatre for April 6, 1796, advertised a Spanish Fandango between the play and the afterpiece; yet the bill for the dance mentions a cast of three, plus four dancers and five singers! [151] Most dances of the time, despite being used merely as entr'acte entertainments, seem to have had several characters in them and to have told a story, however brief. A "comic dance" done in Charleston in 1794 included fourteen characters and a duet.[152] Dickens, albeit writing in the nineteenth century, includes in *Nicholas Nickleby* a description of one of these dance interludes, this one called *The Indian Savage and the Maiden.* A girl came in,

> turned a pirouette, cut twice in the air, turned another pirouette, then, looking off at the opposite wing, shrieked, bounded forward to within six inches of the footlights, and fell into a beautiful attitude of terror, as a shabby gentleman in an old pair of buff slippers came in at one powerful slide, and chattering his teeth, fiercely brandished his walking stick. . . . The savage, becoming ferocious, made a slide towards the maiden; but the maiden avoided him in six twirls, and came down, at the end of the last one, upon the very point of her toes. This seemed to make some impression upon the savage; for after a little more ferocity and chasing of the maiden into corners, he began to relent, and stroked his face several times with his right thumb and four fingers, thereby intimating that he was struck with admiration of the maiden's beauty. Acting upon the impulse of this passion, he (the savage) began to hit himself severe thumps in the chest, and exhibit other indications of being desperately in love, which being a rather prosy proceeding was very likely the cause of the maiden's falling asleep; whether it was or no, asleep she did fall, sound as a church, on a sloping bank, and the savage perceiving it, leant his left ear on his left hand, and nodded sideways, to intimate to all whom it might concern that she *was* asleep, and no shamming. Being left to himself, the savage had a dance, all alone. Just as he left off, the maiden woke up, rubbed her eyes, got off the bank, and had a dance all alone too—such a dance that the savage looked on [in] ecstasy all the while, and when it was done,

plucked from a neighboring tree some botanical curiosity, resembling a small pickled cabbage, and offered it to the maiden, who at first wouldn't have it, but in the savage shedding tears relented. Then the savage jumped for joy; then the maiden jumped for rapture at the sweet smell of the pickled cabbage. Then the savage and the maiden danced violently together, and, finally, the savage dropped down on one knee, and the maiden stood on one leg on his other knee; thus concluding the ballet, and leaving the spectators in a state of pleasing uncertainty, whether she would ultimately marry the savage, or return to her friends.[153]

In 1792 Placide's company was responsible for introducing ballet to the American people; his "Dancing Ballets" or "Pantomime Ballets" were "probably closer to our present-day conception of a ballet than anything which had been seen in the United States up to that time." [154] Placide's New York debut included a dancing ballet, *The Bird Catcher*, fast followed by rope dancing and the dancing ballet *Two Philosophers*, and these were followed by, among others, *Wood Cutters*, based on *Le Bucheron*, a ballet by Philidor in 1763; he brought to Philadelphia in the same year a number of French pastoral ballets, the music coming from French operas. Obviously, there were ballet pasticcios as well as pantomime pasticcios. Most of the early ballets danced here were merely adaptations and Americanizations of those performed successfully in London or Paris; but soon, they began to be created in America. James Byrne, for example, transformed the much-abused *Poor Soldier* into *Dermot and Kathleen*, a ballet with music from everywhere. Soon, too, the music for American ballets began to be composed here.[155]

The music presented with a ballet, however, did not necessarily remain the same; here, as with the pantomime, it was the book which was all-important. Eighteenth-century ballets contained vocal interpolations, and a popular libretto "would hold its attraction over a period of years, and it was not unusual for successive composers to take it over, writing new music for special numbers or for the whole work." [156] Towards the end of the century the drama in ballet became more and more obscured as dancing, scenery, machinery, and dress took over [157] (similar to what happened in pantomime; indeed, by the end of the century the two forms were almost identical). These tendencies can be observed in an announcement in the newspapers written by Susannah Rowson for her benefit bill. The program was to include a "new serious pantomimical ballet called *Shipwreck'd Mariners Preserved; or La bonne petite fille.*" It was one of the first all-American ballets, with choreography by M. Lege set to Raynor Taylor's music.[158] Mrs. Rowson describes her *Slaves in Algiers,* then:

> . . . So much for the Play—the next thing a Dance is,
> Or a Pantomime Ballet, directed by Francis.
> Representing a ship on a rocky coast stranded—
> Her Captain preserv'd, some few mariners landed;
> By a gang of Blood-thirsty banditti surrounded,
> By terror o'ercome, by their danger confounded—
> Experienc'd the care of kind Providence still,
> And were sav'd by an infant—"Le bon [sic] Petite Fille.
> . . ."

Perhaps the most impressive of the pantomime ballets was Delpini's version of *Don Juan* with music by Gluck and songs and choruses by Reeve; the best actors were always used to mouth its risqué dialogue (Hallam and Hodgkinson performed it for the Old American Company), and *Don Juan* was played as far afield as New York, Philadelphia, Charleston, and Savannah.[159]

Philadelphia, in 1794, was treated to the serious pantomime *La Forêt Noire,* "an event of the greatest importance in the history of the ballet in America." [160] With
music probably by Reinagle and choreography probably
by Mme. Gardie (who danced the leading role), it was
an instant success; before the century was over, it was
danced or mimed in New York, Philadelphia, Boston,
Charleston, Hartford, Baltimore, and Norfolk. It was followed by other serious pantomimes, such as *Sophia of
Brabant, The Death of Captain Cook,* and *Jeanne d'Arc.*[161]

Only one serious pantomime is extant from eighteenth-
century America, and fortunately it is *La Forêt Noire.*[162]
It is difficult to say in what way the serious pantomime
was very different from the ballets and pantomimes of the
day. Possibly its novelty lay in being so neat a blend of
ballet and pantomime; possibly, the answer lay in its
similarity to the foetal melodrama; possibly, the con-
tinuous flow of music and the spectacular scenic effects
gave it life. Whatever the reasons for its seeming originality and freshness to an eighteenth-century audience, its
libretto reads today much like a silent-film scenario. *La
Forêt Noire* is in three acts, each broken up into many
brief scenes (Act I alone has sixteen scenes); the cast
has over twenty-five parts. Geronte, Lucille's father, wants
her to marry L'Abbe; she cannot, since she is concealing
both her marriage to an officer, Lauridan, and her son,
Adolphus (played in Boston by the same Miss Harding
who portrayed William Tell's son in the première of *The
Archers*). Geronte discovers the child and sends it out to
be killed. In the second act, servants attempt to kill the
child who is rescued by La Terreur (the Captain of the
Robbers). Lucille is captured by robbers. Her husband
comes at the head of troops, defeats the robbers in pitched
battle (Wood, Mountain, Rocks, Grotto, etc.), saves

Lucille, is united with her by her father; the soldiers then maneuver all over the stage before marching off at the end. A typical scene (Act I, scene 5) wherein Lucille's father has just exited in a rage leaving Lucille and Abbe (the comic relief) alone on stage, reads:

> She looks at him with disdain; he attempts to make his court; she turns her back. He offers her his *bouquet;* she refuses. He offers her some cakes; she refuses. He consoles himself by eating some of them; he takes his snuff box, and offers snuff. *Lucille* vexed, strikes it out of his hand. He menaces to tell her father, and *Exit in a rage.*

When Francisquy joined the Old American Company in 1796 and inaugurated the most brilliant period of ballet the United States had yet seen, *La Forêt Noire,* only a few days before *The Archers,* was one of his first productions.[163]

Still other ballets and dances were performed in eighteenth-century America. Monk Lewis's Gothic plays were converted to ballets here; they originated in America, and were later performed with great success in London. Still another kind of ballet used a narrative basis, and was generally set to a popular ballad.[164] Too, dances were originated for special occasions; one such involved the President's Birthday Ball at Ricketts's Amphitheatre in Philadelphia in March, 1796, and constitutes one of America's first precision routines:

> There were seven sets of dancers, who took their stations in rank from one centre, and verging toward the circumference, of which the dancers composed so many Radii. When the band of music struck up, which was composed of thirty capital performers, all the sets were put in motion at once, and dancing from the circumference toward one general centre, with so much elegance, and keeping

such true time, it was the most enlivening sight that
could possibly be conceived.[165]

The early American dance was responsible, in large part,
for two characteristics peculiar to the American musical
stage even today: pace,[166] and the musical comedy performer who is expected to dance, as well as to act and
to sing.

8

Act II of *The Archers* involved plans for William Tell's
famed bit of marksmanship. A member of the audience,
impatient perhaps with dialogue, and waiting eagerly for
the next song, might have thought of the musical stage as
it assumed still other forms in the repertory of an eighteenth-century American company. The masque, for example. The form of the masque was fairly stable.[167] A poet
was called in to introduce the dancers; later, a grotesque
antimasque, acted by professionals, was introduced; the
entire piece was accompanied by music. Songs (later,
some recitative), dances, poetry, and spectacle—these
formed the backbone. The plot was always based on a
classic story or legend (and frequently featured allegorical figures who never got beyond explaining who they
were and what they stood for).[168]

When musical stage genres began to proliferate after
about 1760, only the ballad opera and the masque remained from among earlier popular lyric stage forms. The
masque, however, was usually reduced to an afterpiece.
In fact,

The musical masque . . . was the result of the demand
made by the managers for afterpieces. . . . The musical
tendency which led towards the introduction of the Italian opera, and the desire on the part of English writers

to compete with the Italians, naturally led to a rapid development of the masque in the first half of the eighteenth century.[169]

Masques continued popular through 1800, but there was no vitality to the form.

Popular masques, both in England and America, included Milton's *Comus* [170] and those masques inserted into Shakespeare's plays.[171] All through the eighteenth century, for example, on both sides of the Atlantic whenever *The Tempest* was given, the *Masque of Neptune and Amphitrite* was always performed right after the play. Neptune, Amphitrite, Oceanus, and Tethys appeared in a chariot drawn by sea horses; on the sides of the chariot were sea gods and goddesses and tritons and nereides; a dance of twelve tritons followed; then the scene changed to a view of the rising sun with spirits in the air and a song by Ariel; then Ariel, hovering in the air, addressed the audience and the masque was over.[172]

> The masque of Neptune and Amphitrite belonged to Shadwell's original version of *The Tempest*, and Purcell's setting is of interest mainly for purely musical reasons. The songs are particularly beautiful, and the Italian influence is very marked, more so perhaps than in any other opera of Purcell, since we find here several examples of the fully developed *da capo* aria, a form hitherto unknown in English music.[173]

The Purcell music crossed the Atlantic with the *Masque of Neptune and Amphitrite* which was seen in America throughout the 1700's.

The first important debut of the masque in America took place at the College in Philadelphia, in 1757; the students recited and sang "as gentlemen played the instrumental parts," to *The Masque of Alfred*.[174] The masque

had been altered by the Provost, William Smith, and
Francis Hopkinson had arranged and accompanied the
songs on the harpsichord, at least one of which he had
written himself.[175] Its importance to the United States is
that it is the "first native dramatic effort, containing original material and known to have been performed on the
stage, that has come down to us. . . ."[176] In addition to
a new Prologue and Epilogue and two hundred new lines,
the American version contained some new hymns and
pieces of music.

The plot begins[177] as Corin and Emma, peasants, are
mystified by the appearance of a stranger. The Earl of
Devon joins the stranger, who turns out to be Alfred, and
the latter plans a battle with the Danes. Alfred, and Corin
rescue a woman from some Danish soldiers (killing them
in the process); the rescuee is discovered to be Alfred's
wife, Eltruda. After a reunion scene, a Hermit advises
Alfred, and the result is a victory over the Danes. The
Danish king loudly takes leave of his senses when he
learns his only son has been killed by Alfred earlier in the
proceedings. The masque ends with an injunction to build
fleets, since that is how to remain powerful. Typical of
the dialogue is the following from Act I, scene 4. Alfred
has just dispatched some men to prepare for battle with
the Danes. Alone, he soliloquizes, then says:

> But soft: the breeze
> Is dumb! and more than midnight silence reigns!
> Why beats my bosom?—Music!—now the measur'd strains,
> In awful sweetness warbling, strike my sense,
> As if some wing'd musician of the sky
> Touch'd his ethereal harp.

The stage directions for scene 5 immediately follow: "Solemn music is heard at a distance. It comes nearer in a

full symphony: after which a single trumpet sounds a high and awakening air." Much singing and dancing immediately take over as the masque wends its tortuous way in the general direction of the final curtain.

Toward the end of the century, the masque catered to a taste for the spectacular. On February 9, 1798, for example, Charleston saw an original "Musical and Allegorical Masque," called *Americania and Elutheria; or, a new Tale of the Genii.*[178] Though the libretto and the music are lost, a program for the masque in a pamphlet of the time is extant:

> Hybla, a mountain nymph, desirous to see a mortal, implores Offa, a satyr, to procure that pleasure. Offa deludes an old hermit up to the summit of the Allegani Mountains to a great rock, inhabited by Genii, or aerial spirits, the chief of whom, called Americania, understanding that the old hermit is ignorant of the American Revolution, commands her domestics to perform an allegorical masque for his information [this masque within a masque shows the defeat of Typhon (the Genius of Tyranny) and Fastidio (the Genius of Pride) by Eltherius (commander of the American forces) and Galiana (the Genius of France) and Fulmenifer (the apotheosis of Franklin)].
>
> In Act First. . . . A Grand Dance of nymphs and satyrs, who will form a group of the most whimsical kind.
>
> In Act Second. . . . A meeting taking place between Elutheria, the Goddess of Liberty, and Americania, who descends on clouds on opposite sides.
>
> A pas de deux, between the satyr Horbla and the nymph Hybla, the whole to conclude with a general dance of the nymphs and satyrs, a pas de deux by a young master and lady; and a pas de trois, by Mrs. Placide, Mr. Placide, and Mr. Tubbs.

The proverbial kitchen sink would not even have been noticed in such a performance.

9

Toward the end of the eighteenth century, the extravaganza became a stage form. From the magic wand of Harlequin which could transform things, a special fillip was added to spectacular displays, as pantomimes "were all announced to be set off with 'new scenery, decorations, and flyings.'" [179]

As early as 1767 newspapers included in their advertisements tempting descriptions of the plays, "complete with views of the sea, ships fighting, sea monsters, etc." [180] Marine scenery became very popular, and grand sea engagements were done over and over again; ships passing and saluting near the Battery, the Arch Street wharf in Philadelphia, the launching of the *Constitution,* were particular favorites.[181] When John Hodgkinson's production of *The Launch* (with music selected from the best composers and orchestral parts by Pelissier) was presented in Boston in 1797, the advertisements announced, "The whole will conclude with a striking representation of Launching the New Frigate *Constitution.* Boats passing and repassing on the Water. View of the River of Charleston, and the neighboring country. . . ." [182] As 1800 approached, scenic realism grew stronger and stronger (especially in pantomimes at first) and extravaganzas became separate conceptions.

> At times these spectacles were integrated with the representation of a drama; at times they were inserted between the play and the farce, or as the concluding feature of the evening's program; but as often as not they were exhibited by themselves as the feature attraction.[183]

One of the early exhibitions at the Park Theatre, New York, for example, included a distant view of Belgrade, the burning of a camp, and a representation of the fortifications on which an attack was made by storm with red-hot cannon balls. The increased popularity of the panorama and diorama helped push almost everything but spectacle to the background.[184] The heyday of the extravaganza began in America about 1795, when "scenery was so elaborate . . . that the actor sometimes found himself crowded entirely off the stage, the manager relying chiefly on the magic of paint and canvas to pack the house." [185]

Another type of musical extravaganza was close to a modern revue. This olio of recitations and songs was given in most cities of the country and by a variety of actors, although Raynor Taylor and his "burlesque olios" or "extravaganzas" were unquestionably the most famous.[186] His program in Annapolis in 1793 consisted of three parts: first, a selection of comic and pastoral songs; second, a burletta called *The Gray Mare's the Best Horse* which contained a duet with Miss Huntley, who appeared with Taylor, called "Mock wife in a violent passion," then Taylor did "A Father's advice to his son-in-law" and "Giles the countryman's grief for the loss of a scolding wife" and "Happy Miller," after which Miss Huntley reappeared with "Dame Pliant's obedience to her husband," and this section of the program was concluded with three duets ("Obedient wife, determined to have her own way," "New married couple reconciled," and "All parties happy"); the third part of the program was a burlesque of Italian opera called *Capocchio and Dorinna* in which the talented duo appeared in costume to sing the requisite recitations, arias, and duets. Taylor played a piece on the piano before each part.[187]

10

With the extensive use of spectacle, with extravaganzas and olios, the repertory of the Old American Company comes full circle, back to legitimate drama. Yet the straight drama of the eighteenth century was frequently made to look like opera.[188] The first decade of the eighteenth century saw singing and dancing and instrumental performances before, in the course of, and after almost every play. The popularity of works such as *The Beggar's Opera* suggested changes in regular plays so that the "regular drama began to popularize itself at times, in its rivalry with the recent musical innovations, by adopting certain operatic features, such as the introduction of songs or dances."[189] The same tendency took place in America, where an advertisement for a play (not an opera) was as likely to mention the composer and arranger as the playwright.[190] Even plays that were not advertised as musical were often accompanied by music. A prompt book of William Dunlap for Kotzebue's *The Virgin of the Sun*[191] shows a music cue at the beginning of Act III, a cue later (in Dunlap's hand) for "Solemn Music Ready," and next to "The Curtain falls" at the end, Dunlap wrote "Slow to Grand Music." The fact that "many plays were so filled with interpolations of songs, dances, or scenic effects that they were little more than variety entertainments,"[192] meant that almost no straight plays were done, either here or in England. Nowhere is this better seen than in the works of Shakespeare.

Three hundred of Shakespeare's stage directions are musical in nature and occur in thirty-six of the thirty-seven plays.[193] Given this initial impetus, Shakespeare's plays soon began to be made into operas. From the interpolation of songs (such as "When daisies pied" of *Love's Labour's Lost* tucked into *As You Like It,* with music by Dr. Arne), Shakespeare's helpers went on to giving various characters songs to sing (Portia was among the more ludicrous recipients) and from there to the "wholesale operatizing" of many of his plays.[194] Garrick is renowned for having wiped many of Shakespeare's plays free of operatic accretions during the time he ruled London's stage (1742-76), but even he left the songs and dances in *Macbeth,* kept the elaborate Act I Masquerade and Act V funeral procession in *Romeo and Juliet,* countenanced a *Tempest* of 1756 which contained thirty-two songs and duets, a dirge with Arne's music in *Cymbeline, A Midsummer Night's Dream* with thirty-three songs, elaborate processions in *Coriolanus,* and tremendous pageantry for the coronation scene and the christening of Elizabeth in *Henry VIII.*[195]

Nor was Shakespeare excused from being chopped up into musical afterpieces. Garrick created *Florizel and Perdita* out of *A Winter's Tale,* and Colman created, again abridged, *A Winter's Tale* out of Garrick's *Florizel and Perdita,* "embellished with several additional songs." [196] The Shakespeare-to-Garrick-to-Colman double play was again executed with *A Midsummer Night's Dream:* it became Garrick's opera *The Fairies* in 1775 (with twenty-seven songs), and Colman abridged the opera to an afterpiece a little later.[197]

In America Shakespeare was no better off. The very first play that Hallam's company performed in Williamsburg was *The Merchant of Venice,* and special mention was made of the songs in character sung by Lorenzo— Jessica's songs were stressed in other productions.[198] The operatic *Tempest* was one of the most popular: Charleston advertised a "Dance of Demons" in Act II of the play, and Purcell's music in Act III; the elaborate machinery utilized and the masque which followed were inevitably stressed.[199] America was equally adept at Shakespearean perversions, and an example is *The Tamer Tamed; or, A Good Wife at Last,* which emerged from *The Taming of the Shrew.*[200] The season of 1796 shows the embellishments Shakespeare had acquired in eighteenth-century America. Two days after *The Archers,* on April 20, *Macbeth* was performed: twelve vocal parts are listed in the advertisements plus the two principal characters in the witches' dance; Locke's music is mentioned.[201] A production in May of *Much Ado About Nothing* featured a masquerade and a dance in Act II and a triple hornpipe at the end.[202]

Although many pageants and processions were given as separate productions in eighteenth-century America, nonetheless a play, and especially a Shakespeare play, was a favorite vehicle for these spectacles.[203] Something of the state of the nonmusical stage at the end of the eighteenth century may be gleaned from an advertisement for a 1799 production of *Coriolanus* in New York:

> In act 2nd, a Grand Triumphal Entry. *The order of the procession as follows:*
>
> Two boys bearing Incense,
> An Officer with a Roman Eagle,
> Eight Senators, Four Trumpets,
> Two Boys bearing Incense,
> Four Priests with Torches,
> Two Officers
> Six Lictors with Fasces,
> Two Officers with Standards,
> Six Soldiers bearing a Bier laden with Spoils.
>
> A CHOIR *consisting of*
> Four Boys, Six Virgins, Four Priests with Torches, Six Lictors with fasces

Senators—Soldiers—Standard Bearers—Fifes—Drums—
   Trumpets—Priests, etc. etc.

A Captive General in Chains
Volumnia, Virgilia, Valeria.

Six Virgins strewing Flowers, before a *Triumphal Car,*
   bearing Coriolanus, drawn by
Two White Horses,
Accompanied by a full band of Instrumental Music, and a
   Grand Chorus,
"See the Conquering Hero Comes." 204

Act V featured another procession, this one of Roman
matrons, virgins, and children.

Almost a dozen different kinds of musical have been
seen parading their way across the stages of eighteenth-
century America. Whether ballads were used or elaborate
orchestrations, whether sung or mimed or danced, they
were similar in their stress on music rather than drama,
in appealing to a popular rather than a limited audience.
The best musicals being performed anywhere in the world
quickly found their way to American stages, became absorbed in an essentially American repertory, and helped
form a broad base for the transmission of the American
musical to the stages of the future.

The Final scene in Act II of Dunlap and Carr's comic
opera, *The Archers,* was placed outdoors, in the mountains, where a waterfall and a distant view of the lake
provided a fine background for a song, a trio, and finally
a chorus of almost the entire cast. Tell had still to shoot
an apple off his son's head, and the audience must have
waited eagerly for Act III of *The Archers.*

VI

Librettists and Composers

Eighteenth-century America was able to provide for its expanding musical stage not only theatres and orchestras and actors and plays, but also a plentiful supply of highly talented librettists and composers to replenish the repertory.

1

William Dunlap caught his audience's attention at the beginning of the third and final act of *The Archers* by having Tell shoot an apple off his son's head. Years of fascination with the theatre had made Dunlap adept at stage effects. By April, 1796, he had already written a comedy, a farce, and a ballad opera, had penned extensive criticism of the stage, and was negotiating with Hallam and Hodgkinson to join with them in a managerial triumvirate.[1] The eighteenth-century playwright who did nothing but write plays was an unheard-of anomaly.

American playwrights, unlike those in England, were seldom connected with the theatre.[2] They emulated, for the most part, such English authors as O'Keeffe, Colman, Prince Hoare, and Sheridan, or merely adapted the work of others for the American stage.[3] They received, as in England, the whole profit of the third night.[4] But here the amateur was somewhat more in demand. In Charleston, for example, the actors encouraged local plays and original songs and music as a means of filling the theatre.[5] A specific event might cause the manager of a theatre to commission an interlude on the subject; the resultant work might or might not be original, since librettists notoriously stole from wherever they chose.[6] The librettos of early American operas were of vastly greater importance than the music,[7] and were attempted by a great many men and women. John Bernard, an actor who arrived in America in 1797, said the playwriting disease was infectious:

> . . . though many philosophers have classed it with yawning, bad habits, and the yellow fever; yet on no other ground can I account for *my* becoming a victim. I had had one or two attacks in England, which had passed off harmlessly enough, and left not the slightest evidence by which the world could have detected it. But I had come to a city [Philadelphia] where it might truly be styled the epidemic. Every one was seized with it, and the literary physicians, who tried to check the inflammation with cold water or wet blankets, were so inefficient that, on the smallest computation, a hundred subjects a day must have yielded to the attack.[8]

No surprise, then, that America's first librettists included a doctor, a lawyer, a painter, a judge, a novelist, a poet, and assorted actors and actresses.

The doctor was ELIHU HUBBARD SMITH.[9] Born in Litchfield, Connecticut, in 1771, Smith was educated at Yale, and then proceeded, in 1790-91, to the College in Philadelphia to study medicine. He wrote a series of lyrics while in Philadelphia, where he also became friendly with Charles Brockden Brown, over whom he exerted considerable influence.[10] In 1791 Smith practiced medicine in Wethersfield, Connecticut. The Hartford Wits were then at their peak and Smith, too, contributed his time, interest, and ability. He met William Dunlap in 1793, the same year he published the very first anthology of American poetry, *American Poems, Selected and Original*. September of 1793 found Smith in New York, and by October he had completed his one and only play, based on Goldsmith's ballad, "Edwin and Angelina." Hodgkinson accepted it in 1794 for production by the Old American Company, and there the matter rested for two years. In 1796, in one month, Smith converted his two-act prose drama into an opera, and it was produced on December 19 of that year.[11]

A few months before his opera was produced the New York *American Minerva* for April 12 announced that "Samuel L. Mitchell Esq. and Dr. Elihu H. Smith are appointed Physicians of the Hospital of the state of New-York." In the same year he was also secretary of the "Society for the manumission of slaves." [12] In 1797, with Doctors Edward Miller and Samuel L. Mitchell, Smith founded and served as editor of America's first medical journal, the *Medical Repository*. When the Park Theatre opened in New York in 1798 he not only wrote the opening address but criticized the first night for the New York *Commercial Advertiser*. A yellow fever epidemic hit New York in the summer of 1798 and Smith remained in the city to help fight it, caught the disease himself, and died on September 19.

Smith "did nothing but by rule," his friend Dunlap wrote later, "and was as strict an economist of his time as of his money." He "was in cleanliness, neatness and attention to the proprieties of dress, a perfect model, and seemed to make the purity of his person, and even of his clothing, an index of the purity of his mind." [13] Dunlap says of his only stage work, his libretto, that it was pure and energetic but not sufficiently dramatic.[14] Nonetheless, as librettist, poet, critic, anthologist, humanitarian, editor, physician, Smith amply demonstrates that one of the most disconcerting things about the eighteenth-century belief that all things are possible to a reasonable man, is that, quite frequently, they were.

FRANCIS HOPKINSON was another eighteenth-century jack-of-all-professions. Born in Philadelphia September 21, 1737, he attended the College of Philadelphia,[15] and ". . . by the time of his graduation he was recognized as poet, musician, and song writer, and two years after composed the music of the first American song—'My Days Have Been So Wondrous Free.'"[16] While at college he was probably responsible for the addition of some words and music to the *Masque of Alfred* when it was performed there in 1757; in addition, he wrote *An Exercise* and a *Dialogue* for the respective 1762 and 1765 commencements of the College of Philadelphia. In 1781 he wrote words and music to America's first serious opera, *The Temple of Minerva*.[17]

But Hopkinson was not only a librettist and musician. He was a lawyer, he served as Delegate to the Continental Congress, and he was a signer of the Declaration of Independence. Later he became a judge and was active in the Constitutional Convention. As a poet, his "Battle of the Kegs" was popular all over the colonies. He composed a number of songs (indeed, wrote both words and music for a collection published in 1788) and played both the harpsichord and the organ. He was responsible for several improvements of the harpsichord, and he invented a musical instrument.[18] His notebooks show he was acquainted with the works of Handel, Purcell, Boyce, Dr. Arne, Hasse, and Pergolesi; indeed, in 1772 he directed a performance of several pieces of church music, including a Grand Chorus from *The Messiah*. Finally, to round off his career, he was a painter and our first Secretary of the Navy.[19]

His son, JOSEPH HOPKINSON, was scarcely less versatile, though not so important to America's musical stage. Born in 1770, he wrote an essay, "On Dancing," in 1787, soon after edited the first American edition of Shakespeare, and wrote a play himself. He was also a lawyer, also a judge, and he served in the Pennsylvania State Constitutional Convention.[20] Perhaps he was best known in his own day, however, for a song. Gilbert Fox, who had gone to school with Joseph and who, in 1798, was an actor at Philadelphia's Chestnut Street Theatre, asked Joseph for a song to be sung at his benefit. The "President's March" was quite popular at the time, and Joseph gave it new words, calling it "The New Federal Song." He later wrote,

> . . . the theatre was crowded to excess, and so continued night after night, for the rest of the whole season, the song being encored and repeated many times each night, the audience joining in the chorus. It was also sung at night in the streets by large assemblies of citizens, including members of Congress. The enthusiasm was general, and the song was heard, I may say, in every part of the United States.[21]

Soon called "Hail Columbia" this song helps keep Joseph Hopkinson's name alive even today.

ROYALL TYLER was another librettist-judge.[22] He was born in Boston in 1758, studied at Harvard, and later became a lawyer (after studying in the office of John Adams). He fought both in the Revolution and in Shays's Rebellion, in 1786. The following year he wrote his famous comedy, *The Contrast*. He was "encouraged by the favour with which this first effort was received"[23] and brought out the pasticcio for which he wrote the libretto, *May-Day in Town, or New York in an Uproar,* the following month. His older brother, Colonel John Steele Tyler, managed the Federal Street Theatre in Boston for awhile and brought out his brother's last play, *The Georgia Spec; or, Land in the Moon,* in 1797, as well as the prologues which Royall wrote for occasional benefits.[24] Writing on a variety of topics, Tyler was a regular contributor to assorted newspapers. In 1800 he was elected Chief Justice of the Supreme Court of Vermont.

MRS. SUSANNAH HASWELL ROWSON was an important distaff addition to America's librettists.[25] Born in Portsmouth, she nonetheless spent most of her life in the United States, and her best work was written here. She was brought to America by her lieutenant father in 1767, at the age of five; in 1778 her father was forced to return to England with his daughter. She married William Rowson, a musician, in 1786; she sang, played the harpsichord and guitar, and could improvise a song. In 1790 she published her famous novel, *Charlotte Temple,* and in the 1792-93 season, she and her husband made their stage debuts in Edinburgh.

Wignell hired the couple for his Philadelphia company in 1793, and Mrs. Rowson returned to America. She first appeared in Annapolis, then Philadelphia (where her husband served chiefly as prompter); and she also acted in Baltimore before retiring from the Boston theatre in 1797.[26] In her few years on the stage she had acted 129 different parts in 126 different productions.[27] She and her husband had also appeared with Ricketts's circus (where she danced hornpipes in the part of a sailor).[28] She established a school for young ladies in Boston and hired some of the most eminent musicians of her day to teach there.

She wrote a sequel to *Charlotte Temple* and continued writing songs and poems until her death in 1828.

Her writings for the stage varied. She began with some occasional lyrics for use in various plays and pantomimes at the Chestnut Street Theatre, and from then on she was in constant demand as a song writer, creating lyrics for such musicians as Reinagle, Hewitt, Van Hagen, and Carr.[29] She wrote several plays, though only two are of interest to the musical stage. Her *Slaves in Algiers*, 1794, was called "A play interspersed with Songs," [30] said songs having been composed by Alexander Reinagle. Reinagle's vocal score for her next work, a comic opera (*The Volunteers*), is extant, but Mrs. Rowson's book is lost. She was the next writer for the stage, after Tyler and Dunlap, to deal with national themes, and her lost libretto leaves a blank in the picture of America's musical stage.[31]

Near the end of 1793 Dunlap remarks,

> . . . one of the Kemble family arrived in New-York, a sister of Mrs. Siddons, John Kemble, Mrs. Whitlock, Charles Kemble, Stephen Kemble, and the other children of that highly talented family. This person was called Mrs. Hatton, and had a husband with her, a vulgar man. She introduced herself to the American world by writing a play called Tammany, which she presented to the Tammany Society, who patronised it, and recommended it to the theatre through Hodgkinson, whose favour the authoress had secured.[32]

This libretto by ANN JULIA HATTON was "The earliest Indian play of which there is any record on the American stage. . . ." [33] In addition to giving occasional readings, she wrote at least one other work for the stage, *Needs Must, or, the Ballad Singers*, though for the most part she remained known, after *Tammany*, primarily as the wife of William Hatton, who became a celebrated musical-instrument maker in New York.[34]

Tammany was first performed in New York, March 3, 1794, with overture and music by James Hewitt. It was repeated three more times in New York that season, twice in Philadelphia, then once more in New York in 1795 and once in Boston in 1796. Book and music are lost, though extant lyrics suggest that even if the libretto were found it would have more value as an anti-Federalist tract than as the backbone of an opera.[35]

A famous actor contributed his talents to the turning out of librettos. JOHN HODGKINSON began his literary career in America with the prologue to Mrs. Hatton's *Tammany;* in 1797 his *The Launch; or, Huzzah for the Constitution,* "a patriotic trifle in honor of 'the Frigate Constitution breasting the curled surge'" was performed in New York, Boston, and Portsmouth with music assembled by Pelissier. It was a one-act pasticcio. He adapted for the American stage Cross and Reeve's opera *The Purse; or, Benevolent Tar,* calling it by a new and original title, *The Purse; or, the American Tar.* He indulged in at least one nonmusical dramatic work, which he literally stole from Dunlap.[36]

Another actor, JOHN D. TURNBULL, served as poet laureate of Sollee's Charleston Company on his arrival from London in 1795, and then as star of West and Bignall's company as it toured the South. He wrote the book for a musical interlude, *The Recruit,* in 1796, and *Rudolph; or, The Robbers of Calabria,* "A Melodrama in Three Acts" (composer unknown), in 1799, several years before the "official" beginning of melodrama.[37]

PETER MARKOE, born in the West Indies, studied law in London and settled in Philadelphia. He contributed poetry to leading periodicals and brought out a book of poems in 1787. He wrote the libretto for a ballad opera, *The Reconciliation,* which was accepted by the Old American Company in 1790 but never performed.[38] A visitor to the United States found his a "remarkable talent" for poetry, but that "he dishonors his writings by an intemperate life." [39]

Finally, the author of *The Archers,* WILLIAM DUNLAP, "the father of the American Stage." [40] He was born in Perth Amboy, New Jersey, February 19, 1766. His father, pro-British, moved the family to British headquarters in New York in 1777, where William saw his first play. The future painter-poet-manager-playwright-historian-novelist-librettist lost the sight of his right eye in a children's game, and this interrupted his studies for a time. In 1784 he went to England to study art with Benjamin West. Three years later he returned and set himself up as a portrait painter in his father's house.

He tried his first play the same year and married Elizabeth Woolsey (sister-in-law of Timothy Dwight, later president of Yale) in 1789. His circle of friends at about this time included the doctors Smith, Miller, and Mitchell, Charles Brockden Brown, Noah Webster, James Kent, William Johnson, Richard Alsop, and the Reverend Samuel Miller.[41] He went into business with his father (they sold china, vases, looking glasses, tea sets, and so forth) until the latter died; then one of the Woolseys joined him, until he left the business to become a manager of the Old American Company in 1796. Meanwhile, he had been doing much writing—poetry, criticism, translations, and plays.[42] He retired from the theatre, bankrupt, in 1805, and was hired as a general supervisor of the Park Theatre in 1806. He served as Assistant Paymaster General of the New York State Militia, he exhibited his paintings in most cities of the United States, and he was founder and vice-president of the National Academy of Design. He continued to write pieces for the stage through 1828, published his *History of the American Theatre* in 1832, and wrote a novel, assorted biographies, *History of the Rise and Progress of Arts and Design in the United States* (1834), and two regional histories before his death in 1839.

He led, evidently, an exemplary life. In fact, it was he who guarded the well-known actor George Frederick Cooke from his near-legendary dissipations when Cooke arrived in America.[43] In 1833 a drama festival was held in Dunlap's honor at the Park Theatre, and the panegyric ended:

> Thus he, whose merit claims this dazzling crowd,
> Points to the past, and has his claims allowed;
> Looks brightly forth, his faithful journey done,
> And rests in triumph—like the setting sun.[44]

The encomium, at least theatrically speaking, was not undeserved.

Writing of himself and his early success in the theatre, Dunlap said, ". . . pleased with the applause of the public and the encouragement of his associates, he thought only of future triumphs; and tragedies and comedies, operas and farces, occupied his mind, his time, and his pen." [45] One of his reasons for taking over the John Street Theatre was the dream of elevating the moral tone of the drama; he hoped to accomplish this by injecting his own plays into the repertory. His agreement with Hallam and Hodgkinson specifically stated that he was to bring out a play each season. He read his plays to his circle of friends, and they discussed and criticized them before Dunlap had them performed in the theatre.[46] Altogether Dunlap was responsible for about seventy different plays, librettos, and translations.[47] His plays and librettos were published in England, too, where they were favorably received:

> America bids fair to equal us in the productions of wit, as well as in science, in arms, and in commerce. With respect to the present little piece [Dunlap's translation and adaptation *Tell Truth and Shame the Devil*], many of our minor dramas of Covent-Garden and Old Drury, which have passed muster tolerably on the boards, are by no means superior to this New-York performance, either in respect of wit, humour, or poignancy of satire.[48]

His librettos were set to music by Carr, Hewitt, and Pelissier; in at least one case his libretto, *Nina,* was used with original Parisian music. He was not above converting even his own plays to operas: his first attempt at native tragedy, *André,* was performed in 1798, and he later converted it to the musical *The Glory of Columbia—Her Yeomanry.* Even Sterne's *Tristram Shandy* became grist for his operatic mill. During the time he wrote, the tentative beginnings of a native drama arose, and it is perhaps fortunate that a man of the stature of William Dunlap was alive to help it in all aspects of its development.[49]

2

Eighteenth-century American composers were also a versatile group, though their activities centered in the theatre.[50] As in Europe, composers worked for local theatre companies. In the beginning, however, the composer travelled with the troupe, selecting and composing music as it was needed.[51] The works of foreign composers were Americanized only as it was found "necessary to write new orchestral accompaniments or new music for the changes in the librettos adopted for the American stage." [52]

As American theatrical companies settled permanently in particular cities, composers for the theatre did likewise. Managers needed new accompaniments to old works and new settings to accepted operas, and the men in their orchestras could now supply this demand. By the end of the eighteenth century much original music was being written for the stage, for plays and operas and pantomimes and the like; each theatre kept its own stable of composers, and these men, aside from whatever other jobs they took on, composed music in every known form. Reinagle, for example, composed sonatas, overtures, preludes, songs, operas, adaptations, accompaniments, and so forth.[53]

Whereas most of America's early librettists had been born in America, most theatrical composers were born and trained in Europe, though the outstanding ones were scarcely less Americans as a result. "A composer is an American," says John Tasker Howard, "if by birth, or choice of permanent residence, he becomes identified with American life and institutions before his talents have had their greatest outlet; and through his associations and sympathies he makes a genuine contribution to our cultural development." [54] Carr, Hewitt, Reinagle, and Taylor, "represented the best of American creative musical ability at this time," [55] and they, with others almost equally able, all wrote mostly for the stage and did some of their best work with musical drama.

JAMES HEWITT, violin in hand, conducted *The Archers* at its première in the John Street Theatre. Born in Dartmoor, England, in 1770, he arrived in New York in 1792.[56] He was "the leading professional musician in New York during the post-Revolutionary period," and his activities included managing concerts, playing the violin and conducting at concerts, publishing music and running a music store, teaching, organizing and conducting orchestras for

Delacroix's summer gardens as well as the Columbia and
Mount Vernon Gardens, playing the organ at Trinity
Church, directing all military bands in New York, con-
ducting the orchestra of the John Street and later the
Park Theatres, and, of course, composing.[57]

The most important work Hewitt did for the theatre
was his score for *Tammany*.[58] He composed "Songs and
Overutre [*sic*]"[59] for *The Patriot; or, Liberty Asserted*, a
play based on the William Tell story, in 1794; he wrote
incidental music for Kotzebue's *Pizarro* (Reinagle did the
same for the work in Philadelphia), and for *The Mysteri-
ous Marriage;* he created additional songs and, probably,
accompaniments for *Robin Hood;* he composed *The Cot-
tagers,* "a little musical piece," for his own theatre benefit;
and he turned out two operas with Dunlap librettos, *The
Spanish Castle* and *The Wild Goose Chase*.[60]

Eventually he left New York and worked awhile in Boston, where he died in 1827; John R. Parker, who was a
friend of his and who wrote brief biographies of eminent
musicians of the time, said Hewitt "is eminent in science
and a gentleman of great experience and versatility of
talent. . . ."[61]

VICTOR PELISSIER was second only to Hewitt as composer and arranger for the Old American Company in
New York.[62] He was the foremost of the French musicians
to arrive in America, and he advertised himself in Philadelphia, his first city of residence, as "first French horn
of the theatre in Cape François." After one year in Philadelphia he moved to New York, where he resided for
many years. He was associated with the concert life of
the city, he played first horn with the orchestra of the
theatre, and by 1800 "had composed incidental music for
eighteen plays, farces, harlequinades, and ballets,"[63] in
addition to his original operas. Pelissier and Dunlap col-

laborated on many works, and Dunlap remembered him as "a short old gentleman, and so near-sighted as to be nearly blind. Always cheerful, and his thoughts as fully occupied by notes as any banker or broker in Wall-street." [64]

Altogether, a listing of his works before 1800 would include at least twenty-eight different pieces for the stage. He composed accompaniments for serious plays, such as *Bourville Castle*, a "serious drama" written by a friend of Dunlap, John Blair Linn, with original music by Carr.[65] He was responsible for arranging the music and providing accompaniments for most operas the Old American Company imported in the last decade of the eighteenth century, sometimes collaborating with another composer on the same opera.[66] He worked both with pantomimes and with serious pantomimes.[67] He arranged the music for Hodgkinson's *The Launch* and composed the score for Smith's *Edwin and Angelina;* in addition, he composed at least one full score for Dunlap, *Sterne's Maria; or, the Vintage* (the opera "pleased and was pleasing, but not sufficiently attractive or popular to keep the stage after the original performers in it were removed by those fluctuations common in theatrical establishments").[68] He wrote the music for an extravaganza, the "allegorical, musical drama," *The Fourth of July; Temple of American Independence.*[69] Finally, according to Sonneck, "In 1797 a form of entertainment was introduced in New York for which I believe the Americans to be peculiarly gifted: the melodrama." [70] The work was *Ariadne Abandoned By Theseus, in the Isle of Naxos;* it was in one act, and the original music for it was written by Pelissier. The advertisement said, "Between the different passages spoken by the actors, will be full Orchestral Music, expressive of each situation and passion." [71] The work was performed in New York and soon after in Boston; Pelissier had dropped the pebble which started an avalanche, and melodrama in nineteenth-century America would crush nearly every other stage form.

Philadelphia's outstanding musician was ALEXANDER REINAGLE. True, Francis Hopkinson wrote the music and words for at least one opera in Philadelphia, but he was an amateur, primarily concerned with other things. Reinagle's whole life was bound to his music and to the theatre. He was born in Portsmouth, England, in 1756; his father, a musician, saw to it that he was trained in the theory and practices of music by Raynor Taylor, who later became a colleague in Philadelphia. He knew Carl Philipp Emanuel Bach and was a member of the Society of Musicians in London.[72] Near the end of 1784 he took his brother Hugh, who was in the last stages of consumption, to Lisbon for his health; Alexander supported them there by giving concerts before the best people, as his notebook laconically suggests: "Rec'd a present from her Majesty [the Queen of Portugal] of 50 Moids." [73] Hugh died in March, 1785, and his brother returned to Portsmouth. Perhaps England no longer held pleasant memories or close ties for him; in any case, Alexander Reinagle arrived in America in 1786 and never left.

In New York he began to show his versatility in an advertisement which offered lessons in singing, the harpsichord, the piano, and the violin as well as use of "the best instruments and music printed from London." He was also adept at the flute, the trumpet, and the violoncello.[74] He gave concerts, too, in New York, even singing in some, managed a concert series, and became associated with the Old American Company with which he shuttled back and forth between New York and Philadelphia before settling in the Quaker city. In Philadelphia he arranged and gave

concerts, taught music in boarding schools, was hired by
Washington to give music lessons to his adopted daughter, Nellie Custis, and may have owned a share in a piano
factory.[75] But, "perhaps his greatest importance lies in the
history of opera," [76] history he helped to make when Philadelphia got its own theatre company and Reinagle was
one of its managers.

Reinagle and Wignell opened the Chestnut Street Theatre in 1794 with the deliberate intention of giving as
many musicals as straight plays. Reinagle, whom Dunlap
found "a very genteel man and skilful musician," collected
an orchestra of "twenty accomplished musicians." [77] From
then on he was busy not only with conducting the orchestra of the theatre but with arranging and adapting musical works for the stage and with composing music for
operas and pantomimes and songs. His principal stage
works include the musical farce, *The Savoyard; or, the
Repentant Seducer*, new music for the serious pantomime,
La Forêt Noire, when it was first performed in America, a
re-setting of the entire libretto of Mrs. Siddon's *Sicilian
Romance*, songs for Mrs. Rowson's play *Slaves in Algiers*,
the opera, *The Volunteers;* and he collaborated with Raynor Taylor on the music to Sheridan's adaptation of
Kotzebue's *Pizarro*.[78]

Reinagle's songs were quite popular, and "as an author,
both his style and subject were always rich and melodi-
ous." When he died in Baltimore at the end of the first
decade of the nineteenth century, he was working on an
oratorio with recitations instead of recitative, the music set
to parts of *Paradise Lost*. "A mind well stored equally
with various attainments and professional knowledge—
with a disposition mild, amiable and conciliating—with
manners bland, polished and engaging—an imagination
lively and accurate—and in heart formed for tenderness

and the charities of the world," was a contemporary's estimate of Alexander Reinagle; [79] today's estimate must place him in the forefront of those who helped bring alive America's lyric theatre.

Reinagle's old teacher, RAYNOR TAYLOR, followed his pupil to America, arriving in 1792.[80] He was born in England in 1747 and studied at the King's singing school as one of the boys of the Chapel Royal. As a student he made his first bid for immortality; at the funeral of Handel, Taylor's hat tumbled into the grave and was buried with the famous composer. In England he worked at writing music, as a vocalist, organist, harpsichord performer, organist at a church in Essex, and teacher. He was hired as composer and director of music at Sadler's Wells and was in large part responsible for the high quality of music served there along with the place's well-known mineral waters.

In America Taylor's first work was in the South. He served as teacher and organist in Baltimore, and then received an appointment as organist of St. Anne's in Annapolis. In 1793 he arrived in Philadelphia, became friendly with Benjamin Carr, and played at concerts with that gentleman. All the while he gave a series of extravaganzas which he both wrote and performed. By 1796 his programs were supplemented by the performances of other musicians.[81] He was organist at St. Peter's Church in Philadelphia. In fact, he was reputedly the finest organist in America, and Reinagle thought Taylor's extemporizing on the organ equal to that of Carl Philipp Emanuel Bach.

As a composer, according to John R. Parker, admittedly a friend, Taylor "stands upon the highest ground both as to science and originality, as well as to knowledge of effect, and in every respect is certainly entitled to public favor." He wrote in almost every musical form, yet despite "shelves groaning under manuscript files of overtures, operas, anthems, glees, etc." [82] he got little money for his compositions and kept alive largely through teaching and his salary as organist. Before he died (in 1825) he was influential in founding the Musical Fund Society in Philadelphia.

Taylor's outstanding theatrical works include, of course, the pieces he threw into his extravaganzas, such as the burlettas, *The Gray Mare's the Best Horse* and *The Old Woman of Eighty Three,* and his burlesque on Italian opera, *Capocchio and Dorinna.* He wrote the music for the melodrama, *The Rose of Arrayon,* and for the serious pantomimes, *La Petite Piedmontesse* and *La Bonne Petite Fille* (the latter had choreography by M. Lege and was performed in Philadelphia, Baltimore, and Boston). He collaborated with Reinagle on *Pizarro.* He wrote music and accompaniments for many importations, including *The Iron Chest* of George Colman.[83] His music for the theatre may not have been sufficient to keep him alive, but Taylor was helpful in keeping the theatre alive, and perhaps that is just as important.

Also active in Philadelphia was the violinist-conductor of the Chestnut Street Theatre's orchestra, GEORGE GILLINGHAM. He was a fine violinist, and in addition managed a series of concerts. Late in his career (he died about 1823) he conducted at the Park Theatre in New York, but meanwhile he had served to arrange and compose music for a pantomime and one or two short pieces in Philadelphia.[84] One other Philadelphia composer ought to be mentioned: MONSIEUR ROCHEFORT, who wrote original music and accompaniments to the "Grand Serious Pantomime," *The Death of Captain Cook.*[85]

By the end of the eighteenth century, and despite a

late start, Boston was also successful in assembling an impressive collection of musicians. The Van Hagen family, for example, had settled there.[86] The family had been quite prominent musically in Europe before PETER ALBRECHT VAN HAGEN, JR., came to Charleston in 1774. He gave concerts in New York in 1789 (where he became "Senior" in order for his son to assume "Junior" in his debut as violin virtuoso). In New York, Van Hagen sold music, taught, played at concerts, managed subscription concerts, and occasionally conducted at the theatre.[87] In 1796 the family settled in Boston, where he opened a music school with his son, taught music at Mrs. Rowson's school, opened a music store, and imported instruments. Van Hagen conducted the orchestra at the Haymarket Theatre (where he was later succeeded by Gottlieb Graupner, "the father of American orchestral music") from January, 1797, to the end of the 1800 season, when he became organist at the Stone Chapel.[88] While conducting at the theatre he was responsible for completely new music written for one opera (*The Adopted Child*, book by Samuel Birch) and incidental music and accompaniments for three others.[89] His son became known as concert performer and publisher and composer, but none of his music was written for the theatre. The mother, too, was active musically, and

> This ambitious trio became the first important publishers of music in Boston, the most competent teachers, and organists of talent; father and son were experienced conductors and were composers and arrangers of theatrical music to boot.[90]

By 1793 one TRILLE LABARRE was in Boston; "professor and composer of music, lately from Paris," he advertised himself.[91] He worked with the orchestra of the Federal

Street Theatre as leader and arranger. He was responsible for additional music and accompaniments to three operas, one of which, Grétry's *Richard Coeur de Lion*, was particularly well received, possibly because of Labarre's simplification of orchestral accompaniments. In addition, a review of the time (1797) praised Labarre for "perfecting the supernumerary vocal performers in their respective choruses." [92]

R. LEAUMONT was a teacher of music in Mrs. Rowson's school in Boston, gave concerts in the same city, introduced a new instrument he had invented, and conducted the theatre orchestra. Before settling in Charleston in 1801 as orchestra leader, he contributed music and accompaniments to at least one opera. [93]

THOMAS BRADFORD and DEMARQUE were associated with the Charleston theatre. In 1791 Bradford came to Charleston, where he founded a music store and was responsible for arranging at least two operas. Demarque was a violoncellist and composer, one of the Frenchmen who escaped from Cape François. He gave concerts in Baltimore before joining Wignell and Reinagle's company and then migrating to Charleston, where he played in the theatre orchestra and was responsible for a series of pantomimes. [94]

Much music for the early lyric theatre was composed by perambulating composers, men who sold their talents from city to city rather than comfortably lodging in the stable of a particular company. JOHN BENTLEY, for example, managed the City Concerts in Philadelphia in 1783, then joined the orchestra of the Old American Company as harpsichordist in 1785. He travelled with the company, acting with them, playing in the orchestra, and composing for them. At least three pantomimes are known to be of his composition. [95] B. BERGMAN, violinist and composer, arrived from England in 1792, played in the John

Street Theatre orchestra, and occasionally acted with the company. He conducted and arranged accompaniments and so forth for the theatre in Charleston, including Storace's pasticcio, *Doctor and Apothecary.* He also appears in Boston records.[96] JEAN GEHOT, known for an overture in twelve movements plus at least one work for the stage, travelled all over Europe before arriving in America in 1792; he meandered between New York and Philadelphia.[97] Another of the wandering composers was MRS. MARY ANN POWNALL, although she was primarily famed as an actress. Born in England in 1751, she was known there as Mrs. Wright in her work as singer and actress. She came to America as a member of Hallam and Henry's company, travelled awhile with it, then left for Charleston, where she died in 1796. She wrote both words and music of many songs featured in concerts (including, of course, her own), operas, and plays. Her one stage work, *Needs Must; or, the Ballad Singers,* was written in 1794.[98]

The last of the peripatetic composers is BENJAMIN CARR, composer of *The Archers.*[99] He made a name for himself in no less than three cities, New York, Philadelphia, and Baltimore. The Carr family had written and published music in England, before Benjamin arrived here in 1793, the first of his family to emigrate to America. Benjamin was born on September 12, 1768, and studied under Dr. Samuel Arnold and Charles Wesley. He was connected with the London Ancient Concerts. A few months after his arrival in America, his father, Joseph, and his brother, Thomas, landed; the family set up music businesses in three cities—Joseph and Thomas in Baltimore and Benjamin in Philadelphia and New York (though he sold the latter to James Hewitt in 1797). The three men speculated successfully in almost every phase of American music. When Francis Scott Key, for example, wrote a series of patriotic verses, it was Thomas Carr who selected, adapted, and arranged the music (an English drinking song, "To Anacreon in Heaven") for "The Star Spangled Banner" in the form in which it exists today. It was Benjamin, in his capacity as music publisher, who first published "Yankee Doodle" (as part of his own "Federal Overture") and "Hail Columbia." Joseph Carr, not to be outdone by his sons, founded and published a *Musical Journal,* which Benjamin edited.

Benjamin's other Philadelphia enterprises on his arrival there included managing the City Concerts, appearing in concerts both as singer and as pianist, writing accompaniments for operas, conducting, and, later, playing the organ for St. Joseph's Church and the Pennsylvania Tea Gardens.[100] In addition, when a singer such as Miss Broadhurst included songs of his composition in her concerts, he sang and played in her benefits. In New York he was scarcely less active. He acted and sang in operas with the Old American Company in 1794-95, appeared in two different sets of concerts in the same year as singer and pianist, operated a music shop ("Carr's Musical Repository on William Street"), composed music for the theatre, and performed on the organ in churches.[101] He retired from the stage in 1795, though he remained in New York for two more years. Even after he left, Dunlap maintained a correspondence with Carr to ask his advice concerning musicians Dunlap wanted to hire.[102] Carr returned, then, to Philadelphia, where he took charge of the music at the Roman Catholic St. Augustine's Church, and continued conducting, publishing, composing, teaching, performing, and so forth, until his death in 1831. The Musical Fund Society of Philadelphia, of which he was a founder, put up a monument to his memory.

The seal Carr used had a treble clef with the notes *b* and *c* engraved on it, and the staff was appropriate to more than his initials. "Any man who can run three different businesses, write operas and perform in public all at the same time will be notable in whatever profession or line of business he takes up." [103] His compositions for the musical stage were no less varied than his other musical activities.

> He had a hand in the American productions of George Colman's English version of Beaumarchais' *Le Barbier de Seville*, of Samuel Arnold's *The Children in the Wood*, a musical version of *Macbeth*, and *The Deserter*. In addition to opera, he took to pantomime, in *The Caledonian Frolic* and *Poor Jack; or, the Sailor's Landlady* as afterpieces. [104]

He composed incidental music for several plays, including *The Patriot*, which dealt with the William Tell story; evidently the subject interested him, for two months later he wrote the score for *The Archers*. He wrote at least three other operas, one of which (*Philander and Sylvia; or, Love Crowned at Last*) was performed in London. A list of Benjamin Carr's compositions in his own hand was found in a book he owned; [105] according to the list, his output for the stage included five operas, thirty songs (the list mentions which stage work each song was written for), seven pantomimes, four overtures, and the accompaniments to fourteen operas! He was as representative of America's composers as Dunlap, his collaborator on *The Archers*, was of America's librettists.

The librettist and composer of *The Archers*, then, represented the best American talent available in the late eighteenth century. When the battle was over on stage of the John Street Theatre on April 18, 1796, the Austrians defeated, and the forces of liberty and freedom triumphant, many in the audience made their way out of the theatre. There was still an afterpiece (the musical, *Edgar and Emmeline*) to come, but the discriminating theatregoer must have felt the need to mull over the important première he had just witnessed.

VII

Performance and Criticism

The Archers was a musical comedy, atypical only in its American origins and stress on liberty rather than love. An inspection of the work and the reception it received, both in the eighteenth century and from modern critics, will help to make clear the form of the early American musical, a form closely allied to the musical comedies on today's stages.

1

After a lively overture, the Prologue of *The Archers* [1] enters, bows, and informs the audience that they are about to witness a "tale of Liberty," and then asks:

> Can liberty with base injustice dwell?
> As well seek virtue in the depths of hell

thereby establishing both theme and tone of the piece.

The traditional green curtain disappears and we are on a street in Altdorf, Switzerland. The young and lovely Cecily enters crying, "Baskets for sale." Unfortunately, no one is about and she is forced to speak to the audience. She tells us that she's out too early in the morning, but if she sings she will wake people to a need for baskets. Sings? Of course, and the orchestra leads her into a Buttercup-like song describing her wares. As the applause dies down, Conrad enters, accompanied by a jackass (always a sure-fire stunt) loaded with wooden bowls, dishes, ladles, and the like; he sings of the merits of his wares. The couple greet each other, she asks for news, and Dunlap slides into exposition by having Conrad's answer involve the likelihood of war, a Swiss revolution against their Austrian oppressors. Cecily is delighted; business will be better with her competitors off to war. Conrad speaks of the dangers to come (his accurate syntax is accounted for primly if illogically by the fact he lived awhile in the house of a lawyer); Governor Gesler is impressing citizens into the Austrian army, and Conrad is about to join a troupe of bowmen outside the city rather than be 'pressed into service. Cecily promises to love him provided he is not killed; she cannot, she claims, be properly appreciative of a dead man, though Conrad insists she ought to like him better for dying for his country. He asks her to come with him: a soldier, he says, is permitted to take no other beast of burden with him but his wife. She agrees, and they sing a charming duet on the advantages of marriage.

A roll of drums breaks in upon their song, and an Austrian Lieutenant and his Guard enter, followed by drums, 'pressed men, and a crowd of Swiss onlookers. Conrad tries to steal away but is stopped by the Lieutenant.

"We wish none but those who freely enter into the service.—Handcuff that rascal till you get him safe to the castle." Then the joke is varied: "We have the greatest tenderness for the rights of the subject. If the rascal attempts to speak gag him."

The Swiss Burghers indignantly berate the Lieutenant and indignantly walk off. Most of them are recognized by old friends in the audience from other roles, or else they are children learning to walk on stage, or they are stage hands taking up space; in any case, their appearance is brief, their departure hasty—there are armies to man and other costumes to don.

Now Cecily, the Lieutenant, and Conrad sing a trio; Conrad complains, Cecily concurs, and the Lieutenant sings that Conrad is only handcuffed to make him more free. In the best tradition of musical comedy, the song neither obstructs the action nor is totally irrelevant to it.

The sparse scenery is removed before our eyes, a table and chairs added (indicating an indoor scene), and William Tell (John Hodgkinson) strides onstage, adjusting his arms; meanwhile his son (the pretty Miss Harding) tries to remove his father's sword from its scabbard. The characters have moved up several classes from Conrad and Cecily as is made evident by their use of perfectly regular, perfectly dull blank verse. Tell's son swears that when he grows up he will use the sword to defend his father and his mother and his neighbors. William catches his precocious offspring up in his arms just as Portia, Tell's wife, enters. She is afraid of the preparations and of the horrors of war. Tell agrees, but when the peasantry is ground down, then "O Switzerland, my country, we *must* rouze!" It is probably a good thing to help one's neighbors, she agrees, and dictators must be destroyed,

> But when the woman stands upon my soul,
> I nothing see but danger to thy life.
> Then in my dreams I view thy mangled corse—
> Or start affrighted at the shouts of war,
> And see thee flying, all oppress'd with numbers.

(It is interesting to hear the adipose Mrs. Melmoth manage the speech without the letter *r*.)

Now Tell wins her so completely to his point of view

that she swears, should he die, to recount to her son his father's glory. Mother and son leave and Tell, alone on stage, ends the scene bravely singing of how "Forever lives the patriot's fame. . . ." A patriotic song and a favorite star with a great voice—surely the show stops here for an encore or two.

Now rush the chairs and table off and slide on grooves a variety of flats for the shores of the Lake of Uri. Across the Lake can be seen hills, hanging rocks, and so forth— the kind of spectacular landscape Charles Ciceri so delighted in painting. The sound of marching feet, and a chorus of Bowmen enter and sing to the genius of the hills, asking for courage, and a solo voice sings five stanzas which tell what life was like before Austrian oppression; the chorus then rounds out the song. Some of the Bowmen gather together and speak of the virtuous Walter of Uri and the youthful Arnold Melchthal, chief of Underwalden, just as the two, coincidentally, enter, their iambic pentameter fitting smoothly into the speech of the noble Bowmen. Everyone speaks very bravely of freedom and liberty and law, and it is perhaps no accident that all the comments about the nascent Swiss revolution are also applicable to the United States. The actors are regularly interrupted by cheers of delight from the gallery gods and more restrained applause from the rest of the house. Considerably more exposition is now indulged in as the tyranny of Gesler is expatiated on, including his latest act, a decree that all must bow to a pole in Altdorf which bears his hat at the top. All mention William Tell with reverence.

Suddenly warriors are sighted approaching, and the Bowmen ready their weapons and arrange themselves for battle. Distant horns, however, pronounce the newcomers friends: the troops of Schweitz, led by their chief, Werner

Staffach. More colorful if somewhat ragged costumes add to those already assembled. The tripartite army is about to assemble, and the Bowmen of Uri greet the Pikemen of Schweitz with a song; the latter march on stage and sing a rousing answering chorus; when the stage is almost full, a chorus of the whole joins in song. The men exchange welcomes and Werner announces his victory over a vanguard of Emperor Albert's men, coming to put down the insurrection. Werner, Arnold, and Walter take turns crossing swords with each other and pledging their words. In case the point has been missed by the American audience, Walter points out that "In federal bonds united we are safe."

Walter's song over, his daughter, Rhodolpha (Miss Broadhurst), dressed as a huntress, arrives and kneels before him. (Miss Broadhurst was known for her fine singing and poor acting, and the role of Rhodolpha enabled her to display both her proclivities.) She begs that she and her fifty virtuous Maidens may be permitted to fight along with the men; when peace comes she and her followers will put off their boldness and become meek and blythe again. Her request is granted, and all bow to her except Arnold who draws her downstage center and in a graceful song inquires "Why huntress, why, wilt thou thy life expose. . . ." She says she and her troop of Virgins will not hear of love until Switzerland is free, and she sings to him, her song telling him to prove his love for her by freeing Switzerland. This subplot dealing with their love for each other is managed throughout the "opera" entirely in their songs and duets. Their voices blend just as her troop of young women enter (armed and in uniform) and range themselves in front of the stage, before the assembled armies. A chorus of the whole sings its determination at the end of the first act.

The orchestra has played some request numbers during intermission, and the changed scenery now indicates that Act II will begin in front of the Castle of Altdorf, where a hat-bedizened pole dominates the scene. The Lieutenant and Guards enter with Conrad. The latter is dressed as a Cuirassier, though his armor is much too large and heavy for him. His duties, he is told, consist of challenging passers-by and forcing them to bow before the pole. The Lieutenant and Conrad (Jefferson and Hallam) now demonstrate the Old American Company's comic strength as they upstage each other in a comic duet on the joys of a soldier's life. The Lieutenant marches the Guard off and returns with Governor Gesler. Conrad, the dutiful soldier, challenges them and insists that they bow. Gesler, in blank verse, declares that it is the fault of William Tell that no one is volunteering for the army; he speaks of the massing of rival forces; he discloses a forthcoming meeting of the Burghers and his decision to call the meeting seditious and to seize Tell. Having delivered himself of all this, he takes the Lieutenant offstage with him. Their place is immediately filled by the virgin-patriot, Rhodolpha, who laughs at Conrad when he challenges her. He complains that even his ass, Dapple, has been impressed. Rhodolpha may be patriotic but she is completely devoid of humor, and her reply, "Thou tell'st a tale of laugh-provoking sorrow," clearly indicates the worst aspect of the musical: the serious characters are one dimensional and have as little flexibility in their dialogue as in their personalities.

The Burgomaster (so low in Dunlap's esteem as to speak in prose), a comic character and a very fat one, now enters. Conrad mocks him, and Rhodolpha calls him traitor. She refuses to bow to the pole, and the Burgomaster appeals to the suddenly deaf Conrad who replies,

"Who comes there?" Rhodolpha is delighted, readies an arrow, and makes the Burogmaster "bow to me,/The representative of Liberty." The sight of the rotund Burgomaster waddling on his knees goads Rhodolpha into song; the lyrics inform him that the men of the town are gluttons and sink to shame, but that peasants are honest men. Unable to get up by himself, the Burgomaster crawls off.

But now enough of frivolity. A rostrum and a bench or two are sufficient scenery as the Burghers gather in the Town Hall to decide whether to resist or to conciliate the Austrians. Tell strides in, and in a long speech stuffed with modest disclaimers, he attempts to convince them to fight. The Lieutenant now enters (as befitting his serious purpose, his speech, for this scene only, is in blank verse) and tells everyone to go home. Tell defies him, and the Lieutenant, disgruntled, leaves. All the Burghers align themselves with Tell before conveniently dispersing. The Lieutenant quickly enters, this time with his Guard, and they surprise and disarm the hero; Tell is even further discomforted by the news that a part of the Emperor's army has won a victory over the men of Underwalden.

Tell: A victory!
Lieutenant: Why, to be sure, it was not so much a *victory*
                as an *advantage;* that is, our troops suffered
                the rascals to cut to pieces a few hundred men;
                while the rest, making a glorious change of
                position, threw themselves, by a forced march,
                into the Castle here.

Tell thanks heaven that the "glorious game's begun" and he is marched off.

Back at the Castle, Tell speaks to the Burgomaster who in turn tries to bribe him. The abstemious Dunlap evidently made some connection between tyranny and gluttony, for the Burgomaster now dilates on the joys of eating; the stage is then cleared except for Conrad, asleep at his post. Cecily enters, having escaped the Lieutenant's non-martial plans for her. She sees Conrad and sings a song ("Come, Conrad, awake from your trance!"); at the end of each verse she tickles his nose with a straw. He awakens and begs her to help him escape so he can be a Bowman and she one of Rhodolpha's Maidens; her help consists of taking his place on guard duty. After he runs off, she amuses herself by singing the ballad-like "There lived in Altdorf city fair." The Lieutenant and Guard come on, discover the trick, and the Guard races off to catch Conrad. The lecherous Lieutenant takes Cecily away with him, and as they walk off she asks, wide-eyed, "Why, you don't 'press women, do you?"

Inside the Governor's palace, Gesler orders Tell's execution. Portia enters to plead for her husband's life and shed a tear or two. But the Lieutenant suddenly rushes in with news of the assassination of Emperor Albert; Leopold of Austria is now commander of the army. Gesler immediately remands his execution order, but fearing to let Tell off too easily, he says Tell will gain his liberty only—here it is at last—by shooting an apple off his own son's head.

The scene now switches back to the mountains. A backdrop, wings, and flats suggest mountains, a waterfall, and a distant view of part of the lake—all of which is, no doubt, designed to satisfy the taste for spectacular scenic views. Walter, Arnold, and the Bowmen are on stage, and Walter is gleeful over the death of a tyrant. Arnold sings a song telling of how too much pride is responsible for man's downfall, probably the least relevant song in *The Archers*. Then Werner and his Pikemen enter from one side and Rhodolphà and her Maidens from the other.

This gives the Old American Company a chance to stage one of those elaborate processions which were used at the drop of the words "Marches on" in any play. Rhodolpha announces Tell's capture, and Werner's comment is one of the few places where Dunlap's language almost catches fire:

> We'll teach these Austrian slaves that full as dear
> To Switzers is the barren pine-clad rock,
> The cataract's roar, the whirlwind's thundering gust,
> The humble cot and honest poverty,
> As are to other men, in milder climes,
> The endless-varied gifts of Art and Nature.

The fierce language inspires Rhodolpha, Arnold, and the first Bowman to sing a trio; they are joined by the full chorus to end Act II.

This intermission may well entail somewhat more elaborate entertainment than merely the band playing request numbers. John Durang probably dances, and if we are especially lucky several others will also dance a story, a story mixed with solos and songs. Behind the dancers, the scenery is changed, and we are again in front of the Castle, where a stake has been driven into the ground. Gesler has an elevated seat which is surrounded by Guards, Burghers, and so forth. Walter and Werner, disguised, mix with the crowd; their discussion of Tell's plight is designed to build suspense. Tell, Jr., is brought in and bound to the stake. Tell is led in, chained, and Portia follows, pleading with her husband not to shoot. Gesler then rounds out the situation by announcing that if the boy is injured, Tell will die. (How the bow and arrow bit was managed is not known, but a good guess is that a wire was stretched across the stage and an arrow hooked onto it.) Tell shoots, the arrow travels along the wire, and lo, the apple is split! Portia leads her son off, but before Tell can be released, news comes of the arrival of Leopold, and Tell is bound again. The opportunity to comment on the promises of tyrants is not ignored, after which Tell is led off again.

The elaborate stage setting for the mountains is now brought out again. The stage directions indicate that this is the place in the opera where the audience's taste for musically-accompanied scenic effects is gratified. Amidst lightning flashes and the sound of thunder and scenery rattling in the wind and the band playing its lungs and hands off, we see a boat containing Guards, Gesler, and the fettered Tell. The boat is out of hand, and the others appeal to Tell to save them. Tell guides the boat to shore, grabs a crossbow, jumps from the boat, kills Gesler, and escapes into the mountains. Now the storm has abated and Arnold comes in and sings a song of the Swiss rising to arms. He is still describing the effects of the storm when Rhodolpha enters with a song telling her Maids to hurry now that the storm is past. The Maidens enter, and all can see, on the distant hills, the Austrian soldiers approaching. Walter and Werner enter, and the latter describes Tell's escape, in case we missed the import of the pantomime. Now all can see Tell approaching from offstage, and Rhodolpha calls out to greet him with a song of triumph. She sings, and the chorus echoes her; Arnold sings, and the chorus echoes him.

Tell enters, followed by the Bowmen and the Pikemen, and all listen as he proceeds alliteratively to milk an image:

Now cease your sounds of soothing melody;
For we must tune our souls to death and discord.

Let us forswear all notes but those that flow
From clanging arms, stout strokes, and twanging bows,
'Till victory is ours, and Switzers free.

He imitates Henry V in rousing the men to battle pitch, and they cry for him to lead them. He says, "Come! let us rather lead on time than follow!" He arranges for Rhodolpha's Maidens to take the town, then turns to the others:

Bend your tough bows, ye archers, draw the cords,
'Til the barb's steel doth touch the stubborn yew.
'Tis for our rights we fight, our country, and our laws!

All eagerly run off but the lovers, Rhodolpha and Arnold, who remain to sing a duet about Tell which sounds strangely like "Joe Hill":

O no, true worth is only found
     Where Liberty doth dwell;
Where none are lords, and none are slaves,
     There look to find a Tell.

The next scene moves us quickly back to the Castle, where Conrad is being tried for desertion, and such time-tested devices are used as having him sentenced before being condemned and condemned before being tried. Conrad is tied to a stake to be shot with arrows; he points out helpfully that it is more honorable to shoot a bird on the wing. Cecily's comment on the proceedings brings the house down: "O, O, O! Have all my prospects come to this? Am I never to be married? Never to be one of the Virgins?"

Just as they are about to shoot, there are arrows from offstage, followed by Rhodolpha, the Maidens, and the Bowmen, to the rescue. The Austrians retreat, and the Lieutenant and the Burgomaster are seized. Rhodolpha evinces her first human sentiment as, seeing Conrad tied to the stake, she says, "What, my friend Conrad, faithful to your post?"

Arnold arrives with the news that the Burghers have been armed, and all goes well. The Lieutenant and the Burgomaster are led off, and Cecily sings a song of thanks to Rhodolpha. Arnold says peace will soon come ("Soon shall the affrighting trumpet cease its blast;/And peace sit smiling on our hills sublime."), and a glee follows. One of the lines of the refrain goes, "Dance around, link'd hand in hand." The Old American Company's formidable ballet corps performs here, and song, dance, and color combine to presage the best that American musical comedy will have to offer for years to come.

The final setting is in the mountains again, and the final scenes are on different parts of the field of battle, requiring no change of scene, but merely exeunt and new entrance. The sound of alarms, or trumpets, precedes the first appearance of Leopold, who enters cursing the Swiss archery, which is decimating his Austrian troops. He makes a fine speech, thereby becoming a worthy foil for Tell.

Now another part of the field. More alarms, horns, and trumpets. Walter finds himself fighting a collection of Austrians, but he is rescued by his daughter and her Virgins. The girls describe the battle, then run off, making way for Leopold and Werner, who enter fighting, then exit with Leopold getting the better of his opponent. Surely, no one other than a William Tell can take the measure of this man. Leopold comes back, looking for the demon who is killing off all his forces. Conrad enters. "Now for a little more honour." He sees Leopold. "By the mass, there's the duke.—Too much honour is dangerous to honesty—'ware honesty," and he runs off. Now a party of Swiss soldiers enter from one side pursued by Leopold, and a party of Austrians from the other pursued by Tell. Leopold and Tell meet, and the latter speaks bravely and well, to Leopold's surprise. Leopold says Tell must be a nobleman, but Tell says yes, he is one of *nature's* noblemen, that is, a man. "Republicans no other nobles know!" These are evidently fighting words, and Leopold is wounded several times before the two exit, still fighting.

Now Conrad bravely beats an Austrian who has churlishly attacked him from behind. Meanwhile, Tell has killed Leopold and enters with the feathers from his helmet. Walter, Arnold, Rhodolpha, the Maidens, the Bowmen, and the Pikemen enter. They discuss the victory, including the fact that Werner was not seriously wounded. Arnold and Rhodolpha plight their troth; Cecily enters, and she and Conrad do the same, thereby neatly tying off plot and subplot. Tell advances to point the moral of the piece. And now a pastiche of songs: Tell sings of laws; Arnold sings of virtue; Rhodolpha sings of patriotism; Cecily sings of going home to make and sell baskets. Finally, the "Chorus of the Whole" sings of the importance of defending laws and rights, and *The Archers* is over.

Soon the applause will die down and another intermission with entertainment will intervene before the afterpiece is presented.

In this inspection of Dunlap and Carr's opera none of the music the eighteenth-century audience heard has been cited, though at least four pieces of music from the work are extant.[2] But as Edward Dent, one of the leading historians of opera, says:

> Yet it is not so absurd as it might seem at first sight to discuss an opera the music of which is entirely lost . . . ;

for it is of comparatively little importance to know what
the music sounded like—we can make a sufficient guess
at that by looking at other compositions of the men who
contributed to it—whereas it is of the greatest interest to
know what relation the music bore to the dramatic action
and how far it intensified the emotional values of the
play. This we can find out to some extent by a careful
examination of the libretto.[3]

Certainly in the solos, duets, trios, and choral music, in
the love songs and comic songs, in the dances, marches,
and descriptive music mentioned in *The Archers* can be
seen much of the nature of America's lyric theatre before
1800.

2

An article in 1794 called "Remarks on the Use and
Abuse of Music, etc. as a Part of Modern Education"[4] said
that opera and drama must be *useful* in "polishing the
manners and correcting the hearts of men." The demand
that music "aid sense," that "operas" be useful as polish
and corrective, were almost the only criteria eighteenth-
century American critics used in viewing musicals. "The
moral of the piece is entirely unexceptionable," says a
typical review of the day, "Virtue is crowned with the
reward which ought ever to be inseparable from the practice of it—and Vice is branded with the disappointment
and disgrace which should ever be its concomitant."[5]
More often than not, when the music is mentioned at all,
it is considered as something apart from the work itself.
A critique of *The Lyar*, for example, says, "The opera is
rich in music, but for plot or dialogue, the most despicable
thing tolerated on our stage."[6] Music, then, did not concern the critic overmuch. He went to the theatre for a
lesson in morality, and review after review completely

ignores the music (and even the singing) in order to
talk about the educational value of the work.[7]

At the time of *The Archers*, New York was blessed with
its first regular circle of theatre critics.[8] William Dunlap,
John Wells, Elias Hicks, Samuel Jones, William Cutting,
Peter Irving, and Charles Adams formed its core, though
Dunlap's fellow members of the Friendly Club probably
contributed on occasion. They met the night after performances to discuss their criticisms and to present one
to the press; they signed the reviews with several initials,
but only the last initial was that of the author. Typical
both of the criticism of the day and of the criticism of
musicals, were the reviews of *The Archers*.

The New York *Diary* for April 19 listed the publication
of *The Archers*, "An Opera in 3 Acts as performed by the
Old American Company in New-York." One day from
production to publication! On April 20, two days after
its première, *The Archers* was reviewed in the New
York *Diary* under "Theatrics, Critique Number XXI,
'. . . nothing extenuate nor set down aught in malice:'"

> On Monday evening were presented to a full house,
> for the first time, *The Archers*, with the afterpiece of
> *Edgar and Emmeline.*
>
> This Opera is the production of an American citizen,
> and as such should meet the patronage of the public.
> The progress of improvement in every description of
> knowledge, must necessarily be slow: imperfect in its
> origin, it derives its future excellence from support and
> encouragement. . . . Motives of policy, equally with
> those of reason, prompt us to give every aid to works of
> this kind. We have too long been accustomed to look up
> to England, as the source of our theatrical entertain-
> ments. . . . The most paltry importations of ribaldry
> and nonsense are too apt to pass for sense and wit; as if

by crossing the Atlantic they had acquired new virtues: whilst the productions of the American muse are disregarded because they are not foreign. The spurious exotic of genius is received and cherished in our soil whilst the real native plant is left to droop without a hand to water it or an eye to pity. Is it not time that this evil should be remedied? Is it not observable that the modern English plays are not applicable to this country, that they are intended either to ridicule fashionable vices which have no existence here, or inculcate principles favorable to their government?

. . . Our stage should represent to us the superior excellence of those manners which result from strict morality and the proper exercise of our political principles. . . .

The piece which has occasioned these observations has a manifest tendency to preserve those principles, which we hope will ever be dear to us. As far as we can judge from its first representation, it appears to be written with great correctness and elegance of language, and filled with that sentiment which must ever inspire freemen with a sense of their rights and a will to preserve them. If we were inclined to enter into a full criticism on the merits of the opera, we might suggest some alterations, in our opinion much to its advantage; although we think it on the whole entitled to credit. We shall however decline any further comments on the piece, until we see it again, or have an opportunity of perusing it. We are inclined to believe it suffered much in the representation.

A final paragraph tearing *Edgar and Emmeline* to shreds, and the review is over. It is signed "H.C.S.A.W.," and was probably written by John Wells. A final sentence apologizes for being a day late with comments, so most reviews were probably published the day following a production.

The next review of *The Archers* appeared only one day

after the second production. Dunlap and Carr's opera was given its second performance on April 22, and the New York *Diary* for Saturday, April 23, contains the following review:

> Last evening was performed, for the second time, *The Archers,* with *The Critic.*
>
> *The Archers* has interested us, from being the production of one of our countrymen. This circumstance has biassed us in its favor, and made us anxious for its success. We were pleased at the first representation. We then believed it possessed *intrinsic* merit to recommend it to public support; and our favorable impressions have not been diminished. Perfection cannot be expected in the commencement of any art or science: but a first attempt will often display genius and talents, which may be improved by cultivation and encouragement. These remarks, we think, apply to the piece before us. It is well written—it contains an interesting plot; the characters are well drawn, and consistent. The plot shows us the gallant resistance of free men against aggression, conducted with perseverance, and crowned with success. We glow with admiration at their determined opposition—we are partners in their danger—we rejoice at their victory. The character of *William Tell* is undoubtedly the best in the piece. He is always the bold asserter of his country's rights. Unawed by the threats or by the lawless power of the tyrant, he pursues with firmness the great object of his soul—the deliverance of his countrymen from oppression. In delineating the characters of *Conrad* and *Cecily,* the author has displayed to great advantage his talents for the comic and humorous. They enliven the piece by their natural and genuine witticisms. Though this piece is entitled to more praise than we have here bestowed on it, yet it was obvious that it did not obtain that decided applause we could have wished;

and before we finish our remarks on the play we will suggest those alterations which may remove the blemishes which appeared most hostile to its success. Could the scenes be more connected and made to arise out of each other—if the choruses, particularly those at the end of the acts, were shortened—if some of the songs were omitted—and less action represented—we are convinced that the piece would appear to much greater advantage. We also think some of the scenes are spun out without any incident to support them, while others are so crowded with it as to render them confused. We doubt not that, after a revisal of the opera, from the proofs of genius and talents which the author has displayed, the representation of *The Archers* may be often attended with much gratification.

We do not think that this piece received due support from all the performers.

The review continues with criticism of each member of the cast, and is then signed "A.D.A.S.M." The doctors Miller and Mitchell, and the Reverend Samuel Miller were friends of Dunlap—his literary critics and advisers; [9] and any one of the three might have been responsible for the review.

Dunlap's own comment on his opera was that it was "received with great applause. The music by Carr was pleasing, and well got up." [10] A letter to Dunlap from T. Holcroft said:

Your friend gave me William Tell to read: it proves you have made some progress; but it likewise proves, as far as I am a judge, that much remains for you to accomplish. Common thoughts, common characters, and common sensations have little attraction: we must soar beyond them, or be contented to walk the earth and join the crowd.[11]

Dunlap was pleased with the critic's favorable review of
The Archers in London, though he found the review
"superficial." [12] It was certainly superficial, though it is
hard to say how Dunlap managed to find it favorable:
"This liberty-play [says the London review of *The Archers*] is well calculated for the soil into which it has been
transplanted." [13]

The only other contemporary evaluation of the work
comes from Dunlap himself, in his preface to the printed
edition of the libretto:

> The principal liberty taken with history, is, that I have
> concentrated some of the actions of these heroic moun-
> taineers; making time submit to the laws of the Drama.
> But the reader will not have that sublime pleasure in-
> vaded, which is ever felt in the contemplation of virtuous
> characters: Tell, Furst, Melchthal, Staffach, and Winkel-
> reid, are not the children of poetic fiction.[14]

The Archers was well received, and Dunlap claims it
"was repeatedly played." [15] It received three performances
in New York in 1796.[16] Robert Gerson, in his *Music in
Philadelphia*, says, "No record has been traced of a performance of the opera in Philadelphia, but it is thought
that in 1797 or shortly thereafter Carr's opera was given
in that city." [17] Nor is there a record of a performance of
The Archers in Hartford, though a letter from Dunlap to
Hodgkinson asking the latter to sell copies of the play
there (at fifty cents each) suggests the possibility.[18] The
musical comedy was definitely performed in Boston at
least twice: once at a benefit for Dunlap (which suggests
the author's confidence in his work), and on another occasion before a small audience.[19] Unfortunately, records are
not complete, and it is difficult to estimate accurately the
total number of performances of *The Archers*. However,

the combination of favorable reviews, Dunlap's assertion about the frequency of its performance, and the fact that he was willing to take the considerable financial risk attached to using his musical for a benefit night, all attest to the popularity of one of America's first musical comedies.

Modern audiences have not had an opportunity to judge *The Archers*, but modern critics have been kind to the work. From the extant music, Granville Vernon deduces that Carr "was a composer evidently well schooled in the music of Handel, which, after all, is not the worst of models." [20] John Tasker Howard, in commenting on the music of *The Archers*, points out that "Carr's score to this adaptation of Schiller's *Wilhelm Tell* antedates Rossini's setting by thirty-three years," [21] apparently overlooking the fact that Schiller, too, was antedated, by seven years. Howard does claim that the few remaining pieces of music from *The Archers* are "so charming as to cause regret at the loss of the others." [22] Gerson says *The Archers* was Carr's "most ambitious work," and Chase says the music proves Carr to have been "a musician of exceptional talent." [23]

Dunlap's book has, on the whole, been less kindly treated. Quinn says the play "is interesting, but not one of his best. The chronicle element is uppermost and, as in nearly all operas, the songs interfere with the dramatic action." [24] Redway says the book's "tendency to display the worthy Tell as a busy and able politician rather than as a hero for a statue is nowadays subject for invidious comment, and it must be admitted that it is far nearer comic opera than Schiller's version makes quite palatable." [25] Again the confusion about who came first, Dunlap or Schiller, seems to have distorted the critic's eye. Coad, Dunlap's biographer, finds *The Archers* "William

Dunlap's chief contribution to American opera." [26] But Sonneck, who did so much work on America's early musical life, feels, after looking at *The Archers,* that:

> Still, we must not censure Dunlap too severely. Others, and greater than he, sinned against good taste by forcing serious themes into the straitjacket of comic opera.
>
> This had to be pointed out, as the origin of the peculiarly spectacular and nonsensical character of the American (so called) comic operas of today . . . must partly be traced back to the beginnings of operatic life in America. The remark will go a good way towards a reasonable explanation of why so far the birth of genuine American opera has been so tardy, for American comic opera is, at its best, a deeply rooted national evil.[27]

The audience on the night of April 18, 1796, had witnessed the origin of this "national evil"; they had seen a production similar in every respect to those performed in America a century and a half later. Perhaps they hummed "Why Huntress Why?" from the show as they turned their steps toward home.

Epilogue

If the audience which attended *The Archers* had been able to attend theatrical productions for another century and a half, they would have seen the tremendous influence the stage as they knew it exerted on all that came after. At the same time in history that musicals became the most prominent feature of the American repertory, the country began to push back her frontier and expand rapidly. The result was that, for America, wherever the stage became known it was known as a musical stage; the musical took root as an indigenous form.

The bridge between early productions and the modern lyric theatre was built by the nineteenth century's contributions to the musical stage. At least four new outlets for musical theatre became prominent in the 1800's: melodramas, showboats, minstrel shows, and vaudeville shows. Our old friend, William Dunlap, will be responsible for introducing melodrama to America,[1] and it will be found that each new form grows from something the eighteenth century introduced, in however tentative a fashion. Serious opera will be re-planted on American soil, and this time it will take (though, oddly enough, in its original tongue).[2] Oh, yes, and *The Black Crook* will be introduced, in 1866. Modern critics will find *The Black Crook* to be the first American musical comedy, and yet an examination of the work and its details of production will show that, far from being the first American musical comedy, *The Black Crook* offered nothing different from *The Archers*.[3]

All these things will be found in another century and another volume. Yet a country that uses musical productions to accompany its political conventions, its circuses, its sports events, its parades; a country that finds its theatre most alive in its musical productions—such a country must have had a long history of musical theatre. And the roots of America's tradition of musical comedy go back to the eighteenth century, at least as far as the performance the audience saw in 1796 of William Dunlap and Benjamin Carr's *The Archers*.

Notes

Prologue

[1] Few primary sources were used in connection with the music itself. The reader who desires to look at eighteenth-century American theatre music will find extant copies listed in the *Bio-Bibliographical Index of Musicians in the United States of America Since Colonial Times* (prepared by the District of Columbia Historical Records Survey, 2nd ed., Washington, 1956) and all extant secular music in the Sonneck-Upton *Bibliography of Early Secular American Music*. Nor have I listed the extensive bibliography connected with the popular songs mentioned in Chap. VI; I do not think a book of this nature need include an extensive analysis or bibliography of patriotic songs except insofar as they are related to the musical stage.

[2] Walter Kerr, *How Not to Write a Play*, New York, 1955, p. 237.

Chapter I

[1] Jacques Barzun, *Music in American Life*, New York, 1956, p. 15.

[2] William Priest, *Travels in the United States of America: 1793-1797*, London, 1802, p. 150.

[3] Michael G. Mulhall, *The Dictionary of Statistics*, 4th ed., London, 1899, p. 454; Isaac Weld, Jr., *Travels through the United States of North America and the Provinces of Upper and Lower Canada During the Years 1795, 1796, and 1797*, London, 1799, pp. 463-64.

[4] Lists assembled from Rita Susswein Gottesman, ed., *The Arts*

and Crafts in New York, New York, 1938 and 1954, Vols. I (1726-1776) and II (1777-1799).

⁵ Maud Wilder Goodwin, *The Colonial Cavalier,* New York, 1894, pp. 143-59. The diary of Mrs. Gabriel Manigault (cited by Eola Willis, *The Charleston Stage in the XVIII Century,* Columbia, South Carolina, 1924, pp. 40, 417), in 1754 recorded the existence in Charleston of dancing assemblies, rope dancers, plays, and so forth; by 1799, a circus, an elephant, a set of clocks, automatons, a troupe of child actors, and a variety of concerts had been seen.

⁶ The *History of the New Haven Theatre,* WPA Connecticut Writers Project, October 23, 1941, MS and typescript in Yale University Library, pp. 20-39, mentions a collection of plays, a variety of dancing schools, concerts, shades, animal exhibits, wax works—all by 1785. Louis B. Wright, *The Cultural Life of the American Colonies: 1607-1763,* New York, 1957, p. 188; Louis Pichierri, *Music in New Hampshire: 1623-1800,* New York, 1960, p. 66.

⁷ *The New-York Magazine,* December, 1794, p. 717.

⁸ George O. Seilhamer, *History of the American Theatre: During the Revolution and After* (Vol. II), Philadelphia, 1889, p. 296. Entertainments related to the musical stage are discussed and described in this chapter; the musical stage entertainments themselves are handled in detail in Chap. V.

⁹ George C. D. Odell, *Annals of the New York Stage,* Vol. I, New York, 1927, p. xi.

¹⁰ Quoted in Odell, I, 377.

¹¹ O[scar] G. Sonneck, *Early Concert-Life in America: 1731-1800,* Leipzig, 1907, p. 24; Odell, I, 153 ff.

¹² Harold Earle Johnson, *Musical Interludes in Boston: 1795-1830,* New York, 1943, p. 45.

¹³ O[scar] G. Sonneck, *Early Opera in America,* New York, 1915, p. 40.

¹⁴ It is important to note the fact that the concerts I shall discuss bore at least some resemblance to what we understand as concerts today. I do not refer here to those theatrical performances disguised as concerts in order to evade laws against the theatre (see Sonneck, *Early Concert-Life,* p. 25); for examples of stars in concerts, see Willis, p. 65, and Chap. III below.

¹⁵ See, for example, Johnson, pp. 172, 76; Sonneck, *Early Concert-Life,* p. 126.

[16] John Drayton, *Letters Written During a Tour through the Northern and Eastern States of America,* in Warren S. Tryon, ed., *A Mirror for Americans,* Chicago, 1952, I, 6.

[17] Johnson, p. 121; Odell, I, 311, 315.

[18] Adam Carse, *The Orchestra in the XVIIIth Century,* Cambridge, England, 1940, pp. 11, 68; Robert Rutherford Drummond, *Early German Music in Philadelphia,* New York, 1910, pp. 65, 68.

[19] Captain Francis Goelet, *Extracts from the Journal of Captain Francis Goelet, Merchant, Relating to Boston, Salem, Marblehead, Etc.: 1746-1750,* Albert H. Hoyt, ed., Boston, 1870, pp. 8, 11. The musical distinction between "consort" and "concert" was blithely ignored in eighteenth-century America. Also see Dr. Alexander Hamilton, who visited New York and Boston in 1744, *Hamilton's Itinerarium,* Albert Bushnell Hart, ed., St. Louis, Missouri, 1907; Jean Anthelme Brillat-Savarin, *The Physiology of Taste,* New York, 1926, p. 51.

[20] Pichierri, p. 56. Also see John Anderson diary, 1794-1798, MS in New York Historical Society. He mentions specifically February 11, 15, and 26, March 9, and May 3 in 1796; and these dates do not include the many times John himself played the violin to entertain either his guests or his hosts.

[21] Manfred F. Bukofzer, *Music in the Baroque Era,* New York, 1947, p. 403.

[22] John Tasker Howard, *Our American Music,* New York, 1939, p. 16; Sonneck, *Early Concert-Life,* pp. 104, 311; Frédérick Louis Ritter, *Music in America,* New Edition, New York, 1895, p. 27.

[23] Hamilton, p. 236.

[24] Howard, *Our American Music,* p. 26. The Society changed the spelling of its name from Coecilia to Cecilia in 1790 (Sonneck, *Early Concert-Life,* p. 28).

[25] Sonneck, *Early Concert-Life,* p. 18.

[26] Carse, p. 68; Sonneck, *Early Concert-Life,* pp. 66, 21; Henry M. Brooks, *Olden Time Music,* Boston, 1888, p. 89.

[27] Sonneck, *Early Concert-Life,* pp. 320, 56, 58, 258, and 317 respectively; also see pp. 320, 321.

[28] *Ibid.,* pp. 201, 205, 207, 203; Odell, I, 416; II, 69.

[29] Sonneck, *Early Concert-Life,* p. 201.

[30] New York *American Minerva,* April 2, 1796.

[31] Elizabeth De Hart Bleecker, MS diary, 1799-1806, in the New

York Public Library, entries for January 24, March 11, and April 11, 1799.

³² Sonneck, *Early Concert-Life*, pp. 13, 65-69, 78; Carl Bridenbaugh, *Cities in Revolt: Urban Life in America, 1743-1746*, New York, 1955, p. 401.

³³ Sonneck, *Early Concert-Life*, pp. 163, 198; Bridenbaugh, *Cities in Revolt*, p. 195; Odell, I, 362.

³⁴ See the New York *American Minerva* for the initial announcements and some of the programs. Other programs are listed in the New York *Argus*, and the New York *Daily Advertiser* carried advertisements for the fourth concert, not listed in other papers.

³⁵ See New York *American Minerva*, November 25 and December 24, 1796.

³⁶ Sonneck, *Early Concert-Life*, p. 166; see New York *American Minerva*, September 13, 1796.

³⁷ Carse, p. 71.

³⁸ Bukofzer, p. 404.

³⁹ Sonneck, *Early Concert-Life*, p. 1. Sonneck feels there probably were earlier public concerts, but these are the first of which we have definite record. A. A. Parker, ed., *Church Music and Musical Life in Pennsylvania in the Eighteenth Century*, III, Part 2, Philadelphia, 1947, p. 431.

⁴⁰ Both references cited in Carl Bridenbaugh, *Cities in the Wilderness: The First Century of Urban Life in America, 1625-1742*, New York, 1938, pp. 294 and 295.

⁴¹ Bridenbaugh, *Cities in the Wilderness*, pp. 455, 462; John Tasker Howard, *The Music of George Washington's Time*, Washington, D.C., 1931, p. 5; T. Allston Brown, *A History of the New York Stage*, I, Part 2, New York, 1903.

⁴² Howard, *Our American Music*, p. 22;Drummond, p. 28.

⁴³ Willis, p. 32; Sonneck, *Early Concert-Life*, pp. 11-13.

⁴⁴ Sonneck's *Early Concert-Life* traces this expansion, and while my own notes list a few concerts not contained in his work, I believe it pointless to duplicate, or at best supplement, this nearly exhaustive study. The points I am concerned with, in any case, do not rely on listing these concerts.

⁴⁵ See, for example, Odell, I, 69.

⁴⁶ Carl and Jessica Bridenbaugh, *Rebels and Gentlemen: Philadelphia in the Age of Franklin*, New York, 1942, p. 158. New York

at this time had, at the very least, weekly concerts given by Leonard and Dienval (advertisement cited in John F. Watson, *Annals and Occurrences of New York City and State,* Philadelphia, 1846, p. 273), the latter of whom is known to have been furnishing music for the theatre as well (William Dunlap, *A History of the American Theatre,* New York, 1832, p. 25). This decade saw Boston begin a practice which was to be essential to the development of the theatre in twenty years: concerts which were really "opera performances in disguise" (Sonneck, *Early Concert-Life,* p. 259).

[47] Paul Leicester Ford, *Washington and the Theatre,* New York, 1899, p. 33.

[48] Charles Durang, *History of the Philadelphia Stage: 1749-1855,* a series of articles from the Philadelphia *Sunday Dispatch,* 1854, arranged and illustrated by Thompson Westcott, 1868, in 6 volumes, in the University of Pennsylvania library, I, 44.

[49] Odell, I, 364.

[50] Priest, p. 52.

[51] Respectively, Brooks, p. 162; Willis, p. 411.

[52] Respectively, J. Max Patrick, *Savannah's Pioneer Theatre from Its Origins to 1810,* Athens, Georgia, 1953, p. 22; Willis, pp. 301-2, 303 ff.

[53] See New York *American Minerva,* November 11, 1796, and New York *Diary,* July 11, 1796.

[54] See, for example, the lists of prices in the New York *American Minerva,* December 24 and 27, 1796.

[55] Parker, pp. 73-74; Bleecker, January 24, 1799; Sonneck, *Early Concert-Life,* pp. 11, 12, 84.

[56] Quoted in Odell, I, 97.

[57] Sonneck, *Early Concert-Life,* p. 20; note George Washington's description of 400 women at a ball, *ibid.,* p. 27; Priest, pp. 60-61.

[58] Carse, p. 13.

[59] Sonneck, *Early Concert-Life,* pp. 73, 180. Mrs. Hodgkinson, Mrs. Pownall, and Benjamin Carr sang solos in *The Messiah* when it was performed in New York in 1796.

[60] Carse, p. 14; Sonneck, *Early Concert-Life,* p. 325.

[61] New York *American Minerva,* November 11, 1796.

[62] Sonneck, *Early Concert-Life,* p. 91.

[63] Johnson, p. 48.

[64] Sonneck, *Early Concert-Life,* p. 69. See Chap. III below for a discussion of the size of eighteenth-century orchestras in America.

[65] Respectively, Ritter, p. 44; Sonneck, *Early Concert-Life*, p. 110.

[66] New York *American Minerva*, April 2, 1796.

[67] New York *Argus*, January 19, 1796; Sonneck, *Early Concert-Life*, p. 58. Sonneck estimated the length of the concerts at four hours, but this seems a little long considering the full dances held afterwards.

[68] New York *Argus*, January 19, 1796.

[69] See Priest, pp. 52 and 61; Patrick, p. 32; Brooks, pp. 62, 98; Johnson, pp. 69, 172; Sonneck, *Early Concert-Life*, pp. 43, 44, 57-63, 156, 247, 248, 312, 317, 320, 322.

[70] Sonneck, *Early Concert-Life*, p. 59.

[71] Isaac J. Greenwood, *The Circus: Its Origin and Growth Prior to 1835*, New York, 1898, pp. 8-9.

[72] *Ibid.*, p. 18; J. Decastro, *Memoirs of J. Decastro*, R. Humphreys, ed., London, 1824, p. 28 ff.

[73] Decastro, p. 28, advertisement quoted on pp. 33-35.

[74] Weld, p. 14.

[75] Decastro, p. 149.

[76] Greenwood, p. 47; Durang, I, 47 (There is no good reason to accept Durang's statement that Faulks was the first equestrian in America); John Rowe, *Letters and Diary of John Rowe, Boston Merchant: 1759-1762, 1764-1779*, Anne Rowe Cunningham, ed., Boston, 1903, p. 221.

[77] Durang, I, 47; Odell, I, 175, 248-49; Rowe, p. 251; Greenwood, pp. 53, 57.

[78] Thomas Clark Pollock, *Philadelphia Theatre in the Eighteenth Century*, Philadelphia, 1933, p. 58 ff.; Odell, I, 336 ff.; Mederic Louis Elie Moreau de Sainte-Mery, *Journal*, in Oscar Handlin, ed., *This Was America*, Cambridge, Massachusetts, p. 91; Willis, p. 196; Greenwood, pp. 75, 69; Marian Murray, *Circus!*, New York, 1956, p. 120.

[79] Lewis P. Waldo, *The French Drama in the Eighteenth Century and its Influence on the American Drama of that Period: 1701-1800*, Baltimore, 1942, pp. 43, 48.

[80] John Bernard, *Retrospections of America: 1797-1811*, ed. from MSS by Mrs. Boyle Bernard, New York, 1887, p. 190; George Washington Parke Custis, in his *Recollections and Private Memoirs of Washington*, New York, 1860, p. 486, claims he heard Ricketts

say, "I delight to see the general [Washington] ride, and make it a point to fall in with him when I hear that he is on horseback—his seat is so firm, his management so easy and graceful, that I who am a professor of horsemanship, would go to him and *learn to ride.*"

[81] Stokes, I, 423. During this period of time he was frequently in competition with Lailson's circuses, and both competed with the theatre: see Willis, p. 424, for competition in Charleston; Pollock, pp. 61-62, for competition in Philadelphia; Odell, II, 31, for competition in New York.

[82] Cobbett, VIII, 145.

[83] Dunlap, *A History of the American Theatre*, p. 212.

[84] Weld, p. 14; see pictures of Astley's in Murray, and of Ricketts's in Durang. Greenwood, p. 71, says the Philadelphia circus of 1795 was 97 feet in diameter; the New York circus was probably approximately the same size.

[85] Murray, pp. 82-83.

[86] Picture on p. 82 of Murray; Wignell and Reinagle's Philadelphia Company, for example, performed in the New York circus building (Odell, I, 450), and later Fennell bought the building for $8,500 in order to give performances there (James Fennell, *An Apology for the Life of James Fennell, Written by Himself*, Philadelphia, 1814, p. 360).

[87] Charles Dickens, *The Old Curiosity Shop*, New York, Heritage Press, 1941, p. 297. Originally published in 1840-1841.

[88] New York *American Minerva*, June 4, 1796.

[89] *Ibid.*, May 5, 1796, and Joseph N. Ireland, *Records of the New York Stage from 1750-1860*, I, New York, 1866, p. 127; Greenwood, p. 69.

[90] Diary of J. Anderson, January 6, 1798.

[91] Greenwood, pp. 19, 24, 29.

[92] Odell, I, 420.

[93] New York *American Minerva*. The additional entertainments are all extracted from this newspaper except where otherwise noted. Ricketts's season probably did not actually get under way until May 10, since a reference in the New York *Argus* for this date mentions the fact that "Ricketts opens this night."

[94] New York *Diary*, July 11, 1796, and diary of J. Anderson, August 2, 1796.

[95] Pollock, pp. 59, 371, 373; Paul McPharlin, *The Puppet Theatre in America: A History,* New York, 1949, pp. 66, 86; Sonneck, *Early Opera in America,* p. 104.

[96] See, for example, Bleecker diary, April 23, 1799: "Mary, Eliza Stuyvesant, Anthony, Peter MacDonald and I went to the Circus to see The Revenge performed." Also see William Dunlap, *Diary,* 1766-1839, ed., Dorothy C. Barck, New York, 1930. Entry for June 1, 1797, in I, 54.

[97] Pollock, p. 61; New York *Argus,* July 18 ff., 1796; Lillian Moore, "John Durang: the First American Dancer," in *Chronicles of the American Dance,* ed. Paul Magriel, New York, 1948, pp. 31-32; Greenwood, p. 67.

[98] *The New-York Magazine,* March, 1795, p. 130.

[99] Sonneck, *Early Opera in America,* p. 129.

[100] Willis, p. 424.

[101] Pollock, pp. 58, 59, 266 ff.

[102] Dunlap, *Diary,* I, 144, entry for September 12, 1797.

[103] Diary of Alexander Anderson, October 17, 1794. Typescript and MS in Columbia University Library.

[104] See picture in Durang; Dickens, *Old Curiosity Shop,* pp. 297-98.

[105] See, for example, New York *Argus,* July 18, 1796.

[106] Carse, pp. 71, 77. While the English eighteenth-century pleasure gardens may be traced to the period between the Restoration and Queen Anne, none of that period lasted into the eighteenth century. Instead, three basic types became prevalent in England, and these were eighteenth-century products. The first type, including Marylebone Gardens, Cuper's Gardens, Ranelagh, and Vauxhall, were all established by 1750 (and all gone by 1859) and depended for their popularity on evening concerts, fireworks, eating, and drinking. There were many imitations of these four, and all featured music. In the second category are those primarily connected with mineral springs, and these were generally day resorts (though Sadler's lost its Wells early in the eighteenth century and began to rely on rope dancing and pantomimes in its theatre. It is interesting to note the fact that Sadler's Wells in London is still located over the boarded-up mineral wells which gave it its name. One of England's most famous amusements still shows its debt to an eighteenth-century origin). The third category embraced mainly tea gardens, and generally only an organ was

used for musical entertainment (W. A. Wroth and A. E. Wroth, *The London Pleasure Gardens of the Eighteenth Century*, New York, 1896, pp. 1-10).

[107] Sonneck, *Early Concert-Life*, p. 19.

[108] Watson, p. 280; Odell, I, 99; Sonneck, *Early Concert-Life*, p. 20.

[109] See, for example, Bridenbaugh's *Cities in Revolt*, p. 360.

[110] I. N. Phelps Stokes, *The Iconography of Manhattan Island*, New York, 1915, I, 384-85; V, 1319, 1341; Willis, pp. 290, 437, 466; Robert A. Gerson, *Music in Philadelphia*, Philadelphia, 1940, p. 30; Pollock, p. 51; Sonneck, *Early Concert-Life*, p. 57.

[111] Gerson, p. 14; Stokes, V, 1341; Sonneck, *Early Concert-Life*, p. 102.

[112] Sonneck, *Early Concert-Life*, pp. 102, 166, 209, 210 ff.; Gottesman, II, 378. Additional enticements to attend these pleasure gardens included waxwork figures (Bridenbaugh, *Cities in Revolt*, p. 360), food (with ice cream a particular attraction, according to contemporary accounts—see Odell, I, 99 and Bleecker diary for August 5 and 8, 1799), illuminated waterfalls (Sonneck, *Early Concert-Life*, p. 99), a circus (Stokes, I, 384), and the like, though the advertisements clearly indicate that the various musical endeavors were the chief attraction. A Vauxhall advertisement in New York for 1793 mentions the fact that in addition to tight and slack-rope dancing and "equilibriums," the orchestra will be "in the middle of a large tree, elegantly illuminated." (cited in Stokes, V, 1298). Also see New York *American Minerva*, September 13, 1796.

[113] Odell, II, 35-36.

[114] Ireland, *Records of the New York Stage*, I, 84, and Daniel Spillane, *History of the American Pianoforte*, New York, 1890, p. 99. Pollock, p. 51, mentions the fact that the Kenna company of actors performed at the Northern Liberties Theatre, Philadelphia, in the summers of 1791 and 1792, alternating with Vauxhall Gardens, thus indicating the possibility of some type of performance at the latter.

[115] Sonneck, *Early Opera in America*, pp. 107, 214; Odell, II, 95, 126.

[116] McPharlin, p. 122.

[117] A puppet is "a theatrical figure moved under human control . . ." by string, hand, or rod, whether it be called marionette

(a fancy name for the same thing) or fantoccini. Early puppet shows assured excellence by calling themselves Prussian or High German, but by the late 1700's Italian extraction seemed more desirable. One possible distinction between fantoccini and puppets lies not in the miniature figures used but in the fact that "fantoccini used a variety of types, whereas Punch and his family came to be associated with puppet shows" (McPharlin, pp. 1, 5, 53, 67, 89). Shadow plays (or *ombres chinoises* or *ombres françaises*) involve figures which are *not* articulated, though many have articulated limbs; dialogue is always used in their presentation (Brander Matthews, "The Forerunner of the Movies," *The Century Magazine,* LXXXVII (April, 1914), 917, 919.

[118] McPharlin, p. 3.

[119] *History of the New Haven Theatre,* unpaginated section; McPharlin, pp. 38-39; Ireland, *Records of the New York Stage,* I, 2n.

[120] Pollock, p. 6; Bridenbaugh, *Cities in the Wilderness,* p. 439.

[121] Pennsylvania *Gazette,* December 30, 1742, cited in McPharlin, p. 41.

[122] T. A. Brown, I, 2; Odell, I, 27, 29; advertisement from New York *Gazette,* September 7, 1747, cited in McPharlin, p. 42; also, McPharlin, pp. 44, 397.

[123] New York *Mercury,* December 29, 1755, cited in Gottesman, I, 144.

[124] Odell, I, 102; Bridenbaugh, *Cities in Revolt,* p. 361; McPharlin, pp. 48, 421.

[125] Pollock, p. 128, McPharlin, pp. 445, 397, 421, 50; Odell, I, 155; Ford, *Washington and the Theatre,* p. 23.

[126] *History of the New Haven Theatre,* p. 39; McPharlin, pp. 58, 397; Moore, p. 16; Durang, I, 25.

[127] McPharlin, pp. 397, 417, 422, 440; Odell, I, 439.

[128] New York *American Minerva,* May 21, June 20, 1796; McPharlin, pp. 90, 422.

[129] Matthews, "The Forerunner of the Movies," p. 917; McPharlin, pp. 58, 60.

[130] Plot taken from Matthews, "The Forerunner of the Movies," pp. 917-19.

[131] Reproduced in McPharlin, p. 58.

[132] Matthews, "The Forerunner of the Movies," p. 919.

[133] Information collated from Sonneck, *Early Opera in America.*

[134] John O'Keeffe and William Shield, *The Poor Soldier: A Comic Opera*, in two acts, as it is acted at the Theatre, Smoke-Alley, Dublin, 1786.

[135] Durang, I, 25.

[136] McPharlin, p. 21.

[137] *Ibid.*, p. 26.

[138] Edwin Duerr, "Charles Ciceri and the Background of American Scene Design," *Theatre Arts Monthly*, XVI, No. 12, December, 1932, p. 989.

[139] Sonneck, *Early Opera in America*, p. 22.

[140] New York *Journal or the General Advertiser*, April 9, 1767, cited in Gottesman, I, 313-14.

[141] Odell, I, 102.

[142] Willis, p. 104. Dancing pervaded even non-theatrical entertainments: for instance, sleigh riding, frequently mentioned as the most popular winter entertainment, had as standard equipment a fiddler, "who is placed at the head of the sleigh, and plays all the way. At every inn they meet with on the road, the company alight and have a dance." (Priest, pp. 47-48. See also diary of John Anderson for January 31, 1795, and John Davis, *The Original Letters of Ferdinand and Elisabeth*, New York, 1798, which contains a brief description of one of these travelling dancing assemblies.)

[143] See, for example, the New York *American Minerva*, May 9, 1796, and Willis, p. 30.

[144] Howard, *The Music of George Washington's Time*, p. 8; see New York *American Minerva*, January 18 and November 30, 1796, and New York *Daily Advertiser*, January 5, 1796.

[145] Dr. Alexander Hamilton, writing on August 16, 1744, in Boston, says, "Assemblies of the gayer sort are frequent here, the gentlemen and ladies meeting almost every week at concerts of musick and balls. I was present at two or three such, and saw as fine a ring of ladies, as good dancing, and heard musick as elegant as I had been witness to anywhere" (Hamilton, pp. 178-79). New York had many balls as far back as the 1730's, and they were still one of the most popular forms of entertainment there in 1800 (Sonneck, *Early Concert-Life*, p. 14. Note the number of entries for Bleecker for 1799 and January 2 and March 3 of 1800. Note, too, the numerous dancing academies in 1800, for which see Odell, II, 92).

[146] Francis Baily, March 15, 1796, cited in Stokes, V, 1329.

[147] A dancing school had been opened and promptly closed in Massachusetts in 1672 (Richardson Wright, *Hawkers and Walkers in Early America*, Philadelphia, 1927, p. 164), and a dancing master had appeared in New England in 1684-1685 (Odell, I, 4); from then on there was no dearth of men and women to teach. After the Revolution dancing masters generally emerged from the travelling troupes of actors (Richardson Wright, p. 167). "Dancing between the play and the farce was a regular part of the evening's entertainment and, when not acting, most of the early managers gave instruction in dancing. . . ." (Willis, p. 104.)

[148] New York *American Minerva,* September 27, 1796; New York *Argus,* January 1, 1796; New York *Daily Advertiser,* January 1, 1796, respectively.

[149] Bernard, p. 189.

[150] Odell, I, 25.

[151] Cited in Gottesman, I, 383-84.

[152] Oscar G. Sonneck, *Francis Hopkinson and James Lyon,* Washington, D. C., 1905, p. 16.

[153] Odell, I, 103. Steven's "Lecture on Heads," the popularity of which probably reflected a craze for phrenology, involved a "set of portraits of famous men, comic characters, and other types"; they were usually shown "in life size; and characteristics of the originals were lectured upon and impersonated, often with musical accompaniment." (Patrick, p. 10.)

[154] Pollock, p. 23.

[155] *Ibid.,* p. 100.

[156] Pichierri, p. 81; Rowe *Diary,* pp. 190, 200.

[157] Willis, pp. 55, 143; Patrick, p. 10; Sonneck, *Early Concert-Life,* pp. 43, 55.

[158] Odell, I, 270; Fennell, p. 360.

[159] Sonneck, *Early Opera in America,* p. 63; *Early Concert-Life,* pp. 143, 152.

[160] Brooke Hindle, *The Pursuit of Science in Revolutionary America,* Chapel Hill, North Carolina, 1956, p. 260; Seilhamer, II, 296.

[161] Stokes, I, p. 386; "Walter Barrett, clerk," *John Pintard,* pamphlet in New York Historical Society, no publishing information. In 1795 Baker took over the museum from the Tammany Society, calling it Baker's American Museum (Walter Barrett; Stokes, I, 386), and running it until his death from yellow fever

in 1798 (George Gates Raddin, Jr., *The New York of Hocquet Caritat and His Associates: 1797-1817*, Dover, New Jersey, 1953, pp. 18-19). A somewhat blurred line of descent (Raddin, p. 39; Walter Barrett, Stokes, I, 386) eventually put the museum into the hands of P. T. Barnum in 1835 with results that, themselves, are not unrelated to America's musical stage. Baker must have been, as Odell calls him, "a kind of early Barnum," for anything which might draw a crowd got itself exhibited in his museum (Odell, II, 33). So respectable were many of his exhibits, paintings for example, that even people opposed to the theatre found themselves exposed to some of its vices which were also on display (see, for example, the MS diary of Rev. John Barent Johnson, April 24, 1798—in Columbia University Library).

[162] Diary of A. Anderson, June 20, 1796.

[163] Rowe, *Diary*, November 23, 1768, p. 180; and diary of A. Anderson, September 26, 1794 respectively; Bridenbaugh, *Cities in Revolt*, p. 194.

Chapter II

[1] Arthur Hornblow, *A History of the Theatre in America*, Philadelphia and London, 1919, I, 10; Hugh Jones, *The Present State of Virginia*, Richard L. Morton, ed., Chapel Hill, North Carolina, 1956, pp. 11, 70; Oral Sumner Coad, "The American Theatre in the Eighteenth Century," *South Atlantic Quarterly*, XVII, No. 3, July, 1918, p. 190; Louis B. Wright, *The Cultural Life of the American Colonies: 1607-1763*, New York, 1957, p. 180.

[2] Francis C. Wemyss, *Chronology of the American Stage: From 1752-1852*, New York, 1852, p. 11; Arthur Hobson Quinn, *A History of the American Drama*, New York and London, 1923, I, 16.

[3] Eola Willis, *The Charleston Stage in the XVIII Century*, Columbia, South Carolina, 1924, p. 7 (unless the rope dancing advertised in Philadelphia in 1724 was performed at a theatre. See Thomas Clark Pollock, *The Philadelphia Theatre in the Eighteenth Century*, Philadelphia, 1933, p. 5).

[4] George O. Seilhamer in his *History of the American Theatre* ably traces the history of the various colonial theatres. However, Seilhamer has been shown to be inaccurate; the next few paragraphs attempt to straighten the record by using local historians

to trace chronologically the placement of theatres in eighteenth-
century America, and in so doing provide a background against
which America's musical stage can be seen most clearly.

⁵ Willis, pp. 16, 21, 38, 43, 61, 75, 104, 144, 145, 155, 237.

⁶ Pollock, p. 6 and John Tasker Howard, *Our American Music,*
New York, 1939, p. 23.

⁷ Pollock, pp. 9, 14, 45, 48, 51; Carl and Jessica Bridenbaugh,
Rebels and Gentlemen: Philadelphia in the Age of Franklin, New
York, 1942, p. 142; Howard, p. 71.

⁸ Pollock, pp. 17, 20, 53; Quinn, I, 16.

⁹ Isaac Weld, Jr., *Travels through the States of North America
and the Provinces of Upper and Lower Canada During the Years
1795, 1796, and 1797,* London, 1799, p. 14.

¹⁰ William W. Clapp, Jr., *A Record of the Boston Stage,* Boston
and Cambridge, 1853, p. 2.

¹¹ Clapp, pp. 3, 4, 6-7, 14, 15, 23; George O. Seilhamer, *History
of the American Theatre: During the Revolution and After* (II),
Philadelphia, 1889, p. 18.

¹² Oscar G. Sonneck, *Early Opera in America,* New York, London, Boston, 1915, p. 139; Clapp, pp. 19, 20, 42, 59, 68; Harold
Earle Johnson, *Musical Interludes in Boston: 1795-1830,* New York,
1943, pp. 30, 186; William Priest, *Travels in the United States
of America: 1793-1797,* London, 1802, p. 165.

¹³ George O. Willard, *A History of the Providence Stage: 1762-
1891,* Providence, 1891, pp. 22, 23, 24, 26.

¹⁴ Andrew Burnaby, *Burnaby's Travels Through North America:
1759 and 1760,* Introduction and notes by Rufus Rockwell Wilson,
New York, 1904, p. 80.

¹⁵ Sonneck, *Early Opera in America,* p. 149.

¹⁶ Rutherford Goodwin, *A Brief and True Report for the Traveller concerning Williamsburg in Virginia,* Richmond, Virginia, 1936,
pp. 60-61, 183; Oral Sumner Coad, *William Dunlap,* New York,
1917, p. 32; Hornblow, I, 47; Sonneck, *Early Opera in America,*
p. 18.

¹⁷ James Fennell, *An Apology for the Life of James Fennell, Written by Himself,* Philadelphia, 1814, pp. 337-38.

¹⁸ Willis, pp. 85, 133; Hornblow, I, 212; quotation from Weld,
pp. 26-27.

¹⁹ *History of the New Haven Theatre,* WPA Connecticut Writers'

Project, 1941. MS and typescript in Yale University Library, pp. 2-5, 20.

[20] Willard, p. 28; Willis, pp. 104, 237; Wemyss, p. 11; Richard Moody, *America Takes the Stage*, Bloomington, Indiana, 1955, pp. 27-28; Louis Pichierri, *Music in New Hampshire: 1623-1800*, New York, 1960, p. 81.

[21] It is not known how successful Hunter was, though Anthony Aston definitely performed in New York in 1703 in *some* sort of structure (Foster Rhea Dulles, *America Learns to Play*, New York, 1952, pp. 53-54; Wright, p. 179; Hornblow, I, 30).

[22] Wright, p. 181; T. Allston Brown, *A History of the New York Stage*, New York, 1903, I, 1, 2; Charles P. Daly, *First Theatre in America*, New York, 1896, pp. 4, 10, 12, 13; George C. D. Odell, *Annals of the New York Stage*, New York, 1927, I, 32, 35.

[23] Daly, p. 14; Joseph N. Ireland, *Records of the New York Stage: 1750-1860*, New York, 1866, I, 29; Odell, I, 75; Seilhamer, *Before the Revolution* (I), 1888, p. 92; Brown, I, 6.

[24] Odell, I, 79; Ireland, I, 32, 41; Brown, I, 6; Daly, p. 15.

[25] Ireland, I, 42; Daly, p. 15; I. N. Phelps Stokes, *The Iconography of Manhattan Island*, New York, Vol. IV, 1922, p. 779; Seilhamer, II, 22, 34; *Receipts of the Treasurer of the "Theatre Royal," John Street, 1779*, MS in New York Historical Society; Odell, I, 184, 189.

[26] Seilhamer, II, 169; Odell, I, 232. This was evidently a courageous act, since anti-theatre sentiment forced such subterfuges as Philadelphia's Southwark Theatre being called an "opera house" (the first time this term was used in America), and Charleston's theatre being called "Harmony Hall" (Edward Ellsworth Hipsher, *American Opera and Its Composers*, Philadelphia, 1927, p. 23; Willis, p. 107).

[27] Odell, I, 285, says these William Street performances were "probably amateurs," but there is more reason to believe that the actors were only "automatons" (see Alexander Anderson diary, MS and typescript in Columbia University, September 20, 1794; John Anderson diary, MS and typescript in New York Historical Society, June 21, 1796); also see Odell, I, 288.

[28] Stokes, Vol. V, 1926, p. 1334.

[29] Hugh Gaine, *The Journals of Hugh Gaine, Printer*, Paul Leicester Ford, ed., New York, 1902, II, 186, entry for Saturday, January 13, 1798.

[30] William Dunlap, *Diary of William Dunlap* (*1766-1839*), ed. Dorothy C. Barck, New York, 1930, p. 215, entry for January 29, 1798, and p. 79, June, 1798.

[31] See advertisements in newspapers and playbills of the time; and New York *American Minerva,* May 30, 1796.

[32] James J. Lynch, *Box, Pit, and Gallery,* Berkeley and Los Angeles, 1953, p. 200; J. Max Patrick, *Savannah's Pioneer Theatre from Its Origins to 1810,* Athens, Georgia, 1953, p. 27; Willis, p. 156; William Dunlap, *A History of the American Theatre,* New York, 1932, p. 13. A playbill of M'Grath's Strolling Company in Reading, Pennsylvania, 1798, gives six thirty as the starting time, close enough to permit my generalization; Daly, p. 52; Joseph Ireland, *Fifty Years of a Play-Goer's Journal,* New York, 1860, p. 9 (Ireland gives six fifteen as starting time for the Park Theatre). Also see Willis, p. 333.

[33] William Eben Schultz, *Gay's Beggar's Opera,* New Haven, 1923, pp. 271-72.

[34] In *Early Opera in America,* Sonneck quotes from a letter of 1794 that the theatre in Philadelphia gave performances from six o'clock to midnight—six hours!

[35] Dunlap, *A History of the American Theatre,* p. 14; Ireland, *Records of the New York Stage,* I, pp. 10, 173; Pollock, p. 56; Daly, p. 5; Lynch, p. 12. In London, after the season was well under way, each theatre gave six performances a week. The only duplication of nights in New York seems to have been on Saturday.

[36] Coad, "The American Theatre in the Eighteenth Century," p. 195; Lynch, p. 12.

[37] See respectively, Clapp, pp. 25, 51; Henry Wansey, *The Journal of an Excursion to the United States of North America, in the Summer of 1794,* Salisbury, 1796, p. 42; Patrick, p. 27; Willis, pp. 156, 333; Pollock, pp. 14, 56; Charles Durang, *History of the Philadelphia Stage: 1749-1855,* clippings from 1854 articles in the Philadelphia *Sunday Dispatch* arranged and illustrated by Thompson Westcott, 1868, in University of Pennsylvania, I, 56; Willard, pp. 24, 29, 31.

[38] Information from 1798 playbill in New York Public Library.

[39] In a letter to William Dunlap in the New York *Mirror,* February 9, 1833, M. M. Noah recalls buying a season ticket as a boy to Wignell and Reinagle's Chestnut Street Theatre for $18.

[40] Respectively, Daly, p. 50; Seilhamer, I, 10; Odell, I, 38; Daly,

p. 4; Brown, I, 3; Ireland, *Records of the New York Stage*, I, 16, 21; John F. Watson, *Annals and Occurrences in New York City and State*, Philadelphia, 1846, p. 282; Odell, I, 114; Ireland, *Records of the New York Stage*, I, 32, 94, 174; also, see playbills and newspaper advertisements of the time.

[41] Ireland, *Records of the New York Stage*, I, 24.

[42] In Harvard University theatre collection.

[43] Alexander Anderson diary, March 26, 1793; see playbill for the John Street Theatre for February 27, 1796, in New York Public Library.

[44] E.g., Clapp, p. 35.

[45] Quoted in Brown, I, 8.

[46] Quoted in Stokes, IV, 779.

[47] Playbill for January 31, 1792, in Harvard University theatre collection.

[48] Royall Tyler, *The Contrast*, in *Representative Plays by American Dramatists*, ed. Montrose J. Moses, New York, 1918, I, 473, Act III, scene 1.

[49] Dunlap, *A History of the American Theatre*, p. 28.

[50] Pollock, p. 24.

[51] Dunlap, *A History of the American Theatre*, p. 22.

[52] Pollock, p. 19.

[53] In a letter dated March 25, 1795, arranging for the building of the Hartford Theatre, Hodgkinson had written, "One thing it will be necessary to mention: the plans of Mr. Wilson, are drawn to the size of our present stage here, and as the Scenery will be supplied *from* here, strict attention should be paid to that circumstance by forming the breadth and height exactly the same." The Articles of Agreement between Hodgkinson and Hallam (managers of the Old American Company at the time) and three men in Hartford, call for the theatre in Hartford to be the 52 by 87 mentioned above (Letter and Articles of Agreement which give size are both in the Houghton Library, Harvard University).

[54] New York *American Minerva*, February 8, 1796.

[55] Weld, p. 153.

[56] Respectively, Coad, "The American Theatre in the Eighteenth Century," p. 190; Brown, I, 2, 6; Henry C. Lahee, *Annals of Music in America*, Boston, 1922, p. 5; Watson, p. 201.

[57] Lynch, p. 303.

[58] Clapp, p. 19.

[59] Wansey, p. 42.

[60] Respectively, Wansey, p. 42; Priest, p. 165.

[61] Pollock, p. 54; Wansey, p. 126; John Bernard, *Retrospections of America: 1797-1811*, ed. from MSS by Mrs. Boyle Bernard, New York, 1887, p. 69.

[62] Willard, p. 26.

[63] Stokes, V, 1334, 1349; Ireland, *Fifty Years of a Play-Goer's Journal*, p. 7.

[64] Odell, II, 4, 5. This is Odell's description of a picture of the exterior of the Park.

[65] Odell's description, above, indicates more than one door to the new theatre, and such comments as Alexander Anderson's (diary, March 12, 1794) speak of *doors* opening prior to the performance.

[66] New York *American Minerva*, January, 1795, quoted in A. M. Nagler, *Sources of Theatrical History*, New York, 1952, p. 521.

[67] Dunlap, *A History of the American Theatre*, p. 248; *The New-York Magazine*, February, 1795, p. 68.

[68] Pollock, p. 212; Ford, *Washington and the Theatre*, pp. 49-58. Johnson, p. 161, gives an advertisement showing that music was occasionally published on the same day as the evening songs were to be sung in the theatre.

[69] Dulles, p. 56; New York *Gazette*, November 19, 1750, cited in Rita S. Gottesman, ed., *The Arts and Crafts in New York*, New York, 1938, Vol. I, 1726-1776, p. 122. *Receipt Book of the Treasurer of the "Theatre Royal"* also includes a bill for "stove and pipe."

[70] William Winter, *Life and Art of Joseph Jefferson*, New York, 1894, p. 85 footnote.

[71] Washington Irving, *Letters of Jonathan Oldstyle*, nine letters from New York *Morning Chronicle*, 1802-1803, New York, 1935, p. 255.

[72] Charles William Janson, *The Stranger in America: 1793-1806*, Introduction and Notes by Carl S. Driver, New York, 1935, p. 255.

[73] Collated from: Alexander Anderson diary, March 12, 1794; Wesley Swanson, "Wings and Backdrops: The Story of American Stage Scenery from the Beginnings to 1875," *The Drama*, October, 1927, p. 7; Irving, pp. 41-42.

[74] Lillian Moore, "John Durang: the First American Dancer," *Chronicles of the American Dance*, ed. Paul Magriel, New York,

1948, p. 24. The description is of the Southwark, but, as pointed out above, the John Street was similar.

[75] New York *American Minerva*, January, 1795, quoted in Nagler, p. 521.

[76] Swanson, November, 1927, p. 64; New York *American Minerva*, February 8, 1796; William Van Lennep, "The So-Called View of New York's John Street Theatre," *Theatre Notebook*, July-September, 1950, p. 87; Dunlap, *A History of the American Theatre*, p. 28. There is a possibility that the gallery was on the same level and behind the upper boxes, since this is the way Moore, p. 24, claims the Southwark was constructed.

[77] Van Lennep, p. 87; Dulles, p. 56; Alexander Anderson diary, March 12, 1794. Anderson and his brother had bought gallery tickets—"The doors were open when we arrived, but we got a pretty good seat. . . ."

[78] Lahee, p. 5; Odell, I, p. 39.

[79] Quoted from Royall Tyler, *The Contrast*, p. 473; also see Willis, p. 153.

[80] Pollock, p. 19, description of the Southwark.

[81] Respectively, Stokes, V, 1349; Clapp, p. 42; *The New-York Magazine*, April, 1794, p. 195; Willis, p. 153; Willard, p. 26.

[82] Lahee, p. 5; Swanson, October, 1927, p. 7; also see *Receipts of the Treasurer of the "Theatre Royal"* to get some idea of the expenses entailed in purchasing and caring for spermaceti candles.

[83] *The New-York Magazine*, April, 1794, p. 195; Irving, pp. 25, 41.

[84] William Dunlap, *Memoirs of a Water Drinker*, New York, 1837, p. 29.

[85] Respectively, Willard, p. 26; Clapp, p. 19; Ireland, *Records of the New York Stage*, I, 69.

[86] Coad, "The American Theatre in the Eighteenth Century," p. 90; Brown, I, 3; Odell, I, 39; Seilhamer, I, 10.

[87] Willis, p. 108.

[88] Brown, I, 6; Ireland, *Records of the New York Stage*, I, 32.

[89] George Washington Parke Custis, *Recollections and Private Memoirs of Washington*, New York, 1860, p. 367 footnote; Dulles, p. 54.

[90] New York *American Minerva*, January, 1795, quoted in Nagler, p. 521.

[91] Dunlap, *A History of the American Theatre*, p. 28.

[92] Coad, "The American Theatre in the Eighteenth Century," p. 193; Odell, II, 8 and Stokes, V, 1349; Pollock, p. 54. It is interesting to compare these figures with the capacity of theaters in smaller cities; the Bow Street Theater in Portsmouth, for example, had a capacity of 400 (Pichierri, p. 92).

[93] Brown, I, 2; Swanson, p. 5; again my sources refer to the Southwark Theatre: Pollock, p. 19, and Moore, p. 24. Early theatres had used candles exclusively, both in the auditorium and upon the stage (Swanson, p. 7). Later, "plain oil lamps illuminated the traditional wings and backdrops of the time. . . . In addition to weak footlights, the house chandeliers and side- or wing-lights were utilized. . . ." (Edwin Duerr, "Charles Ciceri and the Background of American Scenic Design," *Theatre Arts Monthly*, XVI, No. 12, December, 1932, pp. 988-89.)

[94] Odell, I, 140.

[95] Dunlap, *A History of the American Theatre*, p. 28; Moore, p. 24.

[96] *The New-York Magazine*, January, 1795, p. 6.

[97] Respectively, Clapp, p. 19; Pollock, p. 54; Willard, p. 26; Willis, p. 153.

[98] Clifford E. Hamar, "Scenery on the American Stage," *The Theatre Annual*, VII, 1948-1949, p. 84.

[99] Willard, p. 26.

[100] Irving, p. 13.

[101] See Hodgkinson letter, March 25, 1795, in Harvard University, directing the building of the Hartford Theatre. Note the fact that Douglass, former manager of the Old American Company, built theatres in each city to which he brought his troupe.

[102] Brown, I, 2; Swanson, p. 5; Odell, I, 140; Duerr, p. 988; Hamar, pp. 86-87.

[103] Cited in Odell, I, 254.

[104] Swanson, pp. 5-6, 30. For detailed handling of English theatres and their scenery in the eighteenth century, see Richard Southern, *Changeable Scenery*, London, 1952, pp. 177-245.

[105] Wansey, p. 126; also Swanson, p. 30.

[106] See, for example, Bernard, p. 69; Priest, pp. 30-31; Swanson, p. 5.

[107] Hamar, pp. 85, 87-88; Dunlap, *Memoirs of a Water Drinker*, p. 37; Duerr, p. 983.

[108] Hamar, p. 89; Duerr, p. 984.

[109] Swanson, pp. 6, 41, 42; Ireland, *Fifty Years of a Play-Goer's Journal*, p. 8.

[110] Duerr, pp. 985-87.

[111] Dunlap, *A History of the American Theatre*, pp. 109-110.

[112] Duerr, p. 989.

[113] *Ibid.*, p. 987.

[114] See, for example, *The New-York Magazine*, February, 1795, p. 68; New York *Spectator*, March 3, 1798, cited by Gottesman, 1954, II, 1777-1799, p. 340.

[115] Gottesman, II, 345; New York *American Minerva*, June 9, 1796; Duerr, p. 984.

[116] Ireland, *Fifty Years of a Play-Goer's Journal*, p. 8.

[117] Swanson, p. 78.

[118] See, for example, *The New-York Magazine*, January, 1795, p. 3; also, Swanson, pp. 6, 7, 78; Hamar, pp. 84, 87; Dulles, pp. 56-57; Irving, p. 24; Lynch, p. 6.

[119] Carl and Jessica Bridenbaugh, *Rebels and Gentlemen*, p. 141.

[120] Lynch, p. 2.

[121] *Ibid.*, pp. 199, 201, 203-4.

[122] Coad, "The American Theatre in the Eighteenth Century," p. 196.

[123] Dunlap, *A History of the American Theatre*, p. 251.

[124] Lynch, p. 200; Dulles, p. 54.

[125] New York *American Minerva*, January, 1795, quoted in Nagler, p. 521.

[126] Pollock, p. 10.

[127] Frederick Tupper and Helen Tyler Brown, eds., *Grandmother Tyler's Book: The Recollections of Mary Palmer Tyler (Mrs. Royall Tyler), 1775-1866*, New York and London, 1925, p. 118.

[128] *The New-York Magazine*, November, 1794, p. 655.

[129] Arnold Whitridge, "Brillat-Savarin in America," *The Franco-American Review*, June, 1936, Vol. I, No. 1, p. 5.

[130] New York *Argus*, April 8, 1796.

[131] *The New-York Magazine*, February, 1795, p. 69.

[132] Sonneck, *Early Opera in America*, p. 121.

[133] Dunlap, *A History of the American Theatre*, pp. 210-11.

[134] *The Mirror of Taste and Dramatic Censor*, Philadelphia and New York, 1810-1811, II, 296, 381.

[135] New York *American Minerva*, January, 1795, quoted in Nagler, p. 521.

[136] Lynch, p. 304.

[137] Respectively, Willis, p. 261; Irving, p. 18. Full scale riots occurred and audiences frequently swarmed all over the stage when their ire was aroused (James E. Cronin, "Elihu Hubbard Smith and the New York Theatre (1793-1798)," *New York History*, April 1950, XXXI, No. 2, p. 136). In Charleston an audience threw beer bottles on the stage when an advertised dance was not forthcoming; an actor, Godwin, threw one back, and people jumped on the stage after him (Willis, p. 121). Beer bottles were flung in Philadelphia in 1794 (Pollock, p. 57), and in New York, where two drunken sea captains demanded "Yankee Doodle," were refused, and came back to the theatre with their crews (Cronin, p. 145).

[138] Janson, pp. 263-65.

[139] Dulles, p. 56.

[140] Collated from Dulles, p. 56; Swanson, p. 7; Ritter, p. 135; Johnson, p. 35; Irving, p. 18.

[141] Quoted in Laurence Hutton, *Opening Addresses,* New York, 1887, p. 8.

[142] Stokes, IV (1922), 837; William Dunlap, *Memoirs of the Life of George Frederick Cooke, Esq.,* New York, 1813, II, 179.

[143] Willis, p. 64.

[144] Clapp, p. 42.

[145] In 1787 a newspaper correspondent in New York thanked women for reducing the size of these ornaments, thereby making it easier to see in the playhouse (cited in Brown, I, 8); the problem still existed in 1793, when a notice in the Charleston press complained truculently of ladies' feathers and turbans blocking the view of the stage (cited in Willis, p. 167); also see Pichierri, p. 93.

[146] New York *Herald,* April 20, 1796.

[147] Clapp, p. 42.

[148] Irving, pp. 19-20.

[149] Irving, pp. 25, 26; Seilhamer, I, 133; Lynch, p. 203; the New York *American Minerva* for November, 1796, carried two separate advertisements for pocketbooks lost or stolen in the theatre.

[150] J. P. Brissot de Warville, *New Travels in the United States of America: Performed in 1788,* trans. anon., Boston, 1797, p. 87.

[151] Weld, p. 14.

[152] Janson, p. 255.

[153] If a reference in Goethe's *Wilhelm Meister* (first published 1778-1796, New York and London, 1944, I, 78) to "clouds of

tobacco smoke" at an amateur performance is acceptable evidence.

154 Ireland, *Fifty Years of a Play-Goer's Journal*, p. 9; *The Mirror of Taste and Dramatic Censor*, p. 296.

155 Lynch, p. 202; Quinn, I, 15.

156 Willard, p. 16. The procession scene in *Romeo and Juliet*, for example, was held up in New York in 1762 by gentlemen on the stage.

157 Playbill for November 12, 1753, in Harvard University theatre collection; Sonneck, *Early Opera in America*, p. 27.

158 Quoted in Willis, pp. 71-72.

159 E.g., playbill for November 20, 1785, in Museum of the City of New York.

160 E.g., New York *Argus*, November 7, 1796.

161 New York *American Minerva*, November 8, 1796.

162 Respectively, Janson, p. 255; Weld, p. 14.

163 See, for example, Willis, p. 156.

164 Irving, p. 41. Alexander Anderson, February 11, 1795, supplied himself with half a pound of raisins to get through a single performance.

165 Sonneck, *Early Opera in America*, p. 127. In the days when Washington had been a regular theatregoer, however, *any* night he was to attend the theatre was fashionable. The manager waited on him, requesting him to command a play, and "in New York, the play-bill was headed, '*By particular desire*' when it was announced that the President would attend" (Custis, pp. 367-68). In Philadelphia, Wignell himself would escort the President to his specially decorated box (Paul Leicester Ford, *Washington and the Theatre*, New York, 1899, p. 45).

166 Odell, I, 126.

167 Irving, pp. 21, 27; *The New-York Magazine*, February, 1795, pp. 67-68.

Chapter III

1 Royall Tyler, *The Contrast*, Act III, scene 1, in *Representative Plays by American Dramatists*, I, 1765-1819, New York, 1918, pp. 473-74. The reference is to the John Street Theatre.

2 Henry Wansey, *Journal of an Excursion to the United States of North America in the Summer of 1794*, Salisbury, 1796, pp. 42-43.

[3] George O. Seilhamer, *History of the American Theatre: New Foundations* (III), Philadelphia, 1888, p. 86; Frédérick Louis Ritter, *Music in America*, New York, 1895, p. 135.

[4] Washington Irving, *Letters of Jonathan Oldstyle,* reproduced in facsimile from 1824 edition by Columbia University Press, 1941, p. 24. This letter originally appeared in the New York *Morning Chronicle,* December 1, 1802, and described behavior in the Park Theatre, the successor in 1798 to the John Street Theatre.

[5] *The New-York Magazine,* December, 1794, p. 718.

[6] Thomas Clark Pollock, *The Philadelphia Theatre in the Eighteenth Century,* Philadelphia, 1933, p. 28n.; Seilhamer, III, 230-31.

[7] George C. D. Odell, *Annals of the New York Stage,* New York, 1927, I, 254.

[8] New York *Argus,* January 19, 1796.

[9] Adam Carse, *The Orchestra in the Eighteenth Century,* Cambridge, England, 1940, p. 88. Unless other references are given, all generalizations concerning the eighteenth-century orchestra are from this work.

[10] *Ibid.,* p. 90.

[11] Ritter, p. 121.

[12] Charles Durang, *History of the Philadelphia Stage: 1794-1855,* I, 35.

[13] The "Mr. Pelham and His Harpsichord" referred to in William Dunlap, *A History of the American Theatre,* New York, 1832, p. 201, probably supplied all the theatre music there was until Hulett joined the company and established an orchestra.

[14] Odell, I, 58-59, 72.

[15] John F. Watson, *Annals and Occurrences of New York City and State,* Philadelphia, 1846, p. 285.

[16] Odell, I, 69; Oscar G. Sonneck, *Francis Hopkinson and James Lyon,* Washington, 1905, p. 20; both say Charles Love was probably harpsichordist for the company in Philadelphia and New York. Sonneck disagrees with himself in his *Early Opera in America,* New York, 1915, p. 23, and feels that Mr. Love played the violin and *not* the harpsichord, that someone else must have been the keyboard-director.

[17] John Tasker Howard, *Our American Music,* New York, 1939, p. 35.

[18] *Receipts of the Treasurer of the "Theatre Royal," John Street, New York, A.D., 1779,* MS in New York Historical Society.

[19] Dunlap, A History of the American Theatre, p. 248.

[20] William Dunlap, Diary, 1766-1839, ed. Dorothy C. Barck, New York, 1930, June 26, 1798, I, 302.

[21] Sonneck, Hopkinson and Lyon, p. 50; Daniel Spillane, History of the American Pianoforte, New York, 1890, p. 62; Receipts of the Treasurer of the "Theatre Royal"; Durang, I, 31.

[22] Odell, I, 226; Eola Willis, The Charleston Stage in the XVIII Century, Columbia, South Carolina, 1924, pp. 289, 427; Harold Earle Johnson, Musical Interludes in Boston, 1795-1830, New York, 1943, pp. 158-59, 174; Oscar G. Sonneck, Early Concert-Life in America, Leipzig, 1907, pp. 32, 307; Pollock, p. 383.

[23] Both William B. Wood (Personal Recollections of the Stage, Philadelphia, 1855, p. 93) and William Dunlap (Diary, I, 305) mention the fact.

[24] Carse, p. 28.

[25] Ibid., p. 32 ff.

[26] Quoted in Ritter, p. 8. Robert Rutherford Drummond (Early German Music in Philadelphia, New York, 1910, p. 27) finds references as early as 1675 to a drum, trumpet, and jew's-harp in New England.

[27] Louis Pichierri, Music in New Hampshire: 1623-1800, New York, 1960, p. 14; Howard, pp. 20, 22.

[28] Philip Alexander Bruce, Social Life of Virginia in the Seventeenth Century, Richmond, 1907, p. 181.

[29] Drummond, p. 13.

[30] Henry M. Brooks, Olden-Time Music, Boston, 1888, p. 44; Henry C. Lahee, Annals of Music in America, Boston, 1922, p. 3; Willis, p. 48.

[31] Compiled from Rita S. Gottesman, ed., The Arts and Crafts in New York, New York, 1954, I, 1726-1776, pp. 365-68.

[32] Sonneck, Hopkinson and Lyon, p. 54. It is tempting to try to trace the arrival of these instruments into America. That is, it would be tempting if there were any agreement amongst the men who have specialized in the history of musical instruments in America. The organ is a good example. Early in the eighteenth century it was not primarily an ecclesiastical instrument (as late as 1783 vocal music in the Yale Chapel, for example, was accompanied only by a flute; see History of the New Haven Theatre, W.P.A. Connecticut Writers Project, October 23, 1941, MS and typescript in Yale University library), but was used mostly in

amusement gardens and hotels (Robert A. Gerson, *Music in Phila-delphia*, Philadelphia, 1940, p. 14). Louis C. Elson (*The National Music of America and Its Sources*, Boston, 1924, p. 56) says the first organ in America was one in Boston in 1711. Lahee (p. 3) says the first organ in America appeared in Virginia in 1700. Gerson (pp. 2, 3) finds an organ in Philadelphia in 1703, and a new one in 1728. Drummond (p. 13) finds, in journals of the time, organs being *built* in Philadelphia by 1702. Tracing the date each instrument was first constructed in this country represents another problem. Spillane (p. 73) finds the first American-built organ in 1742. George Hood (*A History of Music in New England*, Boston, 1846, p. 152) says Edward Bromfield, Jr., built the first American organ in 1745 (also see Brooks, p. 32, and Louis C. Elson, *The History of American Music*, New York, 1904, p. 43). Dichter says the first organ built here was in 1737, by Johann G. Klemm, for Trinity Church, New York (Harry Dichter and Elliott Shapiro, *Early American Sheet Music*, New York, 1941, p. xxv). Multiply this confusion by the number of different instruments in America by 1800, and the task becomes improbable of fulfillment in a work whose scope is the musical theatre.

[33] Carl Wittke, *Tambo and Bones: A History of the American Minstrel Stage*, Durham, North Carolina, 1930, p. 6.

[34] Thomas Fairfax, *Journey from Virginia to Salem, Mass., 1799*, London, 1936, p. 2.

[35] John Rowe, *Letters and Diary of John Rowe*, ed. Anne Rowe Cunningham, Boston, 1903, p. 180; J. Max Patrick, *Savannah's Pioneer Theatre*, Athens, Georgia, 1953, p. 8.

[36] Sonneck, *Early Concert-Life*, p. 77.

[37] *Ibid.*, pp. 23, 143. In a footnote Sonneck lists the "improvers" as Rollig, Klein, and Wagner in Europe, and Francis Hopkinson in America.

[38] Benjamin Franklin, *Works of Benjamin Franklin*, compiled and edited by John Bigelow, New York, 1904, III, 411-17.

[39] See, for example, Carl and Jessica Bridenbaugh, *Rebels and Gentlemen: Philadelphia in the Age of Franklin*, New York, 1942, p. 146.

[40] Spillane, pp. 50, 51, 61; see Carr's advertisements in the New York *American Minerva* for January 2, 1796, ff. Elizabeth De Hart Bleecker, MS diary, 1799-1806, in the New York Public Library, entry for April 29, 1799.

[41] Gottesman, ed., II, 1777-1799, 369, taken from the New York *Packet*, June 12, 1786.

[42] Bleecker diary, entry for February 15, 1799.

[43] Carse, p. 85.

[44] *Ibid.*, pp. 112-13; Durang, I, 45; I. N. Phelps Stokes, *The Iconography of Manhattan Island*, New York, I, 1915, 327-28.

[45] John Bernard, *Retrospections of America, 1797-1811*, ed. Mrs. Boyle Bernard, New York, 1887, p. 331; Wood, p. 25; New York *Argus*, March 12, 1796.

[46] Odell, I, 178-79, 307; Patrick, p. 7; Seilhamer, I, 64; Watson, p. 285.

[47] See, for example, A. A. Parker, ed., *Church Music and Musical Life in Pennsylvania in the Eighteenth Century*, Philadelphia, 1938, III, part 1, 400-401.

[48] Gottesman, ed., I, 287, from the New York *Gazette and the Weekly Mercury*, April 19, 1773.

[49] See, for example, the competitive subscription concerts running through the month of December, 1796, in the New York *American Minerva*.

[50] See, for example, Carl Bridenbaugh, *Cities in the Wilderness: The First Century of Urban Life in America, 1625-1742*, New York, 1938, pp. 402-3, or Drummond, p. 53.

[51] Sonneck, *Hopkinson and Lyon*, p. 57; Bridenbaugh, *Rebels and Gentlemen*, p. 150; Johnson, p. 265. The German, or transverse, flute is the instrument known today simply as the flute; in the eighteenth century it was called German to differentiate it from the whistle flute, or what we call the recorder.

[52] Captain Francis Goelet, *Extracts from the Journal of Captain Francis Goelet*, Notes by Albert H. Hoyt, Boston, 1870, p. 8.

[53] Diary of John Anderson, MS in New York Historical Society.

[54] Sonneck, *Hopkinson and Lyon*, p. 20; Sonneck, *Early Opera in America*, p. 24.

[55] Bernard (p. 101) recalls visiting the theatre in Annapolis; he speaks of "black fiddlers" playing the overture before the bell rang for the beginning of the play.

[56] Sonneck, *Early Concert-Life*, p. 50.

[57] Quoted in Seilhamer, I, *Before the Revolution*, 33.

[58] Seilhamer, *During the Revolution and After* (II), 55.

[59] See, for example, Patrick, p. 8, where a theatre advertisement

is quoted which mentions gentlemen playing "for their own amusement."

[60] Stokes, V, 1926, 1329.

[61] Odell, I, 98. The only adverse comment I have found concerning the quality of the amateur music of the time came from J. P. Brissot de Warville (*New Travels in the United States of America. Performed in 1788*, Boston, 1797, p. 52), who visited Boston in 1788, and *he* was trying to compliment the amateur: "In some houses you hear the forte-piano. This art, it is true, is still in its infancy; but the young novices who exercise it, are so gentle, so complaisant, and so modest, that the proud perfection of art gives no pleasure equal to what they afford. God grant that the Bostonian women may never, like those of France, acquire the malady of perfection in this art! It is never attained, but at the expence of domestic virtues."

[62] William Priest, *Travels in the United States of America: 1793-1797*, London, 1802.

[63] Dunlap, *A History of the American Theatre*, p. 247.

[64] Sonneck, *Early Concert-Life*, p. 18.

[65] Given in Willis, p. 210

[66] Dunlap, *A History of the American Theatre*, p. 248.

[67] See *Receipts of the Treasurer of the "Theatre Royal."*

[68] Willis, p. 308.

[69] Dunlap, *Diary*, June 18 and 20, 1798, pp. 293-95; Carse, p. 56. Hodgkinson, incidentally, eventually wandered off with a pair of kettle drums, a double bass, and some music belonging to the company.

[70] Irving, pp. 18, 23, 36.

[71] For example, in the 1760's John Penn, Hillages, and David Frank, amateurs, sometimes joined them when they appeared in Philadelphia (Carl Bridenbaugh, *Cities in Revolt: Urban Life in America, 1743-1776*, New York, 1955, p. 401). Joseph N. Ireland (*Records of the New York Stage*, New York, 1866, I, 38) finds three professionals, Harrison, Van Dienval, and a drummer, with the company in the 1760's.

[72] Durang, I, 23-24.

[73] For example, one might add to the New York orchestra of the 1760's William Tuckey, who was a composer, founder of the New York Oratorio Society, and concert-giver and, in addition, a school-

master and singing teacher (Sonneck, *Early Concert-Life,* pp. 176, 179; Ritter, p. 41).

[74] Sonneck, *Early Concert-Life,* p. 78; Lillian Moore, "John Durang: the First American Dancer," *Chronicles of the American Dance,* ed. Paul Magriel, New York, 1948, pp. 19-20; Seilhamer, II, 165; Odell, I, 271, 283; Johnson, p. 63, lists many prominent New York musicians playing in Boston in the early 1800's.

[75] Dunlap, *A History of the American Theatre,* p. 248.

[76] Cited in William Arms Fisher, *One Hundred and Fifty Years of Music Publishing in the United States: 1783-1933,* Boston, 1933, p. 29.

[77] Dunlap, *A History of the American Theatre,* p. 206; Spillane, p. 101; Grenville Vernon, *Yankee Doodle-Doo,* New York, 1927, p. 35; Howard, p. 97; Fisher, p. 28; Sonneck, *Early Concert-Life,* p. 202; Ireland, I, 103.

[78] Sonneck, *Early Opera in America,* p. 87.

[79] Sonneck, *Early Concert-Life,* p. 195.

[80] Dunlap, *A History of the American Theatre,* pp. 136, 208; Johnson, p. 158.

[81] See Frank Crowinshield's introduction to his *The Physiology of Taste,* New York, 1926, p. vii, and Arnold Whitridge's "Brillat-Savarin in America" in *The Franco-American Review,* June, 1936, I, No. 1, 3. Van Wyck Brooks, also, mentions Brillat-Savarin's presence in "the orchestra of a New York theatre" in *The World of Washington Irving,* New York, 1950, p. 14n.

[82] Samuel Miles Hopkins, *Sketch of the Public and Private Life of Samuel Miles Hopkins,* Publications of the Rochester Historical Society: no. 2, 1898, p. 27.

[83] Whitridge, pp. 5-8.

[84] Carse, p. 33.

[85] *Ibid.,* pp. 28, 29 ff. It is probably well to note that the word "orchestra" in the eighteenth century meant both vocalists and instrumentalists; English writers used the word "band" to distinguish that portion of the orchestra made up exclusively of instrumentalists. I have used the two words interchangeably throughout.

[86] Sonneck (*Early Concert-Life,* p. 35n.) mentions the small size of *all* orchestras of the time: for example, even in Beethoven's day, about 1784, the kurkoellnische orchestra at Bonn had only twenty-two musicians.

[87] Patrick, p. 27; Letter from musicians to the Charleston *Gazette,* quoted in Willis, pp. 210, 290.

[88] Durang, I, 35.

[89] Ritter, p. 44.

[90] See Arthur Hornblow, *A History of the Theatre in America,* Philadelphia, 1919, I, 46, and T. Allston Brown, *A History of the New York Stage,* New York, 1903, I, 2; also *Receipts of the Treasurer of the "Theatre Royal."*

[91] John Hodgkinson, *A Narrative of his Connection with the Old American Company from September, 1792, to March 31, 1797,* New York, 1797, p. 5.

[92] Dunlap, *A History of the American Theatre,* p. 135.

[93] *Ibid.,* p. 201.

[94] Olive d'Auliffe, letters written from the family home "Chevilly," Bloomingdale, New York City, MS in French in the New York Public Library.

[95] Sonneck, *Early Concert-Life,* p. 324.

[96] Carse, pp. 44-46.

[97] See, for example, John Drayton, in *A Mirror for Americans,* ed. Warren S. Tryon, Chicago, 1952, I, 6 and Stokes, V, 1329.

[98] Johnson, p. 168.

[99] Willis, p. 277.

[100] The description of the faces of the musicians is from Irving, p. 23.

Chapter IV

[1] William Dunlap, *The Archers, or Mountaineers of Switzerland: An Opera in Three Acts,* New York, 1796, p. vii. According to George C. D. Odell, *Annals of the New York Stage,* New York, 1927, I, 77, usually the leading men spoke the prologues.

[2] George O. Seilhamer, *History of the American Theatre, Before the Revolution* (I), Philadelphia, 1888, 29; Arthur Hobson Quinn, *The History of the American Drama,* New York and London, 1923, I, 4; Arthur Hornblow, *A History of the Theatre in America,* Philadelphia and London, 1919, I, 10; Louis B. Wright, *The Cultural Life of the American Colonies,* New York, 1957, p. 179; Thomas Clark Pollock, *The Philadelphia Theatre in the Eighteenth Century,* Philadelphia, 1933, p. 4; A. A. Parker, ed., *Church Music and*

Musical Life in Pennsylvania in the Eighteenth Century, Philadelphia, 1938, III, 96, 99, 130-36.

³ Pollock, p. 4; Wright, pp. 180, 181; Charles P. Daly, *First Theatre in America*, New York, 1896, pp. 16, 20, 24, 33; Hornblow, I, 10, 22; Quinn, I, 5, 8; T. Allston Brown, *A History of the New York Stage*, New York, 1903, I, 2; William Eben Schultz, *Gay's Beggar's Opera*, New Haven, 1923, p. 52; George O. Willard, *A History of the Providence Stage*, p. 1; Maud W. Goodwin, *The Colonial Cavalier*, New York, 1894, p. 159.

⁴ Seilhamer, I, 4. Walter Murray and Thomas Kean took their troupe to Philadelphia in 1749, then to New York in 1750-1751, calling themselves the "Company of Comedians from Philadelphia." (Quinn, I, 8; Pollock, p. 6; advertisement in New York *Gazette*, February 26, 1750, quoted in Rita S. Gottesman, ed., *The Arts and Crafts in New York*, I, 1726-1776, New York, 1938, 286). The troupe next appeared in Williamsburg, still in 1751, and played in Hobb's Hole, Fredericksburg, and Annapolis in 1752 (Hornblow, I, 76; Paul Leicester Ford, *Washington and the Theatre*, New York, 1899, p. 45; Seilhamer, I, 30); the company stayed together for twenty years, strolling all over the colonies, and changing its name as it went along (Hornblow, I, 79; Seilhamer, I, 30).

⁵ Odell, I, 45; Daly, p. 11. Upton had been sent by William Hallam to prepare the way for a "London Company of Comedians," but the actor used the opportunity to set up shop for himself (Seilhamer, I, 12 ff.; Oscar G. Sonneck, *Early Opera in America*, New York, London, Boston, 1915, pp. 18-19).

⁶ Willard, p. 17.

⁷ Oral Sumner Coad, *William Dunlap*, New York, 1917, p. 39.

⁸ Sonneck, *Early Opera in America*, p. 76.

⁹ William Dunlap, *A History of the American Theatre*, New York, 1832, p. 8; Seilhamer, I, 30, 42; Charles Durang, *History of the Philadelphia Stage, 1749-1855*, I, Chap. III.

¹⁰ Odell, I, 50, 68; Pollock, pp. 9, 13; Reverend Andrew Burnaby, *Burnaby's Travels Through North America*, ed. Rufus Rockwell Wilson, reprinted from third edition of 1798, New York, 1904, p. 80; Eola Willis, *The Charleston Stage in the XVIII Century*, Columbia, South Carolina, 1924, p. 42; Seilhamer, I, 87.

¹¹ Respectively, Seilhamer, I, 248 and Carl Bridenbaugh, *Cities in Revolt: Urban Life in America, 1743-1776*, New York, 1955, p. 211; Ford, *Washington and the Theatre*, p. 20; John Rowe,

Letters and Diary, ed. Anne Rowe Cunningham, Boston, 1903, p. 190; Seilhamer, I, 121; Willard, p. 12; Sonneck, *Early Opera in America,* p. 30; Seilhamer, *During the Revolution and After,* 1889 (II), 121; Willis, p. 42; Odell, I, 79, 91, 146; Pollock, pp. 20, 24-27.

12 Quinn, I, 32; Seilhamer, II, 135; Sonneck, *Early Opera in America,* pp. 66-67.

13 Seilhamer, II, 205, 174; Sonneck, *Early Opera in America,* p. 76; Quinn, I, 62

14 Odell, I, 418, 469; New York *Argus,* March 16, 1796. New York's summer gardens and two circuses provided the only real competition for the Old American Company through 1800.

15 In the summer before *The Archers,* part of the company was in Hartford and part in Providence; in the Fall, the two parts joined and went to perform in Boston (Willard, pp. 28-29). Yellow fever in New York caused them to stay in Boston longer than usual, and they did not open at the John Street Theatre until February 10, 1796 (Odell, I, 400; New York *American Minerva,* February 8, 1796). The season lasted until June 25, when sections of the company went to Newport, Providence, Hartford, and Boston (New York *American Minerva,* June 25, 1796; Seilhamer, III, 370-71, 376).

16 Wignell and Reinagle, for example, respectively actor-singer and musician with the Old American Company, set up a company in Philadelphia (Seilhamer, *New Foundations* (III), 101) which took over many of the cities the Old American Company had been wont to visit, such as Lancaster and Baltimore (Pollock, p. 53; Joseph N. Ireland, *Records of the New York Stage, 1850-1860,* New York, 1866, I, 83).

17 Seilhamer, III, 11, 282.

18 The duties of the manager in England were somewhat similar. He was a patentee of the royal theatre, and all of the financial affairs of the theatre were his concern. He was also the director and was in sole charge of the repertory. He dealt directly with playwrights and actors for their services; he determined costumes and scenery, and he hired seamstresses, wigmakers, carpenters, and painters to carry out his plans; he was press agent for his company; and he usually acted as well. As patentee, he had always to be ready to cater to the royal command or the royal whim; he was a royal servant, but, when not fulfilling royal wishes, was some-

thing of an arbiter of taste himself (James J. Lynch, *Box, Pit, and Gallery*, Berkeley and Los Angeles, 1953, pp. 119, 120, 122-23).

[19] Godwin, for example, taught minuets, allemands, cotillions, hornpipes, and country dances (Willis, pp. 104, 115). For other functions of the manager, see Seilhamer, I, 97; N. M. Ludlow, *Dramatic Life as I Found It*, Saint Louis, 1880, p. 62; Wesley Swanson, "Wings and Backdrops: The Story of American Stage Scenery from the Beginnings to 1875," *The Drama*, XVIII, No. 1, October, 1927, 5; Hodgkinson letter to Hartford in Harvard University, Houghton Library, March 27, 1795; Hornblow, I, 147; Willis, p. 56; John Bernard, *Retrospections of the Stage*, Boston, 1832, II, 213.

[20] Hodgkinson refers to "the theatres, belonging to us," in John Hodgkinson, *A Narrative of his Connection with the Old American Company: From 5 September, 1792—31 March, 1797*, New York, 1797, p. 17. Also see Hodgkinson letter to Hartford, March 25, 1795; William Ames Fisher, *Notes on Music in Old Boston*, 1918, pp. 59, 62; Mary Caroline Crawford, *The Romance of the American Theatre*, Boston, 1913, pp. 107-8; Willis, p. 131.

[21] Hodgkinson, *A Narrative*, pp. 14-15.

[22] *Ibid.*, pp. 20-22.

[23] Quinn, I, 75-76.

[24] Coad, *William Dunlap*, p. 81; Quinn, I, 113; *The New-York Magazine*, November, 1794, p. 654; Frederick H. Wilkins, *Early Influence of German Literature in America*, New York, undated (about 1900), pp. 16, 18; Harold William Schoenberger, *American Adaptations of French Plays on the New York and Philadelphia Stages from 1790-1833*, Philadelphia, 1924, pp. 15-17, 25. Dunlap frequently translated European plays himself or got friends to translate them, and the result was continental plays seen here before their introduction to England (Wilkins, p. 27; John W. Francis, *Old New York*, New York, 1866, p. 46).

[25] See Chap. V below.

[26] Dunlap, *A History of the American Theatre*, p. 6.

[27] Dunlap, *A History of the American Theatre*, p. 6; Pollock, p. 50. The only throwback to the old sharing system was a modified form used by Wignell (and possibly other managers as well) for summer seasons: a sharing plan was put into effect, but was graduated according to winter salaries (William B. Wood, *Personal Recollections of the Stage*, Philadelphia, 1855, p. 58).

[28] Lynch, p. 139; Willis, p. 417.

[29] Schultz, p. 38.

[30] Parker, III, 375.

[31] Willard, p. 25.

[32] Seilhamer, I, 164; Odell, I, 61.

[33] William Dunlap, *Diary*, I, ed. Dorothy C. Barck, New York, 1930, June 21, 1798, 75.

[34] Lynch, p. 144.

[35] Dunlap, *Diary*, April 13, 1798, I, 243.

[36] Willard, p. 17; *The Mirror of Taste and Dramatic Censor*, III, 1811, 62 ff.; Wood, p. 450.

[37] Dunlap, *A History of the American Theatre*, p. 196.

[38] Lynch, pp. 13, 213; Odell, I, 41.

[39] There was some criticism of the practice: the "Theatrical Register" of *The New-York Magazine* tore into a performance of Schiller's *The Robbers*, saying that it was "beyond the strength of the company, and nothing can excuse its being played but *benefit times.*" (April, 1795, p. 259.) If an actor did not clear enough on his benefit night, he occasionally bought a share of another performer's night (see, for example, Pollock, p. 229). Theatre advertisements indicate that frequently less popular actors or husband-wife teams joined together to give a benefit (e.g., New York *Argus*, June 2 and 10, 1796). And big-name actors may occasionally have received extra money from the performer at whose benefit they appeared (Willis, p. 309).

[40] Wood, p. 46.

[41] Seilhamer, I, 137.

[42] Hodgkinson, *A Narrative*, p. 25.

[43] Carl and Jessica Bridenbaugh, *Rebels and Gentlemen: Philadelphia in the Age of Franklin*, New York, 1942, p. 140.

[44] Quoted in Pollock, p. 21.

[45] Dunlap, *A History of the American Theatre*, p. 99.

[46] E.g., Dunlap, *Diary*, May 29, 1797, I, 50; New York *Argus*, February 24, 1796.

[47] *The New-York Magazine*, April, 1795, p. 194.

[48] James Fennell, *An Apology for the Life of James Fennell, Written by Himself*, Philadelphia, 1814, pp. 362-63.

[49] Odell, I, 343; *The New-York Magazine*, February, 1796, p. 116.

[50] Wood, p. 94.

[51] Swanson, p. 30.

[52] Bernard, *Retrospections of the Stage,* II, 213-14.

[53] John Bernard, *Retrospections of America, 1797-1811,* New York, 1887, pp. 263, 49.

[54] Dunlap, *Diary,* June 3, 1798, I, 274-75.

[55] The cast is collated from Dunlap, *History of the American Theatre,* the 1796 edition of *The Archers,* and the New York *American Minerva,* April 16, 1796.

[56] Francis C. Wemyss, *Chronology of the American Stage, from 1752-1852,* New York, 1852, p. 65; Dunlap, *A History of the American Theatre,* p. 96; Bernard, *Retrospections of America,* p. 26n.

[57] Dunlap, *A History of the American Theatre,* p. 97.

[58] Hodgkinson, *A Narrative,* p. 4; Pollock, p. 191; *The Mirror of Taste and Dramatic Censor,* II, August, 1810, p. 104.

[59] Pollock, p. 53.

[60] Dunlap, *A History of the American Theatre,* p. 99.

[61] Listed in *The Mirror of Taste and Dramatic Censor,* II, August, 1810, pp. 106-8.

[62] Dunlap, *A History of the American Theatre,* pp. 99, 102.

[63] Joseph Ireland, *Fifty Years of a Play-Goer's Journal: or Annals of the New York Stage, from A.D. 1798 to A.D. 1848,* New York, 1860, p. 12.

[64] Bernard, *Retrospections of America,* p. 26.

[65] English visitor in Charles Wilson Janson, *The Stranger in America,* 1793-1806, reprinted from London edition of 1807, New York, 1935, p. 258; Washington Irving, *Letters of Jonathan Oldstyle,* facsimile of 1824 edition, collection of letters to *Morning Chronicle,* 1802-1803, New York, 1941, p. 13.

[66] Respectively, Dunlap, *A History of the American Theatre,* pp. 148-49; New York *Diary,* April 23, 1796.

[67] Dunlap, *A History of the American Theatre,* p. 9; Willard, p. 10.

[68] Alexander Graydon, *Memoirs of a Life, Chiefly Passed in Pennsylvania,* Harrisburg, Pa., 1811, pp. 82-84.

[69] Edward Burd, letter to his sister, quoted in Carl and Jessica Bridenbaugh, *Rebels and Gentlemen,* p. 140.

[70] Wood, p. 28.

[71] Respectively, quoted in Pollock, pp. 21, 22; Graydon, p. 84.

[72] Ireland, *Records,* I, 20.

[73] Durang, I, Chap. II; see the list of Hallam's parts to 1774 in Seilhamer, I, 340-42.

[74] Quoted in Pollock, p. 30; Odell, I, 151.

[75] Janson, p. 263; Lillian Moore, "John Durang: the First American Dancer," *Chronicles of the American Dance,* ed. Paul Magriel, New York, 1948, p. 35; Bernard, *Retrospections of America,* p. 265.

[76] Dunlap, *A History of the American Theatre,* pp. 148-49.

[77] Ireland, *Records,* I, 131; William Winter, *Life and Art of Joseph Jefferson,* New York, 1894, p. 47; Dunlap, *A History of the American Theatre,* p. 145.

[78] *The New-York Magazine,* February,1796, pp. 92-95.

[79] Dunlap, *A History of the American Theatre,* p. 145.

[80] Quoted in Winter, p. 92.

[81] *Ibid.*

[82] Dunlap, *A History of the American Theatre,* p. 259.

[83] Winter, p. 59.

[84] See, for example, advertisement in New York *Argus,* June 2, 1796.

[85] Wood, p. 378.

[86] Winter, pp. 53, 99; Edwin Duerr, "Charles Ciceri and the Background of American Scene Design," *Theatre Arts Monthly,* XVI, no. 2, December, 1932, 984; New York *American Minerva,* December 29, 1796.

[87] Winter, p. 71.

[88] Fennell, pp. 412-13.

[89] Respectively, Olive d'Auliffe, Letters written from the family home "Chevilly," Bloomingdale, New York City (in manuscript room of New York Public Library), February 6, 1801; Bernard, *Retrospections of America,* p. 266.

[90] Wemyss, p. 77; Ireland, *Fifty Years of a Play-Goer's Journal,* p. 15.

[91] For comments on his wife, see *The New-York Magazine,* February, 1796, pp. 92-95; New York *American Minerva,* September 28, 1796; Irving, p. 13. For Johnson's ability in old men, see New York *Daily Advertiser,* February 17, 1796.

[92] Ireland, *Records,* I, 130; New York *Daily Advertiser,* February 13, 1796.

[93] Fennell, p. 398; New York *American Minerva,* November 11, 1796.

[94] Bernard, *Retrospections of America*, p. 266; Ireland, *Records*, I, 130.

[95] Pollock, p. 201.

[96] Durang, I, Chap. XXII.

[97] William W. Clapp, Jr., *A Recollection of the Boston Stage*, Boston and Cambridge, 1853, p. 27.

[98] *Ibid.*, pp. 27-28.

[99] Ireland, *Records*, I, 133; Dunlap, *A History of the American Theatre*, p. 147.

[100] New York *Daily Advertiser*, February 17, 1796.

[101] Cited in Pollock, p. 60.

[102] Willis, pp. 369-70.

[103] New York *Diary*, April 23, 1796.

[104] *Greenleaf's New York Journal and Patriotic Register*, April 29, 1796; New York *Argus*, June 10, 1796.

[105] New York *Daily Advertiser*, February 17, 1796; Durang, I, Chap. XVII.

[106] Dunlap, *A History of the American Theatre*, p. 196.

[107] *Ibid.*, p. 100.

[108] Odell, I, 365; Dunlap, *A History of the American Theatre*, pp. 153, 196.

[109] Winter, p. 23; Pollock, p. 191.

[110] Dunlap, *A History of the American Theatre*, p. 100.

[111] *Ibid.*, p. 101; Durang, I, Chap. XVII; Fennell, p. 289; *The New-York Magazine*, June, 1795, p. 327; Odell, I, 334.

[112] *The New-York Magazine*, February, 1796, pp. 115-16.

[113] Dunlap, *A History of the American Theatre*, pp. 193-94.

[114] Pollock, p. 323; Willis, p. 437; Ireland, *Fifty Years of a Play-Goer's Journal*, p. 27.

[115] Pollock, pp. 205, 212; New York *American Minerva*, November 11, 1796.

[116] Respectively, Durang, I, Chap. XXII; *The New-York Magazine*, January, 1795, p. 3.

[117] Dunlap, *A History of the American Theatre*, p. 248.

[118] New York *Diary*, November 4, 1794, cited in Gottesman, ed., II, 1777-1799, 1954, 303.

[119] Dunlap, *A History of the American Theatre*, p. 137.

[120] Pollock, p. 229; Willis, p. 199; Ireland, *Records*, I, 100.

[121] Ireland, *Fifty Years of a Play-Goer's Journal*, p. 27; *The New-York Magazine*, December, 1794, p. 722.

[122] Harold Earle Johnson, *Musical Interludes in Boston, 1795-1830*, New York, 1943, pp. 45-46.

[123] Ireland, *Records*, I, 105; Dunlap, *A History of the American Theatre*, p. 105.

[124] Bernard, *Retrospections of America*, p. 266; Dunlap, *A History of the American Theatre*, p. 105.

[125] Dunlap, *A History of the American Theatre*, p. 105; Pollock, p. 225; George Gates Raddin, Jr., *Hocquet Caritat and the Early New York Literary Scene*, Dover, New Jersey, 1953, p. 40; Ireland, *Fifty Years of a Play-Goer's Journal*, p. 19, and *Records*, I, 106.

[126] Seilhamer, III, 80; Wood, p. 111.

[127] Odell, I, 353; New York *Daily Advertiser*, January 5, 1796.

[128] Dunlap, *A History of the American Theatre*, p. 105.

[129] —— Hodgkinson, *Letters on Emigration*, London, 1794, pp. 40-41.

[130] Respectively, Wemyss, p. 95; Bernard, *Retrospections of America*, p. 266; Wood, p. 111.

[131] Dunlap, *A History of the American Theatre*, pp. 148-49.

[132] New York *American Minerva*, February 11, 1796.

[133] *The New-York Magazine*, February, 1796, p. 93.

[134] Ireland, *Records*, I, 133; *Fifty Years of a Play-Goer's Journal*, p. 13.

[135] December 26, 1794, playbill for John Street Theatre, in Harvard University theatre collection; *The New-York Magazine*, January, 1795, p. 3.

[136] New York *Daily Advertiser*, February 13, 1796; Dunlap, *A History of the American Theatre*, p. 195.

[137] Ireland, *Fifty Years of a Play-Goer's Journal*, p. 38; *Records*, I, 120.

[138] See contracts in Dunlap, *Diary*, I, pp. 75, 243.

[139] Oscar G. Sonneck, *Early Concert-Life in America*, Leipzig, 1907, p. 122.

[140] Johnson, p. 224; Seilhamer, III, 140; Willis, p. 301.

[141] Johnson, p. 223.

[142] See Burton Alva Konkle, *Joseph Hopkinson*, Philadelphia, 1931, pp. 73-77, for story of "Hail Columbia"; Johnson, pp. 218, 46.

[143] Wood, pp. 93-94.

[144] *Ibid.*, p. 77; see, for example, Dunlap, *Diary*, I, 267.

[145] *Euterpeiad or Musical Intelligencer, and Ladies Gazette,*

"Musical Reminiscences no. 7," II, no. 25, March 2, 1822, 194; Ireland, *Records*, I, 133; New York *American Minerva*, January 7, 18 ff., 1796, for concerts; February 11 for theatre debut; Pollock, pp. 60, 398; William Priest, *Travels in the United States of America, 1793-1797*, London, 1802, p. 52 for travels; Frédérick Louis Ritter, *Music in America*, New York, 1895, pp. 151-52 for lessons; *Euterpeiad*, p. 194 for death.

[146] *Euterpeiad*, p. 194.

[147] *Ibid.*, p. 194.

[148] *Thespian Dictionary*, quoted in Ireland, *Records*, I, 133.

[149] Dunlap, *A History of the American Theatre*, p. 124.

[150] *The New-York Magazine*, March, 1796, p. 117; New York *Diary*, April 23, 1796.

[151] Dunlap, *A History of the American Theatre*, p. 194; Philo Theatricus cited in Pollock, p. 60.

[152] Dunlap, *A History of the American Theatre*, p. 100; Pollock, p. 191; Odell, I, 311.

[153] *The Mirror of Taste and Dramatic Censor*, II, August, 1810, 99. For following description see Dunlap, *A History of the American Theatre*, p. 100.

[154] Coad, *William Dunlap*, p. 38.

[155] Dunlap, *A History of the American Theatre*, p. 100.

[156] *The New-York Magazine*, March, 1796, p. 117.

[157] *Ibid.*, December, 1794, p. 720; New York *American Minerva*, September 28, 1796; New York *Argus*, September 29, 1796.

[158] Sonneck, *Early Concert-Life in America*, p. 194.

[159] Dunlap, *A History of the American Theatre*, pp. 148-49.

[160] *Ibid.*, pp. 318-19.

[161] Ireland, *Records*, I, 44; Seilhamer, I, 158; Odell, II, 39; Dunlap, *A History of the American Theatre*, p. 272.

[162] Odell, I, 117, 146.

[163] From list of Woolls' roles in Seilhamer, I, 343-45.

[164] Durang, I, Chap. VIII.

[165] Dunlap, *A History of the American Theatre*, p. 29.

[166] Pollock, p. 159; Ireland, *Fifty Years of a Play-Goer's Journal*, p. 5.

[167] New York *Diary*, April 23, 1796.

[168] Odell, II, 62.

[169] Wemyss, p. 135; New York *American Minerva*, February 8, 1796; Dunlap, *A History of the American Theatre*, p. 146.

[170] New York *Argus,* February 26, 1796; New York *Daily Advertiser,* February 13, 1796; *The New-York Magazine,* February, 1796, pp. 92-95.

[171] See, for example, New York *American Minerva,* November 11, 1796.

[172] Dunlap, *A History of the American Theatre,* p. 145; Ireland, *Records,* I, 130.

[173] Bernard, *Retrospections of America,* p. 266.

[174] Odell, II, 29, 63, 94, 228; Ireland, *Records,* I, 130.

[175] Contract in Dunlap, *Diary,* I, 130; Pollock, p. 220; *The New-York Magazine,* December, 1794, p. 719; June, 1795, p. 328.

[176] Dunlap, *A History of the American Theatre,* p. 135; Ireland, *Records,* I, 118.

[177] Entr'acte entertainment was noted in playbills, though rarely in newspaper advertisements except for benefits. See, for example, the playbill for Mme. Val's benefit (April 21, three days after *The Archers*) in the Harvard University theatre collection; the performance featured an opera, a comic song, a dance, another opera, an overture, a song, a "ballet pantomime," and a dance.

[178] Hornblow, I, 74-76, 80, 92, 35; Dunlap, *A History of the American Theatre,* p. 14; John F. Watson, *Annals and Occurrences of New York City and State,* Philadelphia, 1846, p. 285; J. Max Patrick, *Savannah's Pioneer Theatre from Its Origins to 1810,* Athens, Georgia, 1953, p. 7; Willis, p. 104.

[179] Philip Alexander Bruce, *Social Life of Virginia in the Seventeenth Century,* Richmond, Virginia, 1907, pp. 184-85; Oscar G. Sonneck, *Francis Hopkinson and James Lyon,* Washington, 1905, p. 11; Willis, p. 104.

[180] Seilhamer, III, 282; Patrick, p. 18.

[181] Odell, I, 286, 289; playbill for John Street Theatre, May 24, 1794, in Harvard University theatre collection; Seilhamer, II, 344; Patrick, p. 17; Lewis P. Waldo, *The French Drama in America in the Eighteenth Century and Its Influence on the American Drama of that Period,* Baltimore, 1942, p. 177; Hornblow, I, 188; Seilhamer, I, 204).

[182] Waldo, p. 177; New York *Argus,* March 3 and 16, 1796.

[183] Willis, p. 326.

[184] New York *Gazette Française et Américaine,* January 25, 1796; Willis, p. 109.

[185] Moore, p. 34.

[186] Seilhamer, III, 102; Moore, p. 24.

[187] Moore, p. 31.

[188] Wemyss, p. 43.

[189] She made her stage debut in Philadelphia in 1789 and in New York, dancing with her husband, later the same year (Pollock, p. 146; Odell, I, 278). For John Durang's career see Moore, pp. 15-16, 24; Durang, I, Chap. XIII.

[190] Odell, I, 275.

[191] Placide had been a part of the Nicolet troupe, and Nicolet was "the best known director of spectacles in the boulevard and fair shows of Paris in 1762"; the future Charles X had taken dancing lessons from Placide (Waldo, p. 177). The Placides' training was in classic ballet, acrobatics, tumbling, and tightrope dancing, and there is no question that Durang learned much from them (Moore, pp. 24-25).

[192] Quoted in Odell, I, 319.

[193] Moore, pp. 31-32, 35; Pollock, p. 401.

[194] *Ibid.*, p. 15.

[195] Wemyss, p. 59; Dunlap, *A History of the American Theatre*, p. 194.

[196] Dunlap, *A History of the American Theatre*, pp. 207-208; Pollock, pp. 56, 212; Odell, I, 376.

[197] Durang, I, Chap. XXIII.

[198] *The New-York Magazine*, January, 1795, p. 4.

[199] *Ibid.*, April, 1795, p. 194; May, 1795, p. 258; March, 1796, p. 117.

[200] Dunlap, *A History of the American Theatre*, pp. 208-209.

[201] Willis, pp. 239, 245.

[202] Clapp, p. 52.

[203] Dunlap, *A History of the American Theatre*, p. 147.

[204] Pollock, pp. 175, 180, 187, 204-5; Waldo, p. 177; Durang, I, Chap. XVIII; New York *Daily Advertiser*, February 13, 1796.

[205] Durang, I, Chap. XXII; New York *Diary*, April 23, 1796.

[206] Odell, I, 424, 473.

[207] *Ibid.*, 402, 410, 425; II, 21, 47, 96.

[208] Moore, p. 30.

[209] Seilhamer, III, 325; New York *Argus*, March 3 and 16, 1796.

[210] New York *American Minerva*, March 2 and June 9, 1796.

[211] Dunlap, *A History of the American Theatre*, p. 147; Odell, I, 473; II, 31-32.

[212] Hodgkinson, *A Narrative*, pp. 14, 15, 20; Swanson, XVIII, No. 1, October, 1927, 6; XVIII, No. 3, December, 1927, 78.

[213] Swanson, December, 1927, p. 78.

[214] William Dunlap, *Memoirs of a Water Drinker*, New York, second ed., 1837, II, 32; Durang, I, Chap. XXII; Seilhamer, II, 349.

[215] Durang, I, Chap. VIII; New York playbill for March 24, 1787, in Harvard University theatre collection.

[216] New York *Commercial Advertiser*, December 5, 1799, in Nagler, p. 537.

[217] Dunlap, *Memoirs of a Water Drinker*, II, 24, 29, 32.

[218] See Chap. II above and Dunlap, *A History of the American Theatre*, p. 248.

[219] Ireland, *Records*, I, 94. His name is frequently spelled Falconer.

[220] Dunlap, *A History of the American Theatre*, p. 248; New York *American Minerva*, June 3, 1796; Lynch, p. 212.

[221] *Receipts of the Treasurer of the "Theatre Royal"; The Magazine of History*, "The Songs of T-A-M-M-A-N-Y," XLIII, No. 2, 1931, 59.

[222] Dunlap, *A History of the American Theatre*, p. 248; Durang, I, Chap. XVIII.

[223] Dunlap, *Memoirs of a Water Drinker*, II, 38; Durang, I, Chap. XXIII; Dunlap, *A History of the American Theatre*, p. 248.

[224] Dunlap, *A History of the American Theatre*, pp. 144, 193.

[225] Seilhamer, III, 272, claims that the Old American Company in 1796 was the best in America; Bernard, *Retrospections of America*, p. 266, makes the claim for the Philadelphia company.

[226] Odell, I, 463.

Chapter V

[1] James J. Lynch, *Box, Pit, and Gallery*, Berkeley and Los Angeles, 1953, p. 54.

[2] The English repertory brought over by the early companies was largely drawn from three periods: Elizabethan and Jacobean, Restoration, and early eighteenth-century. Two major new types of English drama, sentimental comedy and bourgeois tragedy, were also performed (Lynch, pp. 36, 219, 301; Brander Matthews,

"The Drama in the Eighteenth Century," *The Sewanee Review,*
XI, No. 1, January, 1903, p. 6).

³ Arthur Hobson Quinn, *A History of the American Drama,*
New York, London, 1923, I, 9; Charles P. Daly, *First Theatre in
America,* New York, 1896, p. 33; Arthur Hornblow, *A History of
the Theatre in America,* Philadelphia and London, 1919, I, 41;
Mary Caroline Crawford, *The Romance of the American Theatre,*
Boston, 1913, p. 58; Paul Leicester Ford, *Washington and the
Theatre,* New York, 1899, pp. 3, 26.

⁴ Lewis P. Waldo, *The French Drama in America in the
Eighteenth Century and Its Influence on the American Drama of
that Period,* Baltimore, 1942, pp. 179, 241-43; Harold William
Schoenberger, *American Adaptations of French Plays on the New
York and Philadelphia Stages from 1790 to 1833,* Philadelphia,
1924, p. 8.

⁵ Waldo, p. 167.

⁶ *Ibid.,* pp. 86, 71; Schoenberger, p. 9; Charles F. Brede, *The
German Drama in English on the Philadelphia Stage from 1794-
1830,* Philadelphia, 1918, p. 4; Quinn, I, 89, 95, 96; Oscar
Wegelin, *Early American Plays: 1714-1830,* New York, 1900, p.
31 ff.; Matthews, "The Drama in the Eighteenth Century," pp.
18-19.

⁷ Paul Leicester Ford, "The Beginnings of American Dramatic
Literature," *The New England Magazine,* N.S. IX, no. 6, February,
1894, 674-76; George O. Seilhamer, *History of the American
Theatre: Before the Revolution* (I), Philadelphia, 1888, 185, 189.

⁸ The five works before the Revolution were: *Prince of Parthia,
Conquest of Canada, Disappointment* (cast and advertised but
withdrawn just before production), the *Mercenary Match,* and
The Masque of Alfred—the last originally English, but with much
new material added here (Seilhamer, *During the Revolution and
After* (II), 1889, 2; Quinn, I, 18). Information concerning drama
during the Revolution is from Quinn, I, 33; Wegelin, pp. 2, 18.
For information concerning popularity of native works, see Hornblow, I, 176; John Bernard, *Retrospections of America, 1797-
1811,* ed. from MSS by Mrs. Boyle Bernard, New York, 1887, pp.
71-72.

⁹ Blanche Elizabeth Davis, *The Hero in American Drama, 1787-
1900,* Ph.D. thesis, Columbia University, New York, 1950, pp. 18-
19. Royall Tyler's *The Contrast* was the source of another popular

American theme, republican ideology; the warmest patriotism always marked the development of these liberty plays (Anon., *Reise von Hamburg nach Philadelphia*, 1800, in Oscar Handlin, ed., *This Was America*, Cambridge, Massachusetts, 1949, p. 104).

[10] George C. D. Odell, *Annals of the New York Stage*, New York, 1927, I, 4; *History of the New Haven Theatre*, WPA Connecticut Writers' Project, 1941, in MSS and typescript in library of Yale University, p. 42; Hornblow, I, 172; Thomas Clark Pollock, *The Philadelphia Theatre in the Eighteenth Century*, Philadelphia, 1933, pp. 35, 44; Oscar G. Sonneck, *Early Opera in America*, New York, London, Boston, 1915, p. 75; Seilhamer, II, 218.

[11] Lynch, p. 213.

[12] Joseph N. Ireland, *Records of the New York Stage from 1750-1860*, New York, 1866, I, 11; Seilhamer, I, 212; Pollock, p. 305. Figure for New York in 1796 collated from Ireland, *Records*, I, 128 ff.; Odell, *Annals*, I, 423 ff.; and Sonneck, *Early Opera in America*, Chart B.

[13] Pollock, pp. 291, 59.

[14] Sonneck, *Early Opera in America*, pp. 183-85, 187, 195, 150.

[15] Sonneck, *Early Opera in America*, pp. 159, 166.

[16] Even before the Revolution, a typical season contained "thirty-five or forty different plays . . . with nearly as many farces, shorter comedies, musical plays and pantomimes." (Pollock, p. 33.) The pre-Revolutionary season of Murray and Kean's company in New York, 1750-1751, for example, included eight musicals in a repertory of twenty-eight different works, in addition to between-the-acts or between-the-play-and-afterpiece songs and dances (compiled from Odell, *Annals*, I, 42-43; Sonneck, *Early Opera in America*, p. 15).

[17] The 1799 season in Charleston saw thirty-nine performances in comedy and tragedy and thirty-nine operas and pantomimes (Sonneck, *Early Opera in America*, p. 78; Eola Willis, *The Charleston Stage in the XVIII Century*, Columbia, South Carolina, 1924, p. 432. Thomas Ridgeway, "Ballad Opera in Philadelphia in the Eighteenth Century," in A. A. Parker, ed., *Church Music and Musical Life in Pennsylvania in the Eighteenth Century*, Philadelphia, 1947, III, Part 2, 432, claims that the Old American Company in 1790 had "more than one hundred operas and musical pantomimes . . ." in its repertory; the discrepancy with Sonneck's

figures is probably accounted for by general indecision about how much music a piece needs or how long it needs to be before it is a musical). In Philadelphia, Wignell and Reinagle *consciously* attempted to make opera equal to drama in the repertory (William B. Wood, *Recollections of the Stage*, Philadelphia, 1855, p. 92; Sonneck, *Early Opera in America*, p. 124). In the years from 1794 to 1800 the repertory of the Boston Federal Street Theatre included more than ninety musicals and of the Boston Haymarket more than sixty (John Tasker Howard, *Our American Music*, New York, 1939, p. 69).

[18] Edmond McAdoo Gagey, *Ballad Opera*, New York, 1937, pp. 6, 12, 29; Oscar G. Sonneck, "Early American Operas," *Miscellaneous Studies in the History of Music*, New York, 1921, p. 16. The eighteenth century felt *The Beggar's Opera* to be a new form, but modern scholarship is somewhat split on the point: see Gagey, p. 4; Frank Kidson, *The Beggar's Opera: Its Predecessors and Successors*, Cambridge, 1922, p. 30; William Eben Schultz, *Gay's Beggar's Opera: Its Content, History, and Influence*, New Haven, 1923, pp. 128-29; Sonneck, "Early American Operas," p. 16; George Tufts, "Ballad Operas: A list and Some Notes," *The Musical Antiquary*, IV, No. 4, January, 1913, p. 63. For launching of form, see Allardyce Nicoll, *A History of English Drama, 1660-1900: Early Eighteenth-Century Drama* (II), Cambridge, 3rd ed., 1952, p. 237.

[19] Gagey, p. 7; Kidson, p. 95; Schultz, pp. 12-13. It was given sixty-two times in its first season, 1728, at John Rich's Theatre Royal in Lincoln's Inn Fields and was played thereafter in every year of the eighteenth century (Schultz, pp. 1, 2, 8, 63). It did, as the saw had it, make Gay rich and Rich gay.

[20] Gagey, p. 4.

[21] Compiled by Nicoll, II, 237n; also Schultz, p. 131.

[22] Quoted in Gagey, p. 4.

[23] Parker, III, 372.

[24] Tufts, p. 85. The March in Handel's opera *Rinaldo*, for example, was used for the chorus of Macheath's gang (Kidson, p. 51).

[25] Tufts, p. 61; Sonneck, *Early Opera in America*, p. 3; J. Brander Matthews, "Pinafore's Predecessor," *Harper's*, LX, March, 1880, p. 501; Gagey, pp. 4, 7; Nicoll, II, 237, 239.

[26] First printed in 1728; I used the edition in *Plays* by John Gay, London, 1772.

27 Schultz, p. 58; Gagey, p. 40.

28 Schultz, pp. 161, 162.

29 Kidson, p. 46; Schultz, p. 157.

30 Schultz, p. 154. Dates for the death of ballad opera (or, rather, its conversion to something else) vary. The relatively pure form (that is, with mostly ballads used) had all but ceased to be written by the late 1730's (Nicoll, II, 251); if the inclusion of *any* old tune is sufficient, the form went on to the 1800's (Tufts, p. 81); if dominance of book over music is the criterion, the ghosts of *The Beggar's Opera* still walk (in *Carousel*, for example). However, the vitality had gone from the form by 1740, and it had stepped down to make way for new genres (Nicoll, II, 237; Kidson, p. 104; Schultz, p. 154).

31 Nicoll, II, 241, 245; Gagey, pp. 100, 107; Kidson, p. 89.

32 Sonneck, *Early Opera in America,* pp. 11, 12; Parker, III, 378. It is probable, however, that ballad operas had been performed in New York from 1732 on.

33 Seilhamer, I, 261.

34 Schultz, pp. 109, 111-12; *History of the New Haven Theatre,* p. 13. It was performed in Jamaica in 1733, Philadelphia in 1749, Upper Marlborough, Maryland, in 1752, New York in 1752, etc. (respectively, Kidson, p. 37; Parker, III, 372; Howard, p. 27; Louis C. Elson, *The History of American Music,* New York, 1904, p. 95).

35 See Tables in Sonneck, *Early Opera in America.*

36 Seilhamer, I, 176.

37 Andrew Barton, Esq., *The Disappointment; or, Force of Credulity,* New York, 1767. Despite Seilhamer's insistence (I, 178) that Andrew Barton was a pseudonym for Colonel Thomas Forrest, I am inclined to accept Sonneck's view ("Early American Operas," pp. 40-45) that more evidence is needed before credit is taken away from Barton.

38 Howard, p. 24.

39 There is some controversy over the possibility of James Ralph's *Fashionable Lady* being the first ballad opera (Sonneck, "Early American Operas," pp. 18-20; Parker, III, p. 161). It is uncertain whether Ralph was born in America, though even if he were, his ballad opera was written and produced in England and the tunes arranged by an English musician. Barton's was written here, is by

an American, has music arranged here, and is about a local situation.

[40] Sonneck, "Early American Operas," p. 37.

[41] Gagey, p. 213.

[42] The Italian pasticcio was a species of lyric drama usually made up of the works of two or more composers. "Really characteristic of the genre and puzzling are only those pasticcios which were an opportunistic afterthought, a mixture of heterogeneous ingredients, an operatic pie, made up of airs from different works by different composers, composed at different times for different cities; and most pasticcios are of this description." (Sonneck, "Ciampi's 'Bertoldo, Bertolino e Cacasenno' and Favert's 'Ninette À La Cour'—A Contribution to the History of Pasticcio," *Miscellaneous Studies,* p. 112.) The result of this system (and it *was* a fully developed system) in Italy was that a libretto by Metastasio might include bits of Zeno, Goldoni, Stampiglia, Rossi, and other writers; a score might include pieces of Gluck, Ciampi, Galuppi, Cocchi, Jommelli, Latilla, Handel, and others (Sonneck, "Ciampi's 'Bertoldo, etc.' " p. 143).

[43] Kidson, p. 104.

[44] Nicoll, II, 242; Tufts, p. 71; Frédérick Louis Ritter, *Music in America,* New York, new edition, 1895, p. 149.

[45] Isaac Bickerstaffe, *Love in a Village: A Comic Opera in Three Acts,* printed from the acting copy, John Cumberland, 2, Cumberland Terrace, Camden, New Town, London, undated. Boswell was one of the pleased first-nighters. His entry in the *London Journal,* 1762-1763, New York, 1950, p. 71, for 7 December, 1762, reads, "At night I went to Covent Garden and saw *Love in a Village,* a new comic opera, for the first night. I liked it much."

[46] Sonneck, *Early Opera in America,* p. 79; Sonneck, "Early American Operas," p. 84.

[47] Willis, p. 51; Sonneck, *Early Opera in America,* p. 34 and Tables.

[48] Edward Ellsworth Hipsher, *American Opera and Its Composers,* Philadelphia, 1927, p. 23.

[49] Odell, *Annals,* I, 259; Sonneck, "Early American Operas," p. 46.

[50] See, for example, descriptions of "plays" in Wegelin.

[51] The history of serious opera goes back only to the beginning of the seventeenth century with the camerata in Italy, and the first

public opera house was not built until 1637, in Venice (Edward J. Dent, *Foundations of English Opera*, Cambridge, 1928, p. 44; Walter McSpadden, *Operas and Musical Comedies*, New York, 1946, p. 89).

[52] Kidson, pp. 9, 17-22; Schultz, pp. 133-34; Nicoll, II, p. 225.

[53] Gagey, p. 17.

[54] J. Aiken, *Letters From a Father to His Son (1792 and 1793)*, Philadelphia, 1796, p. 59.

[55] See, for example, Willis, p. 354; Marian Hannah Winter, "American Theatrical Dancing from 1750 to 1800," *The Musical Quarterly*, XXIV, No. 1, January, 1938, p. 71; Sonneck, *Early Opera in America*, p. 197.

[56] Dunlap, *A History of the American Theatre*, New York, 1832, p. 124.

[57] *Ibid.*, p. 247.

[58] Francis Courtney Wemyss, *Theatrical Biography: or, The Life of an Actor and Manager*, Glasgow, 1848, p. 127.

[59] Sonneck, *Early Opera in America*, p. 197; Sonneck, *Early Concert-Life in America*, Leipzig, 1907, pp. 27-28.

[60] From an article by William Aliburton, 1792, quoted in Sonneck, *Early Opera in America*, p. 140.

[61] Willis, pp. 236-37; Waldo, p. 174.

[62] New York *American Minerva*, March 2, 1796; Pollock, p. 313; Sonneck, *Early Concert Life*, p. 28; Henry C. Lahee, *Annals of Music in America*, Boston, 1922, p. 9.

[63] Seilhamer, *New Foundations* (III), 1891, p. 108; Parker, III, 408.

[64] *The New-York Magazine*, January, 1795, p. 5.

[65] Quoted in Oscar G. Sonneck, *Francis Hopkinson and James Lyon*, Washington, 1905, p. 106.

[66] A copy of the libretto is in the Philadelphia *Columbian Magazine*, April, 1787, and is quoted in full in Sonneck's *Hopkinson and Lyon*, pp. 106-11.

[67] Sonneck, *Hopkinson and Lyon*, pp. 110-11; Oscar G. Sonneck, *Suum Cuique, Essays in Music*, New York, 1916, p. 40; Hipsher, p. 23.

[68] The European course of the comic opera follows a jagged line from about 1285, when Adam de la Halle strung together a collection of Robin Hood ballads in *Le Jeu de Robin et de Marian*

(McSpadden, p. 409); the line weaves drunkenly through most European countries, emerging as intermezzi and the opera buffa in Italy, for example, or opéra bouffe, and parodie in France (McSpadden, pp. 366, 427; Sonneck, "Ciampi's 'Bertoldo, etc.,'" p. 144). In England, the line of comic opera derives from the Elizabethan jig, from drolls, and from ballad operas (Dent, p. 1). French influence, after the success of *La Serva Padrona* in Paris in 1752, also served to stimulate the form (Nicoll, III, *Late Eighteenth-Century Drama,* 1952, p. 192).

[69] For early eighteenth-century examples, see Gagey, pp. 19-20; Parker, III, 62-64.

[70] Gagey, p. 8; Kidson, p. 104.

[71] Matthews, *"Pinafore's* Predecessor," p. 501; Tufts, p. 61; Gagey, p. 100.

[72] Nicoll, III, 197.

[73] Nicoll, III, 251; Gagey, p. 100; Schultz, p. 154.

[74] John O'Keeffe and William Shield, *The Poor Soldier: A Comic Opera in 2 acts, as it is acted at the Theatre, Smoke-Alley, Dublin,* 1786.

[75] Nicoll, III, 293; Odell, *Annals,* I, 239, for first performance by the Old American Company; Sonneck, *Early Opera in America,* Tables A and B for the Old American Company repertory through 1800.

[76] Lynch, pp. 25, 30; Nicoll, III, 207.

[77] The eighteenth century used "farce" to mean almost any short piece, usually of one or two acts, heavily dependent on intrigue, and often bawdy, though soon *any* short afterpiece came to be called a farce (Lynch, pp. 27-28). The second decade of the eighteenth century made up the "years of farce in the history of the stage," (Nicoll, II, 211) but later, when musical farces were the rage as afterpieces, they assumed an essential aspect of the repertory.

[78] Nicoll, III, 194.

[79] Sonneck, *Early Opera in America,* p. 79.

[80] Dr. John Hawkesworth, *Edgar and Emmeline,* in *A Collection of Farces and Other Afterpieces,* selected by Mrs. Inchbald, VI, London, 1809. Typical of eighteenth-century terminology is the fact that *Edgar and Emmeline* is in a collection of farces and is called a "comedy" on its title page; it is also referred to as an "en-

tertainment" (Nicoll, III, 267) and a "fairy tale" (Lynch, p. 193). Critics in 1796 called it "a tale which may amuse children. . . ." (New York *Diary,* April 20, 1796.)

⁸¹ Note their extraction from intermezzi and development into opera buffa (McSpadden, p. 366).

⁸² Nicoll, III, 194. Also see Lynch, p. 30.

⁸³ J. Max Patrick, *Savannah's Pioneer Theatre from Its Origins to 1810,* Athens, Georgia, 1953, p. 12.

⁸⁴ Nicoll, III, 194, 195, 208; Seilhamer, III, 310; Lynch, p. 251.

⁸⁵ Sonneck, *Early Opera in America,* pp. 35-36.

⁸⁶ Hornblow, I, 167; Seilhamer, II, 292.

⁸⁷ Ralph Leslie Rusk, *The Literature of the Middle Western Frontier,* New York, 1926, I, 354-55; Paul McPharlin, *The Puppet Theatre in America,* New York, 1949, p. 30; Charles Durang, *History of the Philadelphia Stage: 1749-1855,* articles in *Philadelphia Sunday Dispatch,* 1854, arranged and illustrated by Thompson Westcott, 1868, in library of University of Pennsylvania, Vol. I, Chap. XIII; Odell, *Annals,* I, 178.

⁸⁸ Howard, pp. 72-74; Sonneck, *Early Opera in America,* pp. 69, 79, 96.

⁸⁹ The usual difficulty with "firsts" occurs again: the first written was not the first performed, and the first performed is not the first extant, and so on. It is perhaps sufficient to know that they were written by a great variety of American librettists and composers and were performed in a great variety of American cities.

⁹⁰ Elihu Hubbard Smith, *Edwin and Angelina; or, the Banditti,* An Opera in Three Acts, New York, 1797. See Sonneck, *Early Opera in America,* p. 100 and Chap. VI below for information concerning the composer.

⁹¹ Quotes from Hipsher, p. 25 and Coad, *William Dunlap,* pp. 162-63, respectively.

⁹² *The Monthly Review; or, Literary Journal Enlarged,* XXIV, London, October, 1797, p. 219. Smith admits using some lyrics of Goldsmith (see p. 6 of his Preface to *Edwin and Angelina*).

⁹³ Hipsher, p. 24.

⁹⁴ Dunlap, *A History of the American Theatre,* p. 104.

⁹⁵ *Ibid.,* p. 108; *The New-York Magazine,* February, 1795, p. 130; Hipsher, p. 24.

⁹⁶ Ann Julia Hatton, *The Songs of Tammany; or, The Indian Chief,* New York, 1794.

[97] Sonneck, *Early Opera in America,* p. 111; Odell, *Annals,* I, 385.

[98] See Wegelin, and Sonneck, *Early Opera in America,* throughout. Coad, *William Dunlap,* and Hipsher both contain partial lists of American musicals of the eighteenth century.

[99] Coad, *William Dunlap,* p. 42; Harold Earle Johnson, *Musical Interludes in Boston: 1795-1830,* New York, 1943, p. 38; Seilhamer, II, 199. Interludes were rarely printed or even named in the theatre advertisements. Newspapers merely noted that "Interludes etc. will be expressed in the bills of the day."

[100] Willis, p. 301.

[101] Dunlap, *A History of the American Theatre,* p. 110; also see John D. Turnbull's *The Recruit* in Sonneck's "Early American Operas," p. 65.

[102] Quoted in *The Magazine of History,* XLIII, No. 2, Extra No. 170, 1931, pp. 71-73.

[103] William Dunlap, *Darby's Return,* complete in Appendix to Paul Leicester Ford's *Washington and the Theatre,* New York, 1899. It was first performed on November 24, 1789 (Odell, *Annals,* I, 279).

[104] See, for example, the New York *Journal or the General Advertiser,* April 9, 1767, quoted in Rita Susswein Gottesman, ed., *The Arts and Crafts In New York,* I (1726-1776), New York, 1938, pp. 313-14; also see Willis, pp. 68, 171, 221; Seilhamer, III, 186, 310, 322; Pollock, pp. 230, 326; Dunlap, *A History of the American Theatre,* p. 62; Ireland, *Records,* I, 58; Odell, *Annals,* I, 406.

[105] "Both 'pantomime' and 'dancing' were referred to by Latin and Roman Christians as *Saltatio,* and 'saltation' is employed down through the eighteenth century by critics and historians of France and England." (Lincoln Kirstein, *Dance; A Short History of Theatrical Dancing,* New York, 1935, p. 48.) Dancing, however, probably referred to social events, while movements *on a stage* were probably always pantomime (R. J. Broadbent, *A History of Pantomime,* London, 1901, p. 42).

[106] Sonneck, "A Description of Alessandre Striggio and Francesco Corteccio's Intermedi 'Psyche and Amor,' 1565," in *Miscellaneous Studies,* p. 270.

[107] Nicoll, II, 251, 253; Thelma Niklaus, *Harlequin, or the Rise and Fall of a Bergamask Rogue,* New York, 1956, p. 139. Panto-

mimes were largely derived from the commedia dell' arte and from intermedi, though these were largely defunct in Italy and France when England began her pantomimical history (Lynch, p. 232; Sonneck, "A Description, etc." p. 271; Niklaus, sections on panto-mimes in France and Italy). Harlequin and his crew had been seen in England before 1700 (Niklaus, p. 190; Broadbent, p. 102; Gagey, p. 58), but the eighteenth century made drastic changes, not only in his person, but in his surroundings.

[108] For controversy, see Broadbent, p. 137; Lynch, p. 26; and especially Nicoll, II, 252; Niklaus, pp. 139, 142.

[109] Broadbent, p. 143; Nicoll, II, 251. Garrick, though disapprov-ing of pantomimes, was forced to include them at Drury Lane, and he hired Henry Woodward as his answer to Rich (Lynch, p. 128; Niklaus, p. 144). Soon such writers as Richard Brinsley Sheridan were contributing their efforts to the form, and its triumphant progress through the eighteenth century was abetted by the minor theatres, such as Sadler's Wells and the Royal Grove (Niklaus, p. 146; Nicoll, II, 208).

[110] Quoted in M. H. Winter, p. 66.

[111] Henry Fielding, The History of Tom Jones, A Foundling, New York, 1952, p. 146.

[112] Niklaus, p. 141; Broadbent, p. 144; Lynch, pp. 27, 232.

[113] Quoted in Niklaus, p. 139.

[114] Niklaus, p. 148. Now four distinct strains could be seen in pantomimes: the influence of classic myth, the influence of com-media dell' arte (Rich himself called his pantomimes "Italian Mimic Scenes" (Broadbent, p. 143), the influence of previous English Farce, and the influence of contemporary satire (Nicoll, II, 253).

[115] Lynch, p. 232; Nicoll, II, 253.

[116] Nicoll, II, 253-54; Broadbent, p. 182.

[117] Niklaus, pp. 146-47. Note, too, the ballet Don Juan (1790), wherein the Don is served by Scaramouch (Nicoll, III, 210).

[118] Nicoll, III, 210; Niklaus, p. 157; Broadbent, pp. 188-90.

[119] Foster Rhea Dulles, America Learns to Play, New York, 1952, pp. 53-54; Carl Bridenbaugh, Cities in the Wilderness, New York, 1938, pp. 435-36; Crawford, pp. 55-57; Willis, p. 14; Seilhamer, I, 28.

[120] Hornblow, I, 80; Dunlap, A History of the American Theatre, p. 5.

[121] Seilhamer, I, 169; Odell, *Annals,* I, 89; Gottesman, ed., I, 313-14.

[122] William Eddis, *Letters from America,* 1769-1777, London, 1792, p. 108.

[123] In the 1796 season, for example, see the New York *American Minerva* for June 9, June 20, June 25, July 4, July 13, and so forth.

[124] M. H. Winter, pp. 60-61; for the 1796 season, see the advertisements for the historical pantomime *The Independence of America,* June 8, in the New York *American Minerva,* June 2 and 8, 1796. (Seilhamer, III, 324, says that this American pantomime "began with an allegorical prologue, included a pastoral dance, and ended with the Declaration of Independence.")

[125] Seilhamer, III, 341.

[126] Laurence Hutton, *Curiosities of the American Stage,* New York, 1891, pp. 94-96; Lillian Moore, "John Durang: the First American Dancer," in Paul Magriel, ed., *Chronicles of the American Dance,* New York, 1948, p. 22.

[127] See, for example, Seilhamer, II, 169; Sonneck, *Early Opera in America,* p. 91.

[128] Charles F. Brede, *The German Drama in English on the Philadelphia Stage from 1794-1830,* Philadelphia, 1918, p. 61; Seilhamer, III, 20, 325, 367; Moore, pp. 24, 30; Isaac J. Greenwood, *The Circus,* New York, 1898, p. 67; Waldo, p. 177; Willis, p. 261.

[129] Sonneck, *Early Opera in America,* p. 198.

[130] M. H. Winter, p. 66; Sonneck, *Early Opera in America,* pp. 128, 217; Willis, p. 254, includes an advertisement for a Grand Pantomime, "with select musical pieces from the French Operas, The Golden Fleece, Iphigénie, Tauride, etc.—none of which has ever yet been performed in America. . . ."

[131] See New York *American Minerva,* June 9, 25, 1796.

[132] Sonneck, *Early Opera in America,* p. 198; Sonneck, *Early Concert-Life,* p. 126.

[133] M. H. Winter, pp. 67-68, 73; Odell, *Annals,* I, 421; Clifford E. Hamar, "Scenery on the Early American Stage," *The Theatre Annual,* VII, 1948-1949, p. 88.

[134] George C. D. Odell, *Shakespeare from Betterton to Irving,* New York, 1920, I, 284; Hamar, p. 103.

[135] Willis, p. 284.

[136] Quoted from New York *Argus,* July 18, 1896; also see Seilhamer, III, 342.

[137] Moore, p. 32; Broadbent, pp. 188-190; M. H. Winter, p. 64.

[138] Quoted in Willis, pp. 306-7.

[139] Kirstein, p. 173. To be sure, the first ballet as the term is still used (that is, a sustained mood in action, music, and decoration) was performed in France in 1581, *La Ballet Comique de la Reine Louise;* its unique contribution was the unification of elements, tournament, masquerade, and pastoral, which had been known separately before. But it was done by amateurs and led slowly to still other amateur forms. The ballet-mascarade and the ballet de cour pointed toward French opera and also helped to establish the classic ballet used at the end of the seventeenth and all through the eighteenth centuries. The *Ballet Comique de la Reine* and its successors were a strong influence on the English masque. The English added an anti-masque which was essentially a second ballet entry, but other than this and some country dances, England remained outside the main developments in theatre dancing. (All of this discussion I have taken from Kirstein, pp. 151-226, except where otherwise noted.)

[140] The introduction of the first ballerina and the beginning of Russia's interest in ballet were developments of the same period. The early eighteenth century saw the formalization and standardization of ballet; Rameau, for example, established the five basic positions. The most typical musical expression of the period in France was the opéra-ballet, each act a little opera but everything in the plot pointing towards the ballet. France provided dance music for the rest of the continent in the eighteenth century (frequently inserted, out of context, as interludes in the drama of other countries) and went ahead constantly with innovations such as looser, shorter costumes and discarding of face masks (though leather-soled shoes with painted heels remained through the eighteenth century).

[141] See Dent, p. 103; Edward W. Naylor, *Shakespeare and Music,* New York, 1896, first revised edition, 1931, pp. 111, 115; Kirstein, p. 224; Gagey, pp. 7, 41.

[142] Robert Rutherford Drummond, *Early German Music in Philadelphia,* New York, 1910, p. 27.

[143] Greenwood, pp. 60, 64; New York *Weekly Museum,* January 23, 1792. Quoted in Gottesman, ed., II, 1777-1799, 1954, p. 396;

William Dunlap, *Diary*, ed. Dorothy C. Barck, New York, 1930, I, 733.

[144] Quoted in M. H. Winter, p. 63.

[145] Willis, p. 14.

[146] Hornblow, I, 76; Ford, *Washington and the Theatre*, pp. 5, 8.

[147] Sonneck, *Early Opera in America*, p. 22; Odell, *Annals*, I, 48; advertisements in Gottesman, I, 313-14; Seilhamer, I, 238; Brede, p. 27; Willis, p. 104.

[148] Moore, pp. 16, 21; William Alexander Duer, *New York As It Was, During the Latter Part of the Last Century*, New York, 1849, p. 35.

[149] Moore, pp. 21-22 (includes the extract from Charles Durang's book, below).

[150] See, for example, Odell, *Annals*, I, 289; Moore, p. 24. The following account of an egg dance is from Wolfgang von Goethe, *Wilhelm Meister*, trans. Thomas Carlyle (first published 1778-1796), New York and London, 1944, Vol. I, Book II, pp. 100-101.

[151] In Museum of the City of New York.

[152] Seilhamer, III, 153; Willis, p. 223.

[153] Charles Dickens, *Nicholas Nickleby* (first published 1838-1839), Boston, n.d., pp. 319-320.

[154] Moore, p. 25; also see Playbill for February 8, 1792 for "Dancing Ballet" as synonymous with "Pantomime Ballet"; also Odell, *Annals*, I, 302; Hornblow, I, 188.

[155] Odell, *Annals*, I, 300-301; Seilhamer, II, 344; Hipsher, p. 432; M. H. Winter, p. 63; Sonneck, *Early Opera in America*, p. 128; M. H. Winter, p. 67; Howard, p. 96.

[156] M. H. Winter, p. 58.

[157] Sonneck, *Early Opera in America*, pp. 95-96.

[158] Quoted in Robert G. Vail, "Susannah Haswell Rowson, A Bibliographical Study," *Proceedings of the American Antiquarian Society*, N.S. Vol. 42, April 20, 1932—October 19, 1932, pp. 54-55; M. H. Winter, p. 65.

[159] Odell, *Annals*, I, 322; Ireland, *Records*, I, 100; Pollock, p. 196; Willis, p. 443; Patrick, p. 40.

[160] Moore, p. 27.

[161] Moore, pp. 27-29, 32; Sonneck, *Early Opera in America*, Tables and p. 190; Seilhamer, III, pp. 71, 165.

[162] *"La Forêt Noire; or, Maternal Affection*. A Serious Pantomime. In 3 Acts. As performed at the Boston Theatre. Boston—

printed and for sale by John and Jos. N. Russell—price 9 pence."
In library of University of Pennsylvania.

[163] Moore, p. 30; New York *The Weekly Museum,* April 9, 1796.

[164] M. H. Winter, pp. 66-67.

[165] Quoted in M. H. Winter, p. 69.

[166] M. H. Winter, p. 73.

[167] Partly thanks to the influence of the French ballet (Kirstein, pp. 174-76), the English masque began to thrive in the early seventeenth century. It began as an elaborate dance in costume by a select body of royalty (though only for the court, masques started the use of scenery in the English theatre; see Dent, p. 19; Odell, *Shakespeare,* I, 90). When the Puritans succeeded in suppressing the drama, the masques, as a means of evasion, began to assume a more definitely dramatic form and English opera began to grow (Dent, p. 3). Although English opera grew out of the masque, the latter form existed side by side with it into the eighteenth century (Parker, III, 58; Dent, p. 3).

[168] Dent, pp. 19-26, 171; Kidson, p. 7.

[169] Quote from Nicoll, II, pp. 258-59. Also see Lynch, pp. 29, 30; Nicoll, III, 212.

[170] Though it "disregards the conventional masque form" (Dent, p. 38 footnote). It was adapted for the stage by Dr. Dalton in 1738, put into three acts, and had additional songs grafted on to it (many drawn from other poems of Milton), and much dancing; in 1773, Colman wrote another version, this one a two-act afterpiece with music by Arne (Lynch, p. 52; Nicoll, II, 260; Ireland, *Records,* I, p. 60; Odell, *Annals,* I, 317; Lahee, p. 9).

[171] E.g., *The Tempest, Timon of Athens, Measure for Measure, The Merchant of Venice, Twelfth Night,* and *A Midsummer Night's Dream* (Odell, *Shakespeare,* I, 36, 48, 73, 78, 82; Dent, p. 216).

[172] Odell, *Shakespeare,* I, 36, 189. Also see Ford, *Washington and the Theatre,* p. 33.

[173] Dent, p. 230.

[174] Carl Bridenbaugh, *Cities in Revolt: Urban Life in America, 1743-1776,* New York, 1955, p. 194. Earlier, in 1606 in Canada, America was first introduced to the masque: Marc Lescarbot's *The Theatre of Neptune in New France* (Parker, III, 86; Odell, *Annals,* I, 2).

[175] Carl and Jessica Bridenbaugh, *Rebels and Gentlemen: Philadelphia in the Age of Franklin,* New York, 1947, p. 109; Pollock,

p. 12; Otto E. Albrecht, *Francis Hopkinson: Musician, Poet and Patriot, 1737-1937*, reprint from Library Chronicle of the University of Pennsylvania, Vol. VI, No. 1, March, 1938, p. 4. Also see Sonneck, *Hopkinson and Lyon*, pp. 22, 76. It had originally been written by Thompson in England in 1740 and was revised by Mallet in 1751 with music by Arne.

[176] Quinn, I, 18; also see p. 19.

[177] Mallet and Thompson, *Alfred: A Masque*, London, 1751.

[178] Willis, p. 382; Sonneck, "Early American Operas," p. 85. The program for the masque is quoted in M. H. Winter, p. 72.

[179] Broadbent, pp. 144, 180. A visitor to one of Rich's pantomimes said that the last, grand scene "is the most magnificent that ever appeared on the English stage—all the gods and goddesses discovered with the apotheosis of Diana, ascending into the air." (Quoted in Broadbent, pp. 155-156.) After Lincoln's Inn Fields, Rich moved to Covent Garden where, for thirty years, he worked with the same twenty pantomimes, constantly reviving and adding more elaborate settings for an audience most interested in the trickery and the scenic wonders of his pantomimes (Odell, *Shakespeare*, I, 312).

[180] Quoted in Gottesman, ed., I, 313-14.

[181] Oral Sumner Coad, "Stage and Players in Eighteenth Century America," *The Journal of English and German Philology*, XIX, 1920, pp. 218-19.

[182] Quoted in Howard, p. 98.

[183] Richard Moody, *America Takes the Stage*, Bloomington, Indiana, 1955, p. 206.

[184] Moody, pp. 212, 218; Odell, *Annals*, I, 286; Sonneck, *Early Opera in America*, p. 91.

[185] Hamar, p. 84.

[186] Willis, p. 146; Sonneck, "Early American Operas," pp. 55-56n. The following program of Taylor is given in Howard's *Our American Music*, pp. 93-94.

[187] In Philadelphia, in 1794, he did two other programs (see Howard, *Our American Music*, pp. 93-94), and they show that his inventiveness was by no means exhausted by his Annapolis efforts. "The Brush," an entertainment in six parts, presented in New York by Mr. Powell at the John Street Theatre in January, 1796, was the same type of musical extravaganza, or review (details of his program are in New York *American Minerva*, January 22, 1796).

¹⁸⁸ In Elizabethan times not only did plays frequently contain songs, but there was much employment of music "generally instrumental, sometimes vocal, as a background to some action which requires emphasis of a special kind." (Dent, p. 8.) By the end of the seventeenth century these uses of music were traditional, and an increasing number of songs were permitted into regular comedy and tragedy.

¹⁸⁹ Quoted in Schultz, pp. 155-56. Also see Nicoll, II, 225-26; Odell, *Shakespeare*, I, p. 159.

¹⁹⁰ See, for example, the playbill for April 6, 1796 (in the Museum of the City of New York), where Colman's *The Mountaineers* is advertised with "Music by Dr. Arnold, Accompanyments by Pelissier." Lee's tragedy, *Theodosius*, was very popular, and "One great reason for its marked success on the American stage was, no doubt, the solemn church music composed for it by Henry Purcell. . . ." (Seilhamer, I, 108.)

¹⁹¹ Dunlap's prompt book for Kotzebue's *The Virgin of the Sun*, trans. Anne Plumtre, London, 1799, in Harvard University theatre collection.

¹⁹² Moody, p. 234.

¹⁹³ Naylor, p. 3.

¹⁹⁴ Lynch, pp. 96, 98, 244. In the seventeenth century both Davenant and Shadwell worked on *The Tempest* (as did many other writers, including Dryden, for a full century thereafter), and other pre-1700 musicals included *Macbeth, Timon of Athens, Henry VIII*, and *A Midsummer Night's Dream* (Odell, *Shakespeare*, I, 28-48; Dent, pp. 128-29, 136-37, 216). In 1700, *Measure for Measure* was added to the list (Odell, *Shakespeare*, I, 73), and *Julius Caesar* would have been, in 1729, but it "was laid aside when the Italian singers, who were to make up the chorus, demanded more than the receipts of the theatre were likely to be." (Lynch, p. 75.) Masques and songs were added to *The Merchant of Venice* and *Twelfth Night*, and even Enorbarbus's drinking song in *Antony and Cleopatra* acquired another verse (Odell, *Shakespeare*, I, 78, 82; Lynch, p. 108).

¹⁹⁵ Odell, *Shakespeare*, I, 340, 345, 362-63, 370, 376, 422, 425, 428; Lynch, p. 113. The end of the eighteenth century and the beginning of the nineteenth still found *The Merchant of Venice* with a collection of songs, *The Tempest* bristling with music, and *Antony and Cleopatra* ending with a funeral procession involving

a chorus, a trio, a solo, and so forth (Odell, *Shakespeare*, II, 26, 59, 69).

[196] Garrick also altered *The Taming of the Shrew* to *Katharine and Petruchio*, and a ballad opera, *A Cure for a Scold*, was based on the same play (Lynch, pp. 97, 104).

[197] Lynch, pp. 106-7; Odell, *Shakespeare*, I, 358. *The Comick Masque of Pyramus and Thisbe* was also extracted, in 1716, from *A Midsummer Night's Dream; The Universal Passion* was a reworking of *Much Ado About Nothing* which contained four songs, one duet, and a dance (Odell, *Shakespeare*, I, 232, 255-56).

[198] Ford, *Washington and the Theatre*, p. 10; Odell, *Annals*, I, 125.

[199] Seilhamer, I, 302; Willis, p. 171; Odell, *Annals*, I, 163; Ford, *Washington and the Theatre*, p. 33.

[200] Willis, p. 264.

[201] New York *American Minerva*, April 19 and 20, 1796. Other productions of *Macbeth* included music by Arne and occasional Scotch songs (Odell, *Annals*, I, 129, 345, 378).

[202] New York *Argus*, May 27.

[203] See, for example, Wegelin, p. 52; Dunlap, *A History of the American Theatre*, p. 75; Waldo, p. 61; Odell, *Annals*, II, 58-59.

[204] New York *Commercial Advertiser*, June 3, 1799, quoted in Coad, "Stage and Players in Eighteenth Century America," p. 218. Information concerning Act V quoted in Odell, *Annals*, II, p. 59.

Chapter VI

[1] For sequence of Dunlap's stage works, see Oscar Wegelin, ed., *Early American Plays, 1714-1830*, New York, 1900, pp. 30-39; for his theatre criticism, see Mary Rives Bowman, "Dunlap and the 'Theatrical Register,'" *Studies in Philology*, XXIV, No. 3, July, 1927, 413-25, and New York *Diary*, 1796; and for his managerial duties, see above Chap. IV.

[2] In England, the playwright was not necessarily a member of a theatre company, but he frequently had a professional connection with the stage. He furnished new plays and alterations of older drama. Every third performance of a play in its first season was a benefit night for the author; these benefits were particularly remunerative if the playwright was also a popular actor appearing

in his own piece. A new play was customarily granted a minimum of nine performances, or three benefits for the author. By 1777 professional playwrights had accepted a change in function and had "largely turned to melodrama, musical farce, and comic opera. Actor-authors and manager-authors thereafter largely confined their efforts to the furnishing of bare scenarios, or mere outlines, which made possible the exploitation of maximum 'sound and shew.'" The result was that operas were turned out even by "serious" writers. (James J. Lynch, Box, Pit, and Gallery, Berkeley and Los Angeles, 1953, pp. 166, 168-69, 182, 179-80.)

[3] Oscar G. Sonneck, Early Opera in America, New York, London, Boston, 1915, p. 96.

[4] At least, such was Dunlap's demand when he took over the John Street Theatre—see William Dunlap, Diary (1766-1839), ed. Dorothy C. Barck, New York, 1930, I, 75.

[5] Eola Willis, The Charleston Stage in the XVIII Century, Columbia, South Carolina, 1924, p. 341.

[6] See Dunlap's account of Cooper's commissioning him to write his Yankee Chronology, in The Magazine of History, XL, No. 2, Extra Number 170, 1931, 73; Grenville Vernon, Yankee Doodle-Doo, New York, 1927, p. 5.

[7] Oscar G. Sonneck, "Early American Operas," Miscellaneous Studies in the History of Music, New York, 1921, p. 18.

[8] John Bernard, Retrospections of America, 1797-1811, ed. from MSS by Mrs. Bayle Bernard, New York, 1887, p. 71.

[9] Information concerning Smith, unless otherwise noted, is from Wegelin, pp. 89-90; Marcia Edgerton Bailey, A Lesser Hartford Wit: Dr. Elihu Hubbard Smith, 1771-1798, University of Maine Studies, Second Series, No. 11, The Maine Bulletin, No. 15, June, 1928; and James E. Cronin, "Elihu Hubbard Smith and the New York Theatre (1793-1798)," New York History, XXXI, No. 2, April, 1950, 136-48.

[10] George Gates Raddin, Jr., Hocquet Caritat and the Early New York Literary Scene, Dover, New Jersey, 1953, p. 51.

[11] Elihu Hubbard Smith, Preface to Edwin and Angelina; or, the Banditti, New York, 1797, pp. 5-6; William Dunlap, A History of the American Theatre, New York, 1832, p. 156.

[12] New York American Minerva, April 26, 1796.

[13] William Dunlap, The Life of Charles Brockden Brown, Philadelphia, 1815, I, 56.

[14] Dunlap, *A History of the American Theatre*, p. 156.

[15] Gilbert Chase, *America's Music*, New York, Toronto, London, 1955, p. 99.

[16] Burton Alva Konkle, *Joseph Hopkinson*, Philadelphia, 1931, p. 5.

[17] Oscar G. Sonneck, *Francis Hopkinson and James Lyon*, Washington, 1905, p. 76; Robert Rutherford Drummond, *Early German Music in Philadelphia*, New York, 1910, p. 48; Wegelin, p. 56. Also see above, Chap. V.

[18] Chase, pp. 99-100; John Tasker Howard, *Our American Music*, New York, 1939, p. 39; Konkle, p. 10; A. A. Parker, ed., *Church Music and Musical Life in Pennsylvania in the Eighteenth Century*, Philadelphia, 1938, III, 438.

[19] Otto E. Albrecht, *Francis Hopkinson: Musician, Poet and Patriot, 1737-1937*, reprinted from the Library Chronicle of the University of Pennsylvania, VI, No. 1, 1938, p. 4; Carl and Jessica Bridenbaugh, *Rebels and Gentlemen: Philadelphia in the Age of Franklin*, New York, 1942, p. 147; Oscar G. Sonneck, *A Bibliography of Early Secular American Music*, revised and enlarged by William Treat Upton, The Library of Congress, Music Division, 1945, p. 512.

[20] Konkle, pp. 12, 21, 48, 51, 28, 259, 309.

[21] Quoted in Konkle, pp. 83-84; also see Sonneck, "The First Edition of 'Hail Columbia!' " in *Miscellaneous Studies*, p. 188.

[22] Unless otherwise noted, the following information is from Wegelin, p. 94.

[23] Dunlap, *A History of the American Theatre*, p. 71.

[24] Frederick Tupper and Helen Tyler Brown, eds., *Grandmother Tyler's Book: The Recollections of Mary Palmer Tyler (Mrs. Royall Tyler), 1775-1866*, New York and London, 1925, p. 257n.

[25] Information concerning Mrs. Rowson is from Elias Nason, *A Memoir of Mrs. Susannah Rowson*, Albany, 1870, and Robert W. G. Vail, "Susannah Haswell Rowson, A Bibliographical Study," *Proceedings of the American Antiquarian Society*, XLII, New Series, April 20, 1932–October 19, 1932, 47-60, except where otherwise noted.

[26] Wegelin, pp. 84-85.

[27] Figures collated from Vail, pp. 56-58.

[28] Charles Durang, *History of the Philadelphia Stage*, collection of 1854 articles in Philadelphia *Sunday Dispatch* arranged and

illustrated by Thompson Westcott, 1868, and in library of University of Pennsylvania, I, Chaps. XXII and XXIII.

[29] Vail, pp. 73-74; Marian Hannah Winter, "American Theatrical Dancing from 1750 to 1800," *The Musical Quarterly*, XXIV, No. 1, January, 1938, 73; Nason, pp. 74-75.

[30] Wegelin, p. 85; Arthur Hobson Quinn, *A History of the American Drama*, New York and London, 1923, I, 121.

[31] Arthur Hobson Quinn, *A History of the American Drama*, New York and London, 1923, I, 121.

[32] Dunlap, *A History of the American Theatre*, p. 104.

[33] Laurence Hutton, *Curiosities of the American Stage*, New York, 1891, p. 8.

[34] George C. D. Odell, *Annals of the New York Stage*, New York, 1927, I, 342, 367; Wegelin, p. 50.

[35] List of performances collated from Odell, I, 346, 348; George O. Seilhamer, *History of the American Theatre, New Foundations* (III), Philadelphia, 1891, 85; Sonneck, "Early American Operas," pp. 57, 59. Also see Dunlap, *A History of the American Theatre*, p. 108.

[36] Sonneck, *Early Opera in America*, p. 97; Edward Ellsworth Hipsher, *American Opera and Its Composers*, Philadelphia, 1927, p. 26; William W. Clapp, Jr., *A Record of the Boston Stage*, Boston and Cambridge, 1853, p. 56; Sonneck, "Early American Operas," pp. 83-84; Hipsher, p. 26; Dunlap, *A History of the American Theatre*, p. 171. For details of Hodgkinson's life and career, see Chap. IV, above. Also see Louis Pichierri, *Music in New Hampshire: 1623-1800*, New York, 1960, p. 105.

[37] Sonneck, *Early Opera in America*, pp. 176, 177, 186; Sonneck, "Early American Operas," pp. 65, 88; Wegelin, p. 93.

[38] Wegelin, p. 68; Sonneck, *A Bibliography*, p. 516; Hipsher, p. 24.

[39] J. P. Brissot de Warville, *New Travels in the United States of America; Performed in 1788*, Boston, 1797, pp. 178-79.

[40] Called so by Wegelin, p. 30. Unless otherwise noted, information concerning Dunlap is from Oral Sumner Coad, *William Dunlap*, New York, 1917.

[41] Joseph N. Ireland, *Records of the New York Stage: From 1750-1860* (I), New York, 1866, 142.

[42] See, for example, Bowman, pp. 413-25; *The New-York Magazine*, January, 1796, p. 49.

[43] James Fennell, *An Apology for the Life of James Fennell, Written by Himself*, Philadelphia, 1814, p. 408.

[44] New York *Mirror*, March 9, 1833.

[45] Dunlap, *A History of the American Theatre*, p. 114.

[46] Dunlap, *Diary*, I, 75; Dunlap, *A History of the American Theatre*, p. 156.

[47] Sonneck, *A Bibliography*, p. 406, gives the total as 70; Wegelin, p. 31 ff. lists 66 different plays of Dunlap; and Coad, p. 284 ff., lists 31 original plays, 18 translations, and 7 of doubtful attribution.

[48] *The Monthly Review; or Literary Journal Enlarged*, London, October, 1797, p. 218.

[49] Quinn, I, 86, 109; Odell, II, 19; Coad, pp. 79, 170. A picture of the gradual assemblage of book and music for an eighteenth-century musical may be achieved through tracing this "opera," *Sterne's Maria*, in Dunlap's *A History of the American Theatre* (e.g., p. 259) and *Diary* (e.g., I, 75, 80, 145, 202, 248, 250, 354); it becomes possible to watch the addition of lyrics by Dunlap, music by Pelissier, and even scenery by Ciceri.

[50] Europe in the 1700's had no musician who functioned exclusively as composer. The composer might also conduct, but almost invariably he doubled as executant; he was expected to write and play his own solos. Composers for the stage in Italy, Paris, or London were generally resident musicians in the sense that they wrote for the resources of a particular theatre (Adam Carse, *The Orchestra in the Eighteenth Century*, Cambridge, England, 1940, pp. 11-12. For details concerning the lives of musicians in the eighteenth century, see above Chap. III).

[51] See, for example, Mr. Bentley with the Old American Company in 1785 (Dunlap, *A History of the American Theatre*, p. 58). The accompaniments for musical pieces were generally not written out; instead, "They had to be supplied from a figured bass by the official composer or arranger of the company and consequently could and would be so arranged as to fit local conditions, that is to say, the size of the orchestra." American composers imitated such musicians as Dibdin, Linley, Arnold, Arne, Reeve, Shield, and Storace (Sonneck, *Early Opera in America*, pp. 71-72).

[52] Sonneck, *Early Opera in America*, p. 96.

[53] Sonneck, "Early American Operas," p. 55; Drummond, p. 75.

[54] Howard, p. xx.

[55] William Treat Upton, "Eighteenth Century American Imprints in the Society's Dielman Collection of Music," *The Maryland Historical Magazine*, XXXV, No. 4, December, 1940, 376.

[56] Sonneck, *A Bibliography*, p. 509.

[57] Quote from Chase, p. 120; also see Howard, pp. 85-86; John R. Parker, *A Musical Biography; or Sketches of the Lives and Writings of Eminent Musical Characters*, Boston, 1824, pp. 193-94.

[58] Howard, p. 90.

[59] Playbill for the John Street Theatre, June 3, 1794, in Harvard University theatre collection.

[60] Howard, p. 91; Odell, II, 112; Sonneck, "Early American Operas," pp. 89-90; Sonneck, *A Bibliography*, pp. 509-10.

[61] John R. Parker, pp. 193-94.

[62] Unless otherwise noted, information concerning Pelissier is from Sonneck, *A Bibliography*, pp. 518-19 and Howard, pp. 97-99.

[63] Lillian Moore, "John Durang: the First American Dancer," *Chronicles of the American Dance*, ed. Paul Magriel, New York, 1948, p. 29.

[64] Dunlap, *A History of the American Theatre*, p. 207.

[65] See Sonneck, *A Bibliography*, pp. 518-19; Odell, I, 429.

[66] He worked with Carr, for example, on Dibdin's *The Deserter* in 1796—see the New York *American Minerva*, April 19, 1796.

[67] In 1796 he worked with the choreographer Francisquy: see their work on *Robinson Crusoe*, New York *American Minerva*, June 9, 1796. When *Sophia of Brabant* was first performed on the New York stage, in 1794, Pelissier wrote the music—see Odell, I, 376.

[68] Dunlap, *A History of the American Theatre*, p. 259.

[69] Howard, p. 99.

[70] Sonneck, "Early American Operas," p. 81.

[71] Quoted in Odell, I, 432. Also see Howard, p. 98.

[72] Sonneck, *A Bibliography*, pp. 521-22; *Euterpeiad or Musical Intelligencer, and Ladies Gazette*, January 19, 1822, p. 170; Chase, p. 113.

[73] Alexander Reinagle, Memorandum Book for 1785, in Library of Congress.

[74] New York *Packet*, June 12, 1786, quoted in Rita Susswein Gottesman, ed., *The Arts and Crafts in New York*, II, 1777-1799, New York, 1954, 369. Also see *Euterpeiad*, January 19, 1822, p. 170.

[75] Howard, p. 75; Odell, I, 248; Oscar G. Sonneck, *Early Concert-Life in America* (1731-1800), Leipzig, 1907, p. 84; Chase, p. 110; *Euterpeiad,* January 19, 1822, p. 170; Drummond, p. 73.

[76] Sonneck, *Early Concert-Life,* p. 46.

[77] Quotes from, respectively, Dunlap, *A History of the American Theatre,* p. 116; Durang, Chap. XIX.

[78] Sonneck, "Early American Operas," pp. 64, 83; Moore, p. 28; Howard, p. 81; Sonneck, *A Bibliography,* p. 522.

[79] *Euterpeiad,* January 19, 1822, p. 170.

[80] Except where otherwise noted, information concerning Taylor is from Sonneck, *A Bibliography,* pp. 527-28; Chase, p. 117; *Euterpeiad,* January 5, 1822, p. 162; John R. Parker, pp. 179-82.

[81] Durang, Chap. XXIII; Robert A. Gerson, *Music in Philadelphia,* Philadelphia, 1940, pp. 41-42; Sonneck, *Early Concert-Life,* p. 144.

[82] John R. Parker, p. 181.

[83] Works collated from Sonneck, *A Bibliography,* pp. 527-28; Howard, pp. 93-96; Sonneck, "Early American Operas," p. 81; Winter, p. 65.

[84] Sonneck, *A Bibliography,* p. 506.

[85] Moore, p. 32.

[86] Except where otherwise noted, information on lives of Van Hagens is from Sonneck, *A Bibliography,* p. 508.

[87] Harold Earle Johnson, *Musical Interludes in Boston: 1795-1830,* New York, 1943, p. 158.

[88] Nason, p. 102; Johnson, pp. 159, 160.

[89] Sonneck, "Early American Operas," p. 82; Howard, pp. 72-74.

[90] Johnson, p. 157.

[91] Information and quotation in Sonneck, *A Bibliography,* p. 514.

[92] *Ibid.*; Sonneck, *Early Opera,* pp. 145, 214-16.

[93] Nason, p. 98; Sonneck, *Early Concert-Life in America,* pp. 302, 304, 305, 307; Sonneck, *A Bibliography,* p. 515.

[94] Sonneck, *A Bibliography,* pp. 500, 503; Howard, p. 113.

[95] Sonneck, *A Bibliography,* p. 499; Odell, I, 233-34; Howard, p. 105.

[96] Seilhamer, III, 89; Sonneck, *A Bibliography,* p. 499; Sonneck, *Early Opera in America,* p. 179.

[97] Sonneck, *A Bibliography,* p. 506.

[98] *Ibid.*, p. 520; Howard, pp. 112-13; Sonneck, *Early Concert-Life*, pp. 198, 295; Odell, I, 342.

[99] Except where otherwise noted, information concerning Carr is from Virginia Larkin Redway, "The Carrs, American Music Publishers," *The Musical Quarterly*, XVIII, No. 1, 1932, 150-77.

[100] Durang, Chap. XXIII; Gerson, p. 51; Jane Campbell, *Old Philadelphia Music*, Philadelphia, 1926, p. 184.

[101] Sonneck, *A Bibliography*, p. 501; William Arms Fisher, *One Hundred and Fifty Years of Music Publishing in the United States*, Boston, 1933, p. 29; New York *American Minerva*, January 2, 1796, and ff.

[102] See, for example, Dunlap, *Diary*, I, November 17, 1798, p. 352.

[103] Redway, p. 163.

[104] *Ibid.*, p. 158.

[105] In the possession of A. B. Hunt, in Brooklyn, according to Redway, p. 175.

Chapter VII

[1] William Dunlap, *The Archers; or, Mountaineers of Switzerland*, New York, 1796.

[2] John Tasker Howard, *Our American Music*, New York, 1939, 3rd edition, 1946, p. 99.

[3] Edward J. Dent, *Foundations of English Opera*, Cambridge, 1928, p. ix.

[4] *The New-York Magazine*, April, 1794, p. 226.

[5] New York *Argus*, February 26, 1796.

[6] *The New-York Magazine*, February, 1796, p. 118.

[7] See, for example, *The New-York Magazine*, December, 1794, review of *Love in a Village*, pp. 718-19, and March, 1796, issue which contains mostly reviews of musicals, yet which talks almost exclusively of the morality of the pieces.

[8] Francis C. Wemyss, *Chronology of the American Stage, from 1752-1852*, New York, 1852, p. 35; William Dunlap, *A History of the American Theatre*, New York, 1832, pp. 193-96.

[9] Joseph N. Ireland, *Records of the New York Stage from 1750-1860*, New York, 1866, I, 142.

[10] Dunlap, *A History of the American Theatre*, pp. 148-49.

[11] Quoted in Dunlap, *A History of the American Theatre*, p. 160.

[12] William Dunlap, *Diary of William Dunlap* (*1766-1839*), ed. Dorothy C. Barck, New York, 1930, I, 219.

[13] *The Monthly Review; or Literary Journal Enlarged,* September-December, 1797, London, pp. 218-19.

[14] Dunlap, *The Archers,* Preface, p. vi.

[15] Dunlap, *A History of the American Theatre,* p. 149.

[16] See New York *American Minerva,* April 16, April 22, and November 24, 1796, advertisements for performances of April 18 and 22 and November 25.

[17] Robert A. Gerson, *Music in Philadelphia,* Philadelphia, 1940, p. 52.

[18] Dunlap, *Diary,* I, 100.

[19] Dunlap, *Diary,* I, October 2 letter to Hodgkinson, p. 154 and October 12 entry, pp. 161, 164.

[20] Grenville Vernon, *Yankee Doodle-Doo,* p. 6.

[21] Howard, p. 99. The error about Schiller as model for the libretto is carried on by others—see, for example, J. Walker McSpadden, *Operas and Musical Comedies,* New York, 1946, p. 329.

[22] Howard, p. 99.

[23] Gerson, p. 52; Gilbert Chase, *America's Music,* p. 119.

[24] Arthur Hobson Quinn, *A History of the American Drama,* New York and London, 1923, I, 82.

[25] Virginia Larkin Redway, "The Carrs, American Music Publishers," *The Musical Quarterly,* 1932, XVIII, No. 1, 159-60.

[26] Oral Sumner Coad, *William Dunlap,* New York, 1917, p. 155.

[27] Oscar G. Sonneck, "Early American Operas," *Miscellaneous Studies in the History of Music,* New York, 1921, p. 75.

Epilogue

[1] For origins of melodrama on the American stage, see Oral Sumner Coad, *William Dunlap,* New York, 1917, pp. 198-200; Arthur Hobson Quinn, *A History of the American Theatre,* New York and London, 1923, I, 102; Harold William Schoenberger, *American Adaptations of French Plays on the New York and Philadelphia Stages from 1790-1833,* 1924, pp. 8, 21.

[2] Oscar G. Sonneck, *Early Opera in America,* New York, London, Boston, 1915, p. 197.

[3] See, for example, Cecil Smith, *Musical Comedy in America*, New York, 1950, p. viii; David Ewen, *Complete Book of the American Musical Theatre*, New York, 1958, p. vii. The libretto for *The Black Crook* was not published; however, Charles M. Barras's original manuscript is in the Harvard University theatre collection, and a prompt copy is in the Players Club, New York.

Bibliography

Books and Plays

Playbills are not included in the following list; too numerous to mention here, they are footnoted when referred to in the text. The playbills used include those in the New York Public Library, the Museum of the City of New York, the Harvard University theatre collection, and the Yale University library.

Aiken, J. *Letters from a Father to his Son.* Philadelphia, 1796.

Anonymous. *La Forêt Noire; or, Maternal Affection. A Serious Pantomime in Three Acts. As Performed at the Boston Theatre.* Boston, 1797.

Barton, Andrew. *The Disappointment: or, the Force of Credulity.* New York, 1767.

Barzun, Jacques. *Music in American Life.* New York, 1956.

Bernard, John. *Retrospections of America: 1797-1811.* New York, 1887.

——. *Retrospections of the Stage.* 2 vols. Boston, 1832.

Bickerstaffe, Isaac. *Love in a Village: A Comic Opera, In Three Acts.* London, 1829.

Blake, Charles. *An Historical Account of the Providence Stage.* Providence, 1868.

Boswell, James. *London Journal: 1762-1763.* New York, 1950.

Brede, Charles F. *The German Drama on the Philadelphia Stage from 1794-1830.* Philadelphia, 1918.

Bridenbaugh, Carl. *Cities in Revolt: Urban Life in America, 1743-1776.* New York, 1955.

——. *Cities in the Wilderness: The First Century of Urban Life in America, 1625-1742.* New York, 1938.

Bridenbaugh, Carl, and Jessica Bridenbaugh. *Rebels and Gentlemen: Philadelphia in the Age of Franklin.* New York, 1942.

Brillat-Savarin, Jean Anthelme. *The Physiology of Taste.* New York, 1926.

Brissot de Warville, J. P. Trans. anon. *New Travels in the United States of America: Performed in 1788.* Boston, 1797.

Broadbent, R. J. *A History of Pantomime.* London, 1901.

Brooks, Henry M. *Olden-Time Music.* Boston, 1888.

Brooks, Van Wyck. *The World of Washington Irving.* New York, 1950.

Brown, Charles Brockden. *The Rhapsodist and Other Uncollected Writings.* Ed. Harry R. Warfel. New York, 1943.

Brown, T. Allston. *A History of the New York Stage.* 3 vols. New York, 1903.

Bruce, Philip Alexander. *Social Life of Virginia in the Seventeenth Century.* Richmond, 1907.

Bukofzer, Manfred F. *Music in the Baroque Era.* New York, 1947.

Burnaby, Andrew. *Burnaby's Travels through North America.* Ed. Rufus Rockwell Wilson. New York, 1904.

Campbell, Jane. *Old Philadelphia Music.* Philadelphia, 1926.

Carse, Adam. *The Orchestra in the Eighteenth Century.* Cambridge, England, 1940.

Chase, Gilbert. *America's Music: From the Pilgrims to the Present.* New York, Toronto, London, 1955.

Clapp, William W., Jr. *A Record of the Boston Stage.* Boston, Cambridge, 1853.

Coad, Oral Sumner. *William Dunlap: A Study of his Life and Works and of his Place in Contemporary Society.* New York, 1917.

Cobbett, William. *Porcupine's Works.* 12 vols. London, 1801.

Colby, Elbridge. *Early American Comedy.* New York, 1919.

Cooper, Thomas. *Some Information Concerning America.* London, 1794.

Cowell, Joe. *Thirty Years Passed Among the Players in England and America.* New York, 1844.

Crawford, Mary Caroline. *The Romance of the American Theatre.* Boston, 1913.

Custis, George Washington Parke. *Recollections and Private Memoirs of Washington.* New York, 1860.

Daly, Charles P. *First Theatre in America.* New York, 1896.

Davis, John. *The Original Letters of Ferdinand and Elisabeth.* New York, 1798.

Davis, Blanche Elizabeth. *The Hero in American Drama: 1787-1900.* New York, 1950.

Decastro, J. *The Memoirs of J. Decastro.* London, 1824.

Dent, Edward J. *Foundations of English Opera: A Study of Musical Drama in England during the Seventeenth Century.* Cambridge, England, 1928.

Dichter, Harry, and Elliott Shapiro. *Early American Sheet Music: Its Lure and Its Lore, 1768-1889.* New York, 1941.

Dickens, Charles. *Nicholas Nickleby.* Boston, undated.

——. *The Old Curiosity Shop.* New York, 1941.

Drummond, Robert Rutherford. *Early German Music in Philadelphia.* New York, 1910.

Duer, William Alexander. *New York As It Was. During the Latter Part of the Last Century.* New York, 1849.

Dulles, Foster Rhea. *America Learns to Play: A History of Popular Recreation, 1607-1940.* New York, 1952.

Dunlap, William. *The Archers, or Mountaineers of Switzerland: An Opera in Three Acts.* New York, 1796.

——. *Diary of William Dunlap.* Ed. Dorothy C. Barck. 3 vols. New York, 1930.

——. *A History of the American Theatre.* New York, 1832.

——. *The Life of Charles Brockden Brown.* 2 vols. Philadelphia, 1815.

——. *Memoirs of the Life of George Frederick Cooke, Esq.* 2 vols. New York, 1813.

——. *Memoirs of a Water Drinker.* 2 vols. New York, 1837.

——. *Yankee Chronology, or Huzzah for the Constitution: A Musical Interlude, In One Act. The Magazine of History.* XLIII, ii (1931), 71-73.

Dwight, Timothy. *Travels in New England and New York.* 4 vols. London, 1823.

Eddis, William. *Letters from America.* London, 1792.

Elson, Louis C. *The History of American Music.* New York, 1904.

————. *The National Music of America and Its Sources.* Boston, 1924.

Evans, Bertrand. *Gothic Drama from Walpole to Shelley.* Berkeley and Los Angeles, 1947.

Ewen, David. *Complete Book of the American Musical Theatre.* New York, 1958.

Fairfax, Thomas. *Journey from Virginia to Salem, Massachusetts (1799).* London, 1936.

Fennell, James. *An Apology for the Life of James Fennell, Written by Himself.* Philadelphia, 1814.

Fielding, Henry. *The History of Tom Jones, A Foundling.* New York, 1952.

Fisher, William Arms. *Notes on Music in Old Boston.* Boston, 1918.

————. *One Hundred and Fifty Years of Music Publishing in the United States.* Boston, 1933.

Ford, Paul Leicester. *Washington and the Theatre.* New York, 1899.

Francis, John W. *Old New York; or, Reminiscences of the Past Sixty Years.* New York, 1866.

Franklin, Benjamin. *The Works of Benjamin Franklin.* Ed. John Bigelow. 12 vols. New York, 1904.

Gagey, Edmond McAdoo. *Ballad Opera.* New York, 1937.

Gaine, Hugh. *The Journals of Hugh Gaine, Printer.* Ed. Paul Leicester Ford. 2 vols. New York, 1902.

Gay, John. *The Beggar's Opera.* In *Plays Written by John Gay.* London, 1772.

Gerson, Robert A. *Music in Philadelphia.* Philadelphia, 1940.

Gilbert, Douglas. *American Vaudeville: Its Life and Times.* New York, London, 1940.

Goelet, Francis. *Extracts from the Journal of Captain Francis*

Goelet, Merchant, Relating to Boston, Salem, Marblehead, Etc.: 1746-1750. Ed. Albert H. Hoyt. Boston, 1870.

Goethe, Wolfgang von. *Wilhelm Meister.* Trans. Thomas Carlyle. 2 vols. New York, London, 1944.

Goodwin, Maud Wilder. *The Colonial Cavalier, or Southern Life Before the Revolution.* New York, 1894.

Goodwin, Rutherford. *A Brief and True Report for the Traveller concerning Williamsburg in Virginia.* Richmond, Virginia, 1936.

Gottesman, Rita Susswein, ed. *The Arts and Crafts in New York.* 2 vols. New York, 1938, 1954.

Graham, Philip. *Showboats: The History of an American Institution.* Austin, Texas, 1951.

Greenwood, Isaac J. *The Circus: Its Origin and Growth prior to 1835.* New York, 1898.

Halline, Allan Gates, ed. *American Plays.* New York, 1935.

Hamilton, Dr. Alexander. *Hamilton's Itinerarium.* Ed. Albert Bushnell Hart. St. Louis, 1907.

Handlin, Oscar, ed. *This Was America.* Cambridge, Massachusetts, 1949.

Hatton, Ann Julia. *The Songs of Tammany; or The Indian Chief: A Serious Opera.* New York, 1794.

Hawkesworth, John. *Edgar and Emmeline.* In *A Collection of Farces and Other Afterpieces.* Ed. Mrs. Inchbald. London, 1809.

Hindle, Brooke. *The Pursuit of Science in Revolutionary America: 1735-89.* Chapel Hill, North Carolina, 1956.

Hipsher, Edward Ellsworth. *American Opera and Its Composers.* Philadelphia, 1927.

Hodgkinson, ——. *Letters on Emigration.* London, 1794.

Hodgkinson, John. *A Narrative of his Connection with the Old American Company, from 5 September, 1792—31 March, 1797.* New York, 1797.

Holyoke, Samuel. *Harmonia Americana.* Boston, 1791.

Hood, George. *A History of Music in New England.* Boston, 1846.

Hornblow, Arthur. *A History of the Theatre in America.* 2 vols. Philadelphia, London, 1919.

Howard, John Tasker. *The Music of George Washington's Time.* Washington, D. C., 1931.

——. *Our American Music: Three Hundred Years of It.* New York, 1939, and third ed., 1946.

Hutton, Laurence. *Curiosities of the American Stage.* New York, 1891.

——, ed. *Opening Addresses.* New York, 1887.

Ireland, Joseph N. *Fifty Years of a Play-Goer's Journal; or Annals of the New York Stage, from A. D. 1798 to A. D. 1848.* New York, 1860.

——. *Records of the New York Stage.* 2 vols. New York, 1866.

——. *T. A. Cooper.* New York, 1888.

Irving, Washington. *Letters of Jonathan Oldstyle,* New York, 1941.

Janson, Charles William. *The Stranger in America: 1793-1806.* Ed. Carl S. Driver. New York, 1935.

Johnson, Harold Earle. *Musical Interludes in Boston: 1795-1830.* New York, 1943.

Jones, Hugh. *The Present State of Virginia.* Ed. Richard L. Morton. Chapel Hill, North Carolina, 1956.

Kerr, Walter. *How Not to Write a Play.* New York, 1955.

Kidson, Frank. *The Beggar's Opera: Its Predecessors and Successors.* Cambridge, England, 1922.

King, Grace. *New Orleans: The Place and the People.* New York, 1937.

Kirstein, Lincoln. *Dance: A Short History of Theatrical Dancing.* New York, 1935.

Konkle, Burton Alva. *Joseph Hopkinson.* Philadelphia, 1931.

Lahee, Henry C. *Annals of Music in America.* Boston, 1922.

Liancourt, Duke de la Rochefoucault. *Travels Through the United States of North America in the Years 1795, '96 and '97.* 2 vols. 1799.

Ludlow, N. M. *Dramatic Life As I Found It.* St. Louis, 1880.

Lynch, James L. *Box, Pit, and Gallery: Stage and Society in Johnson's London.* Berkeley and Los Angeles, 1953.

McPharlin, Paul. *The Puppet Theatre in America: A History.* New York, 1949.

McSpadden, J. Walker. *Operas and Musical Comedies.* New York, 1946.

Magriel, Paul, ed. *Chronicles of the American Dance.* New York, 1948.

Mallet, David, and James Thomson. *Alfred: A Masque.* London, 1751.

Moody, Richard. *America Takes the Stage: Romanticism in American Drama and Theatre, 1750-1900.* Bloomington, Indiana, 1955.

Moses, Montrose J. *The American Dramatist.* Boston, 1911.

——, and John Mason Brown. *The American Theatre as Seen by its Critics, 1752-1934.* New York, 1934.

Mulhall, Michael G. *The Dictionary of Statistics.* London, 1899.

Murray, Marian. *Circus!* New York, 1956.

Nagler, A. M., ed. *Sources of Theatrical History.* New York, 1952.

Nason, Elias. *A Memoir of Mrs. Susannah Rowson.* Albany, 1870.

Naylor, Edward W. *Shakespeare and Music.* New York, 1931.

Nicoll, Allardyce. *A History of English Drama: Early Eighteenth Century Drama.* Cambridge, England, 1952.

——. *A History of English Drama: Late Eighteenth Century Drama.* Cambridge, England, 1952.

Niklaus, Thelma. *Harlequin; or the Rise and Fall of a Burgamask Rogue.* New York, 1956.

Odell, George C. D. *Annals of the New York Stage.* 16 vols. New York, 1927.

——. *Shakespeare from Betterton to Irving.* 2 vols. New York, 1920.

O'Keeffe, John, and William Shield. *The Poor Soldier: A Comic Opera, in Two Acts, as it is acted at the Theatre, Smoke-Alley, Dublin.* London, 1786.

Parker, A. A., ed. *Church Music and Musical Life in Pennsyl-*

vania in the Eighteenth Century. 3 vols. Philadelphia, 1938, 1947.

Parker, John R. *A Musical Biography: Sketches of the Lives and Writings of Eminent Musical Characters.* Boston, 1824.

Parton, James. *Life of John Jacob Astor.* New York, 1865.

Patrick, J. Max. *Savannah's Pioneer Theatre from Its Origins to 1810.* Athens, Georgia, 1953.

Pichierri, Louis. *Music in New Hampshire: 1623-1800.* New York, 1960.

Pollock, Thomas Clark. *The Philadelphia Theatre in the Eighteenth Century.* Philadelphia, 1933.

Priest, William. *Travels in the United States of America: 1793-1797.* London, 1802.

Quinn, Arthur Hobson. *A History of the American Drama.* 2 vols. New York and London, 1923.

Raddin, George Gates, Jr., *Hocquet Caritat and the Early New York Literary Scene.* Dover, New Jersey, 1953.

———. *The New York of Hocquet Caritat and his Associates: 1797-1817.* Dover, New Jersey, 1953.

Redway, Virginia Larkin. *Music Directory of Early New York City.* New York, 1941.

Ritter, Frédérick Louis. *Music in America.* New York, 1895.

Rourke, Constance. *American Humor.* New York, 1953.

Rowe, John. *Letters and Diary of John Rowe, Boston Merchant: 1759-1762, 1764-1779.* Ed. Anne Rowe Cunningham. Boston, 1903.

Rusk, Ralph Leslie. *The Literature of the Middle Western Frontier.* 2 vols. New York, 1926.

Schoenberger, Harold William. *American Adaptations of French Plays on the New York and Philadelphia Stages from 1790 to 1833.* Philadelphia, 1924.

Schultz, William Eben. *Gay's Beggar's Opera: Its Content, History, and Influence.* New Haven, 1923.

Seilhamer, George O. *History of the American Theatre.* 3 vols. I, *Before the Revolution* (Philadelphia, 1888); II, *During the Revolution and After* (1889); III, *New Foundations* (1891).

Smith, Arthur D. Howden. *John Jacob Astor: Landlord of New York*. Philadelphia, 1929.

Smith, Cecil. *Musical Comedy in America*. New York, 1950.

Smith, Elihu Hubbard. *Edwin and Angelina; or the Banditti. An Opera in Three Acts*. New York, 1797.

Smith, Sol. *The Theatrical Journey-Work and Anecdotal Recollections of Sol. Smith*. Philadelphia, 1854.

Sonneck, Oscar G. *A Bibliography of Early Secular American Music*. Revised and enlarged by William Treat Upton. Washington, D. C., 1945.

———. *Early Concert Life in America*. Leipzig, 1907.

———. *Early Opera in America*. New York, London, Boston, 1915.

———. *Francis Hopkinson and James Lyon*. Washington, D. C., 1905.

———. *Miscellaneous Studies in the History of Music*. New York, 1921.

———. *Suum Cuique Essays in Music*. New York, 1916.

Southern, Richard. *Changeable Scenery: Its Origin and Development in the British Theatre*. London, 1952.

Spaeth, Sigmund. *A History of Popular Music in America*. New York, 1948.

Sper, Felix. *From Native Roots: A Panorama of Our Regional Drama*. Caldwell, Idaho, 1948.

Spillane, Daniel. *History of the American Pianoforte; Its Technical Development, and the Trade*. New York, 1890.

Stokes, I. N. Phelps. *The Iconography of Manhattan Island*. 6 vols. New York, 1915-1928.

Tryon, Warren S., ed. *A Mirror for Americans*. 3 vols. Chicago, 1952.

Tyler, Mary Palmer. *Grandmother Tyler's Book: The Recollections of Mary Palmer Tyler (Mrs. Royall Tyler, 1775-1866)*. Ed. Frederick Tupper and Helen Tyler Brown. New York and London, 1925.

Tyler, Royall. *The Contrast*. Introduction by Helen Tyler Brown. Boston and New York, 1920.

Vernon, Grenville. *Yankee Doodle-Doo*. New York, 1927.

Waldo, Lewis P. *The French Drama in America in the Eighteenth Century and Its Influence on the American Drama of that Period: 1701-1800.* Baltimore, 1942.

Wansey, Henry. *The Journal of an Excursion to the United States of North America, in the Summer of 1794.* Salisbury, 1796.

Watson, John F. *Annals and Occurrences of New York City and State.* Philadelphia, 1846.

Wegelin, Oscar. *Early American Plays: 1714-1830.* Ed. John Malone. New York, 1900.

Weld, Isaac, Jr. *Travels through the States of North America and the Provinces of Upper and Lower Canada During the Years 1795, 1796, and 1797.* London, 1799.

Wemyss, Francis C. *Chronology of the American Stage: from 1752-1852.* New York, 1852.

———. *Theatrical Biography: or, The Life of an Actor and Manager.* Glasgow, 1848.

Whitton, Joseph. *An Inside History of "The Black Crook."* Philadelphia, 1897.

Wilkens, Frederick H. *Early Influence of German Literature in America.* New York, 1900.

Willard, George O. *History of the Providence Stage: 1762-1891.* Providence, 1891.

Willis, Eola. *The Charleston Stage in the XVIII Century.* Columbia, South Carolina, 1924.

Winslow, Ola Elizabeth. *American Broadside Verse.* New Haven, 1930.

Winter, William. *Life and Art of Joseph Jefferson: Together with Some Account of his Ancestry and of the Jefferson Family of Actors.* New York, 1894.

Wittke, Carl. *Tambo and Bones: A History of the American Minstrel Stage.* Durham, North Carolina, 1930.

Wood, William B. *Personal Recollections of the Stage.* Philadelphia, 1855.

Wright, Louis B. *The Cultural Life of the American Colonies, 1607-1763.* New York, 1957.

Wright, Richardson. *Hawkers and Walkers in Early America.* Philadelphia, 1927.

Wroth, W. A., and A. E. Wroth. *The London Pleasure Gardens of the Eighteenth Century.* New York, 1896.

Periodicals and Pamphlets

Albrecht, Otto E. *Francis Hopkinson: Musician, Poet and Patriot, 1737-1937.* Reprinted from the *Library Chronicle* of the University of Pennsylvania, VI, i (March, 1938).

American Minerva, New York, file of 1796.

Argus, New York, file of 1796.

Bailey, Marcia Edgerton. *A Lesser Hartford Wit, Dr. Elihu Hubbard Smith, 1771-1798.* University of Maine Studies, second series, No. 11. Reprinted from *The Maine Bulletin* (June, 1928), No. 15.

Barrett, Walter. *John Pintard.* Pamphlet in New York Historical Society, no publishing information, 24 pp.

Bowman, Mary Rives. "Dunlap and the 'Theatrical Register,'" *Studies in Philology,* XXIV, iii (July, 1927), 413-25.

Coad, Oral Sumner. "The American Theatre in the Eighteenth Century," *South Atlantic Quarterly,* XVII, iii (July, 1918), 190-97.

———. "The Dunlap Diaries at Yale," *Studies in Philology,* XXIV, iii (July, 1927), 403-12.

———. "Stage and Players in Eighteenth Century America," *The Journal of English and Germanic Philology,* XIX (1920), 201-23.

Columbian Centinel, Boston, file of 1794.

Cronin, James E. "Elihu Hubbard Smith and the New York Theatre (1793-1798)," *New York History,* XXXI, ii (April, 1950), 136-48.

Cudworth, C. L. "Baroque, Rococo, Galant, Classic," *Monthly Musical Record,* LXXXIII, No. 949 (September, 1953), 172-75.

Daily Advertiser, New York, file of 1796.

Diary, New York, file of 1796.

Duerr, Edwin. "Charles Ciceri and the Background of American Scene Design," *Theatre Arts Monthly*, XVI, xii (December, 1932), 983-90.

Euterpeiad, or Musical Intelligencer, and Ladies Gazette, Boston, file for 1822.

Ford, Paul Leicester. "The Beginnings of American Dramatic Literature," *The New England Magazine*, n. s. IX, vi (February, 1894), 674-87.

Gazette Française et Américaine, New York, file of 1796.

Greenleaf's New York Journal and Patriotic Register, New York, file of 1796.

Hamar, Clifford E. "Scenery on the Early American Stage," *The Theatre Annual*, VII (1948-1949), 84-103.

Herald: A Gazette for the Country, The. New York, file of 1796.

Hopkins, Samuel Miles. *Sketch of the Public and Private Life of Samuel Miles Hopkins*, Publications of the Rochester Historical Society, II, 1898.

Hutchins, Abraham. *Father Hutchins Revived; Being an Almanack and Ephemeris for the Year of our Lord, 1796.* New York, 1796.

Matthews, Brander. "The Drama in the Eighteenth Century," *The Sewanee Review*, XI, i (January, 1903), 1-20.

———. "The Forerunner of the Movies," *The Century Magazine*, LXXXVII, vi (April, 1914), 916-24.

———. "*Pinafore's* Predecessor," *Harper's*, LX, ccclviii (March, 1880), 501-8.

Mirror, The. February 9, March 9, 1833.

Mirror of Taste and Dramatic Censor. 4 vols. Philadelphia and New York, 1810-1811.

Monthly Review; or Literary Journal Enlarged. London. XXIV (September-December, 1797), 218-19.

Moore, Thomas. *Gaine's New-York Almanack, for the year 1796.* New York, 1796.

Moses, Montrose J. "Early American Dramatists: No. 2—William Dunlap," *Theatre Magazine*, 1916, p. 276.

M'Robert, Patrick. *A Tour Through Part of the North Provinces of America.* Ed. Carl Bridenbaugh. The Historical Society of Pennsylvania, I (April, 1935).

New-York Magazine; or, Literary Repository, V, iv (April, 1794), 224-29, xi (November, 1794), 653-56, xii (December, 1794), 717-22; VI, i (January, 1795), 1-8, ii (February, 1795), 65-69, iii (March, 1795), 129-31, iv (April, 1795), 194-95, v (May, 1795), 258-59, vi (June, 1795), 327-28, viii (August, 1795), 449-51; N. S. I, ii (February, 1796), 92-95, iii (March, 1796), 113.

Redway, Virginia Larkin. "The Carrs, American Music Publishers," *The Musical Quarterly,* XVIII, i (1932), 150-77.

Sonneck, Oscar G. *A Survey of Music in America.* Washington, D. C., 1913.

Sunday Herald, Boston, June 24, 1917.

Swanson, Wesley. "Wings and Backdrops: The Story of American Stage Scenery from the Beginnings to 1875," *The Drama,* XVIII, i (October, 1927), 5-7, 30; ii (November, 1927), 41-42, 63-64; iii (December, 1927) 78-80; iv (January, 1928), 107-10.

Tufts, George. "Ballad Operas: A List and Some Notes," *The Musical Antiquary,* IV, iv (January, 1913), 61-86.

Upton, William Treat. "Eighteenth Century American Imprints in the Society's Dielman Collection of Music," *The Maryland Historical Magazine,* XXXV, iv (December, 1940), 374-81.

Vail, Robert G. W. "Susannah Haswell Rowson, A Bibliographical Study," *Proceedings of the American Antiquarian Society,* N. S. XLII (April 20, 1932—October 19, 1932), 47-160.

Van Lennep, William. "The So-Called View of New York's John Street Theatre," *Theatre Notebook,* IV, iv (July-September, 1950), 86-88.

Weekly Museum, New York, file of 1796.

Whitridge, Arnold. "Brillat-Savarin in America," *The Franco-American Review,* I, i (June, 1936), 1-12.

Winter, Marian Hannah. "American Theatrical Dancing from 1750 to 1800," *The Musical Quarterly*, XXIV, i (January, 1938), 58-73.

Manuscripts

Anderson, Alexander. *Diarium Commentarium Vitae Alexander Anderson*. MSS and typescript, 1793-1799, in Columbia University.

Anderson, John. Diary, 1794-1798, in New York Historical Society.

Auliffe, Olive d'. Letters written from the family home "Chevilly," Bloomingdale, New York City, in New York Public Library.

Barras, Charles M. *The Black Crook*. Autograph MS dated June 1, 1862, in Harvard University; prompt copy in Players Club, New York.

Bleecker, Elizabeth De Hart. Diary, 1799-1806, in New York Public Library.

Dunlap, William. Promptbook for Kotzebue's *The Virgin of the Sun*, London, 1799, with Dunlap's handwritten comments, in Harvard University.

Durang, Charles. *History of the Philadelphia Stage: 1749-1855*. Arranged and illustrated by Thompson Westcott, 1868, and in library of University of Pennsylvania.

History of the New Haven Theatre. WPA Connecticut Writers' Project, 1941, in Yale University.

Hodgkinson, John. Letter, March 25, 1795, in Harvard University.

Hodgkinson, John and Lewis Hallam. Articles of Agreement with Hartford, August 18, 1795, in Harvard University.

Johnson, Reverend John Barent. Diary, 1787-1803, in Columbia University.

Kilroe, Edwin Patrick. *The Opera "Tammany,"* undated, in Columbia University.

Receipts of the Treasurer of the "Theatre Royal," John Street, New York, A.D. 1779, in New York Historical Society.

Reinagle, Alexander. Memorandum book, 1784-1785, in Library of Congress.

Wilburn, Elizabeth, *American Theatre Buildings in the Eighteenth Century,* M.A. thesis, Cornell University, August, 1940.

Index